# REMINISCE®

# LIFE ON THE FARM

# TABLE OF CONTENTS

5    **INTRODUCTION**

6    **CHAPTER 1** Family Values & Traditions
Let hardworking farm families inspire you.
Recollections of lovable grandparents passing
down the farming gene, accounts of unforgettable
barns and reflections on life lessons learned are
sure to warm your heart.

30    **CHAPTER 2** Farm-Raised Kids
Children who grow up on a farm are taught
responsibility at an early age. They learn how
to make do, and they truly appreciate what others
take for granted. Enjoy these delightful stories
of kids living life to the fullest and having a lot
of laughs along the way.

60    **CHAPTER 3** Farmhouse Fun
Living on a farm isn't all hard work. There's
plenty of fun to be had sledding behind the
tractor, making mud pies for Dad or just hanging
out at the swimming hole.

76    **CHAPTER 4** Cultivating Romance
Falling in love in the country can definitely
be romantic—just take a look at these tales
of courtship and the mishaps that go with it.

86    **CHAPTER 5** Animal Tales
Farm life wouldn't be the same without animals,
be they loyal and true or willful and mischievous.
Thoughts of horses, cows, chickens, pigs, dogs
and more will bring a smile.

COVER: CLASSICSTOCK/ALAMY STOCK PHOTO
PREVIOUS SPREAD: A.M. WETTACH; THIS SPREAD, CHICKEN: TSEKHMISTER/
SHUTTERSTOCK; NEXT SPREAD, BARNWOOD: ROBERT_S/SHUTTERSTOCK

108   **CHAPTER 6**  Hard, Honest Work
Farm work is never really done. Here you'll find accounts of hard times that demonstrate the tenacity of early farmers. Included are impressive stories of the Great Depression and the Dust Bowl.

140   **CHAPTER 7**  A Love of the Country
Peruse the recollections of those who've lived in the country or on a farm, or just kept it with them in their hearts. One woman describes it as her father's fountain of youth.

158   **CHAPTER 8**  Pastoral Scrapbook
Take an armchair view back into the lives of farmers and other country folks in these pages full of photos from the past. Enjoy this walk down memory lane featuring a family with 15 children, 4-H club fun and more.

180   **CHAPTER 9**  Farm-to-Table
There is nothing quite like country cooking. Garden-fresh ingredients, comforting flavor and plenty of family fun were the specials of the day at these farm kitchens.

194   **CHAPTER 10**  Holiday Cheer
Sharing any holiday on the farm, be it Christmas or Halloween, was certainly a pleasure. Filled with special traditions, joy and laughter, these memories are sure to tug at your heartstrings.

© 2017 RDA Enthusiast Brands, LLC.
1610 N. 2nd St., Suite 102, Milwaukee, WI 53212-3906

International Standard Book Number: 978-1-61765-685-9
Library of Congress Control Number: 2017935149
Component Number: 117300054H

# LIVING A SIMPLER LIFE

Whether you live in or long for the country, you'll enjoy this delightful new book, *Reminisce: Life on the Farm*. This collection will have you waxing nostalgic for simpler times. The stories here are sure to warm your heart and get you talking about the good ol' days with family and friends. The book is a terrific keepsake to share with grandchildren and to hand down through generations.

Enjoy memories of what it was like to be a farm-raised kid, learning country values and traditions passed down by loving grandparents. Read about the importance of a good barn and a good tractor, how to correctly pick pole beans, and how to turn a snowstorm into an adventure.

You'll laugh at the sense of humor that comes with working long days on the farm, from stories of stubborn cows to catching pigs on the loose, and even accounts of outhouse mishaps. Romance blossoms in the country, too, and we included musings on country love, with all its follies.

But no one will tell you that life on a farm is easy. This book is a tribute to those who laid the groundwork before us to make a life on the land. You'll read first-hand accounts of farming during the Great Depression and the Dust Bowl. Through hard work and perseverance, farmers—young and old, past and present—have earned our respect.

Those who live in the country certainly have a strong connection to it. We're glad to share that sentiment with you in these memories, whether delightful recollections of farm food, or holiday fun. We also included a special scrapbook section full of photos of farm life.

We're happy to say that the wonderful stories in *Life on the Farm* come to you from *Reminisce, Country, Country Woman* and *Farm & Ranch Living* magazine contributors—those who truly know country life best. We'd like to thank our loyal readers for sharing their lives with us, and we hope you enjoy their incredible recollections.

Thanks for the memories!

The editors of *Reminisce* magazine

**CHAPTER 1**

# FAMILY VALUES
# & TRADITIONS

*Whether your relatives had farming in their blood or
you simply enjoy heartwarming stories of hardworking
homesteads, you'll love reading about these
farm families.*

# FARMING GRANDPARENTS
### They taught the true meaning of hard work

### FOUR-GENERATION FARMSTEAD

Grandpa Neal and his brother Bert moved from Iowa to northeastern South Dakota in 1902. Together they purchased a half-section of land for $9,000, which was quite a sum of money in those days. They built a simple building to live in that first year and started work on a proper home the following spring. They completed the new house by fall with help from neighbors.

The temporary first home became a granary to store the oats, wheat and flax that they grew. The brothers added a barn in 1903 with room for cows and their six horses. Two or three more outbuildings followed, and soon they had a full-grown farmstead.

The granary was the center of attention each harvest, when the brothers filled it with grain. They sold an occasional wagonload but stored most of the grain to feed their own livestock.

Within a few years, Grandpa and my great-uncle had each married, so they split up their partnership. Great-Uncle Bert and his new bride moved back to Iowa. My grandpa and grandma stayed on the farm, where they had five children. The oldest, my father, was born in 1906. Tragedy struck when Grandma died of tuberculosis at 35. The children lived with neighbors while the house was treated to remove all traces of the disease.

After Dad grew up, he ran the farm until he was drafted into the Army prior to World War II. He spent five years in the Army, then returned home to continue farming. By that time, the granary had been standing more than 40 years and was still used to store the harvests.

The granary was a source of entertainment for my cousins and me when we were growing up. We spent hours climbing across the tops of the grain bins on imagined adventures, fighting off bandits and wild animals. As I got older, I helped Dad on the farm while working at another job. After Dad died in 1973, I farmed for five more years. Then I sold out but stayed on the family farm. In 1979, I married a beautiful nurse, and we had four daughters.

We tore down the old house and built a new one to make room for our growing family. But the granary still stands. It's one of two buildings that remain from my grandpa's era. It has been repainted a few times, the roof leaks and there are holes in the sides. But for 114 years it has stood against the prairie sun, rain, windstorms and blizzards. It's been a home, granary, chicken house, storage shed and childhood playground. It holds many lifetimes of memories from four generations of our family, and we have our ancestors to thank.

**MALCOLM DIRKSEN**
**TWIN BROOKS, SD**

Neal and Bert Dirksen (right) built the granary in 1902 and lived in it until they finished their house.

Much like the hikers at right, Ralph and Diana walked through the snow on their way to Grandma's. Above: Grandma Mae's big smile.

## FULL BELLIES AND WARM MEMORIES

My brother, Ralph, and I were two very lucky kids in the early 1960s because our paternal grandparents, Matt and Mae Werven, lived a half-mile north of our farm in Svold, North Dakota. Though we could see their home through the trees, it seemed miles away to an 8- and a 9-year-old.

To get there we dressed warmly in hooded parkas, thick homemade mittens and four-buckle boots. Mom wrapped dish towels around our faces to protect us from the cold, sometimes so tightly that our flattened noses made us laugh at each other.

If we were fortunate, we'd find a path cut deeply through the snow by the cows. The scariest part of the journey was making our way past the small herd of cattle, dense steam coming from their nostrils and off their backs. They stared at us intently, further cementing the idea in our young minds that they would eat us in a heartbeat if we let our guard down.

Arriving at the old log house, we used the porch broom to sweep the snow from each other before entering. I remember being surrounded by the warmth of the Monarch cookstove, the smell of poplar wood smoke and the sound of cast-iron stove lids being lifted and set back down in their recesses. Grandma laid our wet mittens on the open oven door to dry.

Papa would be sitting in his big oak rocking chair. If we made too much noise during the Paul Harvey radio program, the old Norwegian would glare at us and say, "Shoosh!"

There was always a hot pot of coffee and sometimes a simmering kettle of soup bubbling away on the stove. On some days Grandma toasted thick slabs of homemade bread on the stovetop and slathered them with farm butter—the best toast ever.

Our special treat in Grandma's kitchen was our own cups of coffee at the much-used wooden table, made bright by a colorful flowered tablecloth. Oh, the aroma that wafted up from that sweet treasure! We sipped ever so elegantly, never noticing that it was mostly milk.

Sometimes the table centerpiece was a plate of oatmeal raisin cookies, perfect for dunking in coffee.

Grandma asked us about school, friends and family. She asked our opinions on matters that no one ever asked us about. She never criticized our comments or ideas, always nodding approval by closing her eyes and saying, "Umm-hmm." We felt so important because she was interested in our little stories.

Satisfied in body and soul, we were ready to trudge back home. Grandma wrapped us like mummies and sent us on our way, waving from the porch until we arrived at our doorstep with full bellies and warm memories.

**DIANA YEADO**
**WALHALLA, ND**

Now a man of 30, Adam hangs on to the orange shovel (left). Above, Adam, age 6, helps on the farm.

## SCOOP YOUR WAY TO HAPPINESS

I'm 30 years old—a man, on most days. But I was recently reminded that at certain moments, I'm still just a boy.

From the age of 4 until my first year of high school, I spent almost every day with my grandparents. My mother dropped me off at their farm in the morning and picked me up after work.

The hours in between were filled with lessons that I learned while helping Grandpa. He was a hard worker who taught me that anything worth doing was worth doing right. I shoveled pig manure, baled hay, picked rocks in the field—I wanted to do everything Grandpa did. He even bought me a little orange shovel that I wore down almost to a nub over the years.

After Grandpa retired, he and Grandma moved to town. Every morning he'd give me a ride to school. We listened to Big Red on AM 540 Fort Dodge, and I wouldn't get out of the car until I'd heard the joke for the morning. He still kept some cattle on the farm, so I baled hay during the summers. We sat at the dinner table listening to Paul Harvey or talking about what I was doing that day. Grandpa never missed the chance to tell me that he was going to start charging me for all the ketchup I was using.

Even when he could no longer do farm work, Grandpa still went to the farm every day. Often I found him sitting with his old equipment, watching the wind whip through the cornfields. He'd regale me with stories from when he was a kid. I loved listening to them.

If I had to describe Grandpa in one word, it would be stubborn. He did things his way and had no qualms about it. He was stubborn even in his passing, living a week longer than the nurses thought he would.

I had prepared myself for our last conversation, and when my sister put the phone to his ear I began to speak with the confidence of a 30-year-old man. But when I realized that I would never sit with him watching the cattle graze in the pasture, or hear him say, "Thanks for stopping, Big Boy. You come back again," I was a little boy again. I wanted to thank him for everything he'd taught me and for being such a good man, but all I could muster was "I love you, Grandpa."

At Christmas a few years ago, Grandpa had presented me with the same little orange shovel he'd given me all those years ago. Attached to it were three notes: "Manure builds character," "Scoop your way to happiness" and "Thanks!" I gave him a big hug and let him know how much that meant to me.

I can't wait to put that orange shovel to use again when I see him in that big farm in the sky.

**ADAM MEEKER**
**OGDEN, IA**

## WANT TO SEE WHERE MILK COMES FROM?

As a little boy in Southern California, I would often stare out the classroom window and dream about visiting my grandparents Bert and Rosella Daley. We were very close, and I loved them very much.

Plus, they lived on a little farm in Payson, Utah, with cows, pigs, chickens, dogs, cats and, best of all, horses. In those days, children dreamed of being cowboys. There was no *Star Wars*, and the closest thing to *Dancing with the Stars* was *The Lawrence Welk Show*. We watched Roy Rogers on television and John Wayne on the big screen. You knew who the good guys were, and their values were the same as yours.

It seemed that my grandparents were always just about to eat a meal when we arrived. This troubled me, because my grandmother was not a good cook, and I just wanted to get out there with the animals. Grandpa would say, "As soon as we're done eating, we need to milk the cow," which made me even more impatient.

Luckily, Grandma Rosella's Pomeranian, Penny, loved her cooking. I'm sure that dog gained a few pounds whenever we visited.

Milking the cow was an adventure. Grandpa would carry two tin pails in his big, strong hands—one for the milk and one to sit on. To get to the barn, we had to cross the creek and pass by the horse-drawn farm equipment graveyard and several old wooden outbuildings. It was exciting stuff for a kid.

Then Grandpa would yell, "Hey Betsy, hey Betsy, come along now," and Betsy would hear him no matter where she was on that 10-acre farm. The barn had two milking stations, a ton of hay and a bunch of wild stray cats. I say they were wild, but I think Grandma had a name for each of them, and she always sent saucers out with us so Grandpa could give them fresh milk.

Before the milking began, Grandpa would always look at us kids—Chris, Lilly, Randy and me—and say, "Do you want to know where the milk comes from?"

Now, my grandpa was a real kidder, and he loved to laugh. But we were onto him. We would reply, "Grandpa, you showed us last time!"

Somehow, though, he always convinced us that this time was going to be different. Then he would say, "Now, get real close." We'd edge closer. "No," he would insist, "you can't see from there." So we would move even closer.

And with the powerful squeeze and aim of a real professional, he would spray us all in the face with warm milk. Then he'd laugh until he could hardly sit on his bucket. The cats lined up by their saucers seemed to get a kick out of it as well.

Grandpa and Grandma were happy. They treated each other with respect, and they were true friends to their neighbors. We started each day by thanking the Lord for our bounteous blessings, and the lessons I learned from them are invaluable to me.

My grandparents and their little farm have been gone for a while now. But in my heart, I can still hear Grandpa saying, "Want to see where milk comes from?"

**ROBERT O'HARA
RIVERTON, UT**

Rosella and Bert Daley (above) were happy, Robert says. With Grandpa, farm chores seemed like adventures instead of work.

Gramps let Robert drive (right). Now Robert, with his first son (above), hopes to keep the tractor tradition going.

## FARMER IN TRAINING

The second Monday of October was fall break in our tiny Pennsylvania town. As a 10-year-old boy, I couldn't wait to swap out days in the classroom for the blue skies and golden leaves above a woodlot known as Berrisford's Woods.

Funny how waking up at 6:30 a.m. didn't seem to matter too much when I was sleeping over at my grandparents' house. After a hot breakfast, it was time to head to the garage with Gramps.

The Farmall Cub, Gramps' pride and joy, sat in the usual spot—where the car would have gone had it not been reduced to parking outside. After he inspected and fueled the saws, I remember my grandfather standing to the far side of the Cub to engage the choke at the carburetor. Following a quick wiggle of the gearshift, he fired the old tractor up.

Because the muffler had been removed some time before, the snap and crack of the four-cylinder engine got the blood flowing. It was my job to place the pin in the drawbar after Gramps backed up to the wood trailer. Then I'd hop in the trailer and away we went to Berrisford's Woods.

The winding path cut through grapevines and wild rose bushes, and periodically opened up to reveal fiery maple branches overhead. I watched the rear tires as they cut through the ruts that had been left by a log skidder a few years earlier. The Cub climbed in and out with little difficulty.

Once we were in an area that was relatively flat, it was my turn. Gramps would stop and set the brake so we could switch places. "First gear and easy on the clutch," he would say, and away we would go. Let me tell you: The purr of a working Farmall Cub is music to an appreciative ear.

Dividing the work, Gramps would cut and I would load. I remember hearing a grouse's drumming when the saw stopped for refueling, and I would watch for antler rubs from deer.

Near lunchtime, when we had our load, we'd drive out of the woods. My stomach would be growling for a ham and cheese sandwich and soup prepared with love by my Gran. After the noon news, we'd unload at the woodpile.

On a good day we could bring out three loads before the long shadows of late afternoon drew our work to a close. The Cub pulled the trailer to its spot, and I'd do my duty of pulling the pin and centering the trailer tongue on a block of wood.

Before dinner, Gramps and I shook the sawdust out of our cuffs so Gran's cleaning day wasn't a waste of time. Around 6 p.m., the headlights of my dad's 1974 Impala would shine into the driveway, signaling it was time to go home.

I would so enjoy just one more day with my grandparents. The farm is still in my family, and I've refurbished the Cub. My hope is that my young sons and I too will be able to spend a day together in Berrisford's Woods.

**ROBERT B. FOUST
STONEBORO, PA**

## A PECK OF PUMPKINS FOR SALE

From about 1955 until 1963, my grandfather L.C. Smith had a plot of land outside Kaukauna, Wisconsin, where he grew apple and pear trees, raspberries, currants, carrots, cucumbers and pumpkins. My family—Mom and Dad (Jack and Carol Forster), my sisters Marilyn, Susan and Jackie, and I—would go out to his field and help him weed and pick produce. But of course tasting was what we liked best.

My Grandmother Helen did a lot of canning, as well as making jams and jellies. Any extra produce we picked would go to neighbors and friends from church. Grandma's basement pantry was always well-stocked. I remember heading to the pantry to get a jar of whatever she decided would go well with the day's meal.

In the fall of 1961, Grandpa told us we could pick as many pumpkins as we wanted and take them home to sell at our house in Appleton, Wisconsin. Mom and Dad helped us set up a stand at the end of the driveway, and we made signs for different sizes and pricing.

I don't remember how many pumpkins we sold or how much money we made, but we sure had a lot of fun. The local newspaper, the *Appleton Post-Crescent*, even sent a photographer to take our picture. Some of our neighborhood friends came over to see what was going on, and they happily joined the photo. We were really excited to see ourselves in the paper.

KATHY ZIVICKI
OAK CREEK, WI

Selling pumpkins attracted the neighbors while the Forster girls learned lessons in entrepreneurship. From left: Marilyn Forster, Terri Brewster, David Hoffman, Lynn Wenzel, Susan Forster, Susan Adams, Kathy Forster and Jackie Forster.

Cindy, Megan, Margaret—known as Bobo—and Greta are four generations of crafters. Bobo and her sister Jean (below) tend to lambs on their farm in 1936.

## STITCHED WITH LOVE

These days, everyone is getting on board with upcycling, or creating something unique from existing materials rather than buying more. My granny Margaret Shervey—affectionately called Bobo—has spent 92 years doing just that out of necessity.

Wasting time and resources was never an option in the world she grew up in. By the time her husband returned from the coal mine, she had bottle-fed the lambs—with seven children under 10 at her apron strings. She had picked filberts at the nearest farm, earning a little more money for her family. Her dinner rolls had been set to rise first thing that morning, and her potatoes soaked all day to make a supper side dish and a treat of lefse for later. As the roast finished in the oven, she scrubbed the floors on her hands and knees, using a rag made from the shirt Grandpa wore out the year before.

Bobo has been upcycling since the day Great-Granny Annie put a needle in her hand and taught her how to give new life to every fabric in their Minnesota farmhouse. Granny didn't salvage grain sacks and work pants to craft. She did it to survive. There was always a job for a scrap, even when there wasn't a scrap to be had.

Just like Bobo, my mother, Cindy Curry, grew up making her clothes. She planned her homecoming dress and bought the fabric with money she earned working at a cannery. One generation passed on to the next the art of creating something beautiful and useful by hand.

Granny's and Mom's sewing skills meant that no matter the budget, Christmas, birthday and wedding gifts were possible. From a baby blanket hand-appliqued by Bobo to a bib sewn by Mom, each treasure carries a special touch of personalization.

In my home I am surrounded by upcycling at its best. Quilts, wall hangings, stockings and more are cherished family keepsakes. My son Wilhelm is 2 and about to welcome a little brother into his room, which is filled with Bobo's pillows.

Bobo made many woodland pillows (above) for her great-grandson. Cindy and Megan (right) also sell handmade wares at local craft sales.

Moose, bear, fish, deer, plaids and evergreen trees are perfect for a little Paul Bunyan. Someday he and his sibling will use her creations as the walls of forts, mighty shields and weapons for pillow fights.

Coupons and conveniences have made the budget a little less stingy, so Mom and Bobo have turned their sewing skills into a hobby. They scour garage sales and thrift stores for Pendleton blankets and shirts that open a million possibilities to their artistic eyes.

You won't find their creations online or in a megastore, only at craft sales found by chance down a country road. With totes full of gifts and necessities for kitchen, couch and baby, they offer their wares to those seeking homemade goods.

Thanks to Bobo's old-fashioned ways, the artistry of handwork lives on in four generations of crafters. Granny Bobo lived it. Mom carried it on. I am picking it up by listening and observing. Now my daughter Greta is also learning to use those skills.

I sit and watch closely as Bobo's hands weave needle and thread. In 92 years, her hands have known and cherished life, home and family.

Age has brought the loss of some memories, and her stitching is not as tight as it used to be. But if you listen to her stories while she sews, stories she knows by heart, you'll journey back to the old farm with her. And you'll understand that the wobblier the stitch, the finer the work of art.

**MEGAN GRAMZOW
SPRINGFIELD, OR**

## TWO GRANDMOTHERS

Eleanor Joyce was not related to us, but she and my grandmother Esther Solseng were as close as sisters for 57 years. Eleanor was born in 1919 on her parents' farm in Thief River Falls, where she lived for 94 years. She loved everything about her homestead and even fell in love with and married her father's hired hand, George Joyce. The couple stayed there for decades, raising chickens, cattle and grain.

Eleanor and Esther became fast friends as soon as my grandparents moved nearby. They were almost inseparable, but even more so after they both became widows. It was rare when they weren't together, especially in the kitchen. They loved to cook and bake side by side. One of my favorite memories is watching them make lefse. There was no recipe, just teamwork.

My grandmas were always there with advice and even hands-on help. When I wanted to impress my husband by making his family recipe for the Norwegian cookie called *fattigman*, Eleanor and my grandmother, both in their 80s, came to the rescue. We spent a fun-filled day rolling out and frying the cookies in lard—and sampling them, too!

My grandmother never drove, but Eleanor did, so when they weren't in the kitchen, they would hop into Eleanor's Rambler and drive all over the countryside looking for wildlife to watch or seeking a nice dress shop or a lunch café. After my grandmother turned 70, she and Eleanor took their first plane trip, to Arizona, and they both caught the travel bug. They visited Arizona several times, took an Alaskan cruise and even traveled to Germany to see my Uncle Harold.

In 2000, my grandmother passed away at age 90, and Eleanor was heartbroken. She had always worried about who'd take care of her in her old age, since she had no children. She didn't need to worry. Neighbors and close friends were there to help, especially my dad and mom. Everyone who was connected to Eleanor swooped in, taking her shopping and to doctor appointments, and helping her with home repairs and finances.

Eleanor lived life to its fullest right up to her death. She spent her last weekend celebrating Mother's Day with my family, lavishing us with attention and an enormous feast, which she called "a little lunch." We always left her side with full hearts and warm hugs.

**MICHELLE BENTON**
**THIEF RIVER FALLS, MN**

Eleanor shared her kindness with all around her, including her dog, Pal (top), in the 1960s. When Eleanor was a young farmer (middle), she bonded with Michelle's family. Life was a party when best friends Esther and Eleanor were together (right). Through the years, Eleanor stayed close to Michelle and her sister (left).

## TIN LIZZIE WORKHORSES

My favorite photograph from our family album shows my grandfather Arley Smith with his twin brother, Farley, proudly standing next to their Model T's (above). Like the brothers, the cars are virtually identical. The one-digit difference on the 1925 Indiana license plates is the only way to tell the vehicles apart.

Arley and Farley worked sunup to sundown on their family farm in central Indiana. Like my ancestors, Henry Ford had a understanding of rural life challenges. His mission was to make an inexpensive and dependable workhorse for all Americans; the Model T fit the bill.

The Smith boys look pretty dapper in their straw hats and Sunday suits. I can imagine my grandfather and great-uncle wiping the dust from the black lacquered fenders and giving the brass a shine, too. In the sunlight, these Tin Lizzies must have looked pretty elegant.

**DAVID LADD**
**CICERO, IN**

## GRANDMA'S APRON

The other day, I found my old apron, which brought to mind my grandma's apron. I don't think my kids really know what an apron is. The principal use of Grandma's was to protect her clothes. But it did so much more.

It was wonderful for drying tears and wiping a perspiring brow caused by the hot woodstove. It carried eggs or fussy chicks from the coop, as well as vegetables from the garden. It hauled out hulls after the peas had been shelled. When unexpected company drove up the lane, that old apron could dust a surprising amount of furniture before Grandma answered the door. And when visitors came in, the apron was an ideal place for a shy child to hide.

At harvesttime, Grandma and her apron worked hard to feed the hungry men. When dinner was ready, she walked onto the porch and waved it, and the men knew it was time to come in. Nothing will replace the old-time apron. And nothing will replace my memories of Grandma's apron.

**LORETTA M. ORENDER**
**PLAINVILLE, IN**

## NOSTALGIA

### SPARE HANDS

"I've always enjoyed this photo of my father, J.D., holding his little sister Carol in the family cucumber patch near McAlester, Oklahoma, during the summer of 1949," says Ken LaRue of Tustin, California. "Dad and his five siblings all helped pick cucumbers for my grandfather to sell."

### A HORSE MADE OF HEIRLOOMS

"My father, James, my sister Amber and I created this piece of art in memory of my grandfather Gene Gibson, who passed away in 2014," writes Jade Lovvorn of Ranburne, Alabama. "We built it using old farm tools and equipment from my grandparents', great-grandparents' and great-great-grandparents' farms. While working on the horse, we reminisced about our family and wondered about the uses of the tools. With that in mind, we named it *Reminisce*. We're proud to have used pieces of our family's heritage to create a monument we can treasure."

In the 1930s, Elizabeth's great-grandmother Virginia Anderson Brodbeck lived in Cromwell Township, Pennsylvania. One of Virginia's great-grandsons has her egg basket in his home.

## GREAT-GRANDMOTHER RAN THE SHOW

It is dark on this late-November morning. Excited about the day's events, I snuggle under soft quilts. I hear the murmuring voices of my parents and grandmother.

Mother is quite firm: "I do not want her out there now."

Grandma gives the hoped-for answer: "I'll take her with me."

From my bedroom window, I see Daddy's flashlight beam bobbing through the yard and out the lane. He is going to Great-Grandmother Brodbeck's farm to work on butchering day. The Saturday before or after Thanksgiving is the traditional date for butchering at the Brodbeck farm.

After breakfast, I'm bundled in long, warm stockings, sturdy boots, a warm coat and a bonnet like Grandma wears. We are ready for our walk out the lane. As Grandma Hancock and I approach the barnyard, we hear conversations and chuckles from familiar voices: "Morning, Lizzie; see you brung your little helper."

"Mornin', Lizzie; sleepin' in on Saddidy?"

"Hey there, lil' Lizbeth; you gonna stir the pots today?"

My great-grandmother Virginia Brodbeck stands on her kitchen porch. She and her husband, William, moved to this farm in 1880, when she was 20 years old. She wears her usual dark, long-sleeved, high-necked dress and deep-brimmed bonnet. Age has robbed her of strength but not astuteness. "Raymond, you git that fer higher. Wilson, that the wrong bucket. Gale, you git Pap's knives." Two younger generations are doing the work, but there is no doubt who is the general of this campaign.

I am forbidden to be around the butchering. Hovering in the doorway, I see the men working with glistening, sharp knives. I'm surprised and proud of Daddy when I realize the others defer to him when the most skillful knife work is needed.

During the day, I also learn to say "damn" and "Gol darn" and "sum-of-a-bitch." Mother would not be pleased.

In the packed dirt area outside the barn, fires are built. Huge black kettles hang over fires, cooking "puddin' meat" and "pon-haus," which is local dialect for scrapple. A mixture of meat, "leavin's," cornmeal and special black pepper is cooked and stirred for hours. When I am first allowed to turn the long wooden handle that controls the kettle's paddles, I feel like a grown-up. Grandma Hancock stands behind me, one hand on my shoulder, the other over mine on the stirring rod.

**ELIZABETH ROBINSON**
**SAN MARCOS, CA**

## THE HEART OF THE FARM

In 1875, my great-great-grandfather Christian and his brothers hauled Lake Erie stone up the bank by horse and sledge to lay the foundation of our family barn. Cattle, work horses, goats and pigs were raised to supplement income from the vineyards on their 200-acre farm.

Seven generations later, my brother John still farms the land with his son Andy, and they use the barn for tools, tractors and storage. Andy's son Dawson is the seventh-generation Ziesenheim to farm the same land.

Growing up, my brothers and I didn't have a playground or park, but we had the barn. And, oh, what fun we had! Grandpa Joe slung a Tarzan rope over a rafter in a 20-foot hayloft designed to hold a thousand bales of hay. We whooped and hollered as we swung in wide arcs, daring one another to go higher and faster, before dropping into piles of soft hay. Out of those bales, we built villages—complete with homes, churches and stores—that even made Uncle Cal the engineer proud.

The pure pleasure of exploring the maze of bins, chutes, hidden compartments, wall ladders, lofts and trapdoors kept us small kids busy for hours on end. The chute that slid our corn from the corncrib to the pigsty was our worn-smooth sliding board. On a good day, we stopped short of the pigs on our rapid descent and landed headfirst by the toolbox instead.

My father, John, installed basketball hoops at either end of the first-floor tractor bay. We still laugh about the neighborhood playoff series we held one rainy day at the urging of our mother, Kathy, who supplied us with makeshift uniforms: dungarees, T-shirts and white Keds.

That old barn inspired us to create imaginative, inventive fun that still, 55 years later, resonates as the best of childhood memories.

**TRILL DREISTADT**
**GIRARD, PA**

Andy, Dawson, John and Great-Grandma Kathy represent four generations on this Pennsylvania farm.

# THE GREAT AMERICAN BARN

## The center of building a life on the land

### BUILT TO LAST...AND LAST

My husband, Jim, and I live on his grandparents' farm. Grandpa George Sr. and Grandma Jennie moved here from Iowa with 11 children in 1928 and had one more child here. Jim's dad, Ole, was the second-oldest son.

After helping to build a brick library in a nearby town, Grandpa decided to replace the farm's original barn with a new brick one. He designed it himself and built it with the help of his five sons and a few friends. They used field rock picked from the farm to build a foundation, and then they poured a concrete floor over that. They mixed their own mortar and laid brick walls 9 feet high. The barn is 33 by 56 feet, so it took a lot of bricks and hard work.

The gable ends of the hayloft are made of wood; one end has a large door for loading hay into the loft. Each end also has a smaller door to pitch the hay out. Grandpa topped off the roof with a big cupola holding up a weather vane with a glass ball and cow on it. Inside, the barn has stanchions for 12 milk cows, a calf pen, a bull pen and a calving pen. All the pens were made of steel pipe set in the concrete floor. Grandpa built a very solid barn.

We put on a new green metal roof 13 years ago—and that's the only thing we've had to replace in 68 years. The milk cows are long gone, but we still use the barn for beef cattle. We usually keep about 10 cows, and we put the calves in the calf pen after they're weaned.

We feed out the yearlings on the side of the barn where the stanchions used to be. Grandpa's steel pipes are still solidly sunk into the concrete floor, so the yearlings eat hay through the old stanchion pipes as if they were a hay feeder.

The barn has served its family well, and in many ways. There was never a dull moment with 12 brothers and sisters feeding and milking together. As kids have for five generations now, they built forts in the haymow, played with kittens and swung on the big rope that opened and closed the haymow door. They were pirates, cowboys and circus performers, as well as young farmers.

Grandpa's barn has been a place for good times, a place to learn and a place for kids to grow up into hardworking, efficient, dependable adults. We feel very honored and fortunate to live here.

**LUELLA LUPKES**
**WHEATON, MN**

Grandpa Lupkes (above) laid the barn's brick walls with the help of his five sons and a few friends.

## RESTORING THE FAMILY BARN

Our farm had a large two-story log barn when my grandparents moved to it around 1922. Grandpa farmed with workhorses and had to clear several acres. Because of tight finances, they sold milk and eggs to pay interest on the mortgage. My dad could not afford to attend college, so he stayed home and helped farm the land.

We have a copy of a newspaper article from 1936 showing Grandpa and Dad dismantling the old log barn, which dated back to 1850 or earlier. They probably burned all those walnut, cherry and poplar logs! That same year, Grandpa built an impressive barn. It had special stalls for workhorses, a modern concrete area with stanchions for milk cows, two large mows for hay, and upper storage rooms for oats and wheat.

After my dad inherited the farm, he had the family name, Ammerman, spelled out on the roof when it needed reshingling. Years later, after his death, my mother thought it was too ostentatious and expensive to keep, but we were saddened to see the name go.

Ten years ago, my brother and I inherited the farm. Time had taken its toll on the barn. An Amish builder repaired or replaced the windows and rebuilt the Dutch doors on the horse stalls, reusing the original latches and hardware. Last year we had the barn painted, reproducing the original green trim and name on the barn: Ammerman Cold Water Stock Farm.

When the barn needed a new roof, we contacted the company that had originally put the Ammerman roof on. It still had the pattern, and the name went back on. Now the barn looks great once again.

In later years my grandfather removed the stanchions and raised Hereford feeder calves. Today my great-niece, her husband and their little boys raise goats in the barn, and make and sell goat's milk soaps. I've often wondered what Dad and Grandpa would say if they knew their barn now housed goats.

My grandmother instilled a love of irises in me. For several years I've been developing large iris beds beside the former milk house in the front yard of the old homesite as a memorial to her. It is my prayer to be a good steward of the farm.

**BOB AMMERMAN**
**NEW ALBANY, IN**

The barn proudly shows its family ties.

One of two large haymows awaits the new hay crop.

The barn dates to the early 1800s. It's in the background (left) as Laura's Great-Aunt Marolyn and Grandma Geneva show off one of their horses.

## IF ONLY THIS BARN COULD TALK

The old barn draws my eye each time I walk out to my Great-Aunt Marolyn's shed. My family has gathered to stack green wood to dry for the coming winter. While the others finish clearing out the shed to make room for more wood, Cousin Hannah and I stroll through the open barn door. Her children Annie and Matthew are swinging from a rope tied high on a rafter. Oh, the fun, the excitement and the mystery the old structure seems to embody.

My mother and her siblings used to spend summers here on the family farm in Raymond, Maine, when they were growing up. They worked hard helping Aunt Marolyn and their grandmother with weeding, berry picking and drawing water from the hand pump. When they weren't doing chores, they dreamed, talked, read and played.

The old barn was a place of intrigue, and they explored every inch—from the mysterious and scary hole in the back corner to the two huge haymows, the left one higher than the right.

This old barn has seen many changes over the years. Uncle Rich notes that some timbers used for its beams and posts show signs of having been repurposed. They contain joinery notches and holes that now have no apparent function.

The barn was likely built when the house was erected, around 1823. The War of 1812 had been won less than a decade before, and the Civil War was over 30 years in the future. Hurricanes in the 1930s and '50s damaged it significantly, and it's now only a third of its original footprint—but it's still impressive nonetheless.

I hope my children can someday have the fun of growing up with the old barn, too.

**LAURA PRICE
BELMONT, NH**

## A PLACE FOR WORK AND PLAY

Our family's farm, Forest Oaks (right), was built in 1866, just after the Civil War ended. Four generations of McConnells have farmed the land in Washington County, Virginia.

The barn was built in the era of oxen, mule and horse power. In 1920, a self-supporting roof was put on so more loose hay could be stored. Soon after, a rope and pulley system was installed in the top of the barn to pull hay from wagons. Now our grandchildren enjoy swinging on the rope and falling onto the hay bales.

Through the years, our family has enlarged the barn—built dairy stalls to milk Guernsey cows, a silo to store silage, and stables for the baby calves, horses, sheep and hogs. Our family also added two granaries. In early years, grain was threshed there. A lot of burley tobacco has hung in this barn, too.

So much hard work and sweat has gone into our barn, but we've had good times too—like finding baby kittens to play with, searching for hen eggs in the hay, bottle-feeding cute calves and lambs, and playing hide-and-seek. We love seeing the barn swallows come back in early spring to their mud nests in and around the rafters. A barn is the hallowed heart of a farm, and we are blessed to have this one.

**TOM AND EDNA MCCONNELL**
**ABINGDON, VA**

Four generations have expanded the barn to its current state. Young Tom McConnell poses with his family in 1944 (bottom) as the team of horses pulls a wagonload of loose hay to the barn.

## DAD'S HANDMADE BARN

Our barn is not huge, but its smaller size fits its humble beginnings. When my mama and daddy moved to what is now our Poverty Ridge Farm in East Texas in 1947, they were two poor kids. Daddy was just back from the war and Mama was a sharecropper's daughter.

The first few years, they grew cotton, corn and tomatoes. By 1950, Dad decided they needed a real barn. A portable sawmill was being dismantled down the road, so he stopped to ask what they would take for the wood. One guy said, "$50." Dad said, "I'll give you $25." Sold! Dad doodled the wood home a little at a time on an old single-axle trailer he had made.

Amid farming, doing odd jobs and attending school on the GI Bill, Dad steadily built our barn by hand, all by himself.

The lumber was so hard that neighbors from miles away said they heard Dad pounding those 16-penny nails. He hand cut and nailed every board, none of it uniform, but he made it all fit together. Dad said, "You didn't waste a nail. If it got bent, you straightened it out and used it."

For the foundation, Dad dug down 4 feet and poured slabs for his main forms to sit on. He made his concrete mix using gravel he hauled from our creek over a quarter of a mile away.

Using cast-off wooden nail kegs, he made the foundation forms for the main beams to rest on. It's been 65 years and the barn hasn't settled an inch. You can still see the ridges and metal rings of the nail kegs. The barn has withstood tornadoes, winters, five kids, nine grandkids and 13 great-grandkids. It's held corn, hay, lumber, cow medicine, calves, possums and a few skunks.

In the 1980s Dad gave the barn a face-lift with new siding over the boards and added loft doors.

Our barn is a testament to Dad's thriftiness and ingenuity, and an enduring legacy of the fruits of hard work, perseverance and love for his family.

Dad is 92 and Mom is 88. He still runs the farm, now with my brother Shaun's help, just as he's done for the past 68 years.

**TAMRA BOLTON**
**JACKSONVILLE, TX**

# LIFE LESSONS

## What better way to learn about life than living on the farm

### HEART OF A HOME

A house can be a house or a house can be a home. A house is made of wood, brick or stone; a home is made of memories and love. Aunt Lizzie and Uncle Hike worked every day to make their house a home.

I spent lots of time at that home in Polk County, Missouri. On weekends I traveled there from Arkansas along with my mother and sisters. And my cousin Lee brought his family from Kansas City.

Aunt Lizzie was mom, grandma, great-grandma, great-aunt and aunt to many. Hers was the place to go for Easter, the Fourth of July, Memorial Day or any ordinary day. No need for notice to drop in.

The house was 6 miles off the highway on a dirt road and up a rocky driveway. Water came from a well just a few feet from the back door. We used an outhouse instead of a bathroom, and the ill-tempered rooster attacked anyone walking to the "facility." I had to run so fast in order to protect my legs from his painful pecks! I don't know why he didn't just stay in the coop keeping the hens happy.

Then there was the cow that Uncle Hike patiently tried to teach me to milk. I was lacking either the strength or the technique, but Uncle Hike managed to fill the bucket every morning and every night. He delivered it to Aunt Lizzie, who knew how to get the most out of it. We had fresh cream for coffee, and she taught me to churn butter. Sometimes we drank buttermilk, and in the summer we made ice cream from scratch.

Each year, Uncle Hike hid his watermelon patch to keep ornery teenagers from vandalizing it. "You know, I wouldn't care if they just took a watermelon and ate it," he said. But they made a game of finding the patch and destroying every melon.

I tagged along on strolls of the property

Clockwise from above left: Debra's dad and sister play cards on Christmas; Lizzie and Hike at the house; Lizzie and her sisters.

to search for arrowheads. Occasionally we found one, but I suspect Uncle Hike already had rounded up most of them, judging from the number of arrowheads he had mounted in frames.

When we returned, I helped Aunt Lizzie fix lunch, and then she showed me how to make a peach or apple pie from scratch. But my favorite thing to do with her was to get up early and help her fix breakfast—biscuits, gravy, eggs, pancakes, sausage, bacon—for everyone who'd stayed overnight. She did most of the fixing, and I set the table. Aunt Lizzie always put together a delicious spread.

A brisk breeze blew in from the bedroom and made up for the lack of air conditioning. After dark I could hear June bugs slam against the screen, crickets chirp and other critters making sounds that I could never identify. And, of course, in the morning we awakened to the crow of that aggressive rooster and the elegant singing of the birds. Uncle Hike taught me to listen to one in particular as it whistled *wet year, wet year,* announcing that it would rain that day.

Please don't think we were ever uncomfortable for the lack of a few modern conveniences. Aunt Lizzie decorated beautifully. She kept her home spotless. Lovely flowers were abundant in the yard close to the house. Aunt Lizzie was the epitome of the noble wife in Proverbs 31. She and Uncle Hike put so much life and love in that home.

**DEBRA IRENE**
**KANSAS CITY, MO**

## COUNTRY SUMMER SCHOOL

When I was a little girl, my extended family in Dahlonega, Georgia, invited me to visit. Dropped off by my dad and stepmom, I soon discovered that seven days in that sanctuary wasn't going to be nearly enough. Thus began my summer tradition of calling home and begging, "Can I stay just one more week?"

I spent the time in the company of my maternal grandparents, Garland and Birdie Calhoun; their son and daughter-in-law, Ray and Ellie; and Ray and Ellie's children, Carolyn and Don. My cousins and I walked countless times up and down the dirt road between Granny and Pop's house and Uncle Ray and Aunt Ellie's.

I only wish I could see their faces once more and recapture the joy I felt when I was with them.

Growing up in suburban Atlanta, I knew nothing about country life. By the time I was headed home, however, I had soaked up the beauty of the countryside and the loving, positive influence of my mother's family.

As I witnessed three generations living within walking distance of each other, working alongside each other and praying in the same little church, my life was transformed. My relatives never instructed me with pencil and paper. They simply lived a "do unto others" philosophy every day.

At home, I thought that food came from grocery stores and restaurants. In the country I learned that farm families eat what they grow and that eating beans and corn one day and corn and beans the next tasted awfully good when you were enjoying them in an atmosphere of love and laughter.

I came to understand that husbands and wives or parents and children could have differing opinions and still get along, and that a sense of humor would put out most

Judy poses with her cousin Don. Visiting the farm was the highlight of her summer, particularly playtime with cousins. She learned country values and the rewards of hard work.

fires. If forgiveness was called for, it was freely extended and graciously accepted.

All of us worked hard, from gathering eggs to snapping beans. But we played hard as well. Swimming, riding horses and learning to drive the old truck were all part of a typical week. And on weekends, Carolyn would take me along on her dates. I'm not certain how her boyfriend felt about that arrangement, but it was the treat of a lifetime for me.

I'm still a creature of the suburbs, but when I get a chance to travel along a dirt road, I take it. I can almost see my granny look up from her gardening and wave in greeting.

If I'm ever fortunate enough to be awakened by a rooster crowing, I'm in Carolyn's room once again, listening to the muted conversation and laughter of Uncle Ray and Aunt Ellie as they prepare breakfast. I don't even mind rounding a bend in the road and catching the pungent aroma of somebody's chicken house. It smells like pure happiness to me.

**JUDY FOSTER**
**MARIETTA, GA**

The Zonver family (below), was happy to be sitting at the table together in their warm sanctuary, pictured at left in 1978.

## YES, CHICKENS EAT GRAVEL!

My father taught me the meaning of having someone pull your leg. Dad told me that the way to catch a bird was to sneak up on it and put salt on its tail. So my cousins and I spent hours trying to catch blue jays and chickadees, to no avail. Much later, I realized there was no magic in this trick: If you were close enough to a bird to salt it, you were close enough to grab it!

My dad also advised us kids about fishing: "If it's winter, and you're going ice fishing," he said, "always hold the worms in your mouth for a few minutes to warm them up. Fish don't like cold food." I can't imagine what Mom would have done if we had!

So I was skeptical when he asked me to get a pan of gravel for the chickens to eat. Huh? I had seen chickens eat corn and grain, but I had never seen them eat gravel! But my mom was holding out an old metal pie plate, so I went out to the edge of our dirt road, filled the pan with gravel, and put it in the coop.

To my surprise, the chickens were thrilled! They hopped and pushed one another out of the way, unable to get enough of the gravel bits. My dad explained this as it had been explained to him as a child: "Chickens don't have stomachs full of digestive juices like we do. They have gullets. They need gravel to rub against the corn or grain to break it down and get nutrition from the food."

**CHERYL LAWRENCE**
**SPRINGFIELD, VT**

## BELOVED ILLINOIS HOMESTEAD

Nestled in the hills of northwestern Illinois stands a large 100-year-old white framed house with black shutters and small-paned glass windows. We bought this farmhouse and 2 acres in Elizabeth, Illinois, in 1975.

The tall cedar trees shield the front of the house from cold winter winds. A welcome mat greets anyone who knocks on the shiny walnut-stained front door—the same door my husband and I installed side by side.

Inside, the laughter of children fills the living room, while adults sip hot rum by the hearth, feeling the warmth and serenity brought by a crackling wood fire.

Spring yields a budding of giant oak trees in the yard, where peonies grow along the fence every other year—the same fence we built and painted white, the perfect frame for our life.

Reminiscing on the past, I look to the season when I can go back and capture all that was shared in the place I call Our Home.

**JUDY WALTERS ZONVER**
**ALBANY, GA**

## POUNDS OF WISDOM

Because of several heart attacks, my father could no longer work a regular job. To make ends meet, he and I picked pole beans every summer on farms in Oregon's Willamette Valley. It was hot, hard work, and they paid by the pound, not the hour. I don't remember exactly how much, but it was only pennies.

Like most things, pole beans have a season. The vines wind higher and higher as the season progresses. The blossoms and beans begin to sprout near the bottom at first and gradually work their way up the vine.

Bottom beans are harder to pick. It is literally stoop labor. So, of course, I had a youthful inclination to pick at shoulder height. My father and I always picked on opposite sides of the same row, and his constant, gentle reminders to "pick from the bottom up" still ring in my ears. There was a workman's wisdom in those words. The day goes easier when you get the hard tasks out of the way first.

We had row bosses who would part the vines and step into your world unannounced. They would inspect the area you had picked, and if it wasn't picked clean, they sent you back. When you pick for pennies per pound, you want to pick where the beans are thick, not spend your time retracing your steps.

At first, I got sent back a lot. When that happened, my father would step through the vines and pick back toward me until we had cleaned up my mess.

The vines were so thick that we couldn't see each other, but we always talked back and forth while we worked. His voice would come through the vines, as in a confessional: "Are you picking clean?"

He taught me that anything worth doing—jobs, hobbies, relationships—should be picked clean.

The rows were 7 feet high and only 4 feet apart. No breeze could penetrate those dense green walls. Irrigation kept the ground muddy and the air muggy. Sometimes it was hard to maintain my enthusiasm. As it waned, I'd fall behind, and I'd hear Dad say: "Are you picking with both hands?"

How did he know? He couldn't see through the vines, but he always knew! I'm right-handed, and when I dawdled, only my right hand was picking. No scolding. No sharp words. Just the quiet question.

In the years since, there have been tasks that seemed too large, deadlines that seemed impossible, challenges that seemed more than I could possibly meet. It's then that I still hear him: "Are you picking with both hands?"

The money we earned in the bean fields was barely enough to be worthwhile. But the lessons I learned—pick clean, bottom up, both hands—were principles of my father's life that shaped mine. He taught me the right things, and he taught them well. They have been enough for what life has sent my way.

**R.L. BUTZ**
**LEESBURG, FL**

R.L.'s dad takes a dog-petting break circa 1956.

## FARM ALARM CLOCK

In 1939 my great-great-uncle bought one of the first Ford 9N tractors. It was the first tractor my grandpa was allowed to drive by himself.

Eventually, Grandpa bought the Ford from his uncle, and he farmed with it for over 40 years. His sons—including my dad—also learned to drive on the Ford. My sisters and I learned to drive on it, and my nephew learned to run it last summer while helping us pick up rocks.

The Ford raked thousands of acres of hay over those 40-plus years. It also ran the elevator to put those bales into the barn and pulled the fence-building wagon, the rock wagon and parade floats. It even pulled a few stubborn 4-H calves that did not want to learn to lead. (No animals or 4-H'ers were injured in the writing of this story.) On nice mornings when the windows were open, we would awaken to the putt-putt of the 9N accompanied by Grandpa belting out "Buffalo Gals." What an alarm clock!

In time, Grandpa decided that he had too many tractors and sold the 9N. But it almost broke his heart, I think. A few years later, Grandpa and I went to an auction, and there sat his Ford. We got so excited that we forgot all about the machinery we'd gone to bid on, and Grandpa's 9N came home with us.

From left: Tom Cook, Bryan Cook and Duncan Schott

With the exception of those few years, the Ford has been in our family for 75 years. Five generations of Cooks have worked the land with this great tractor. When summer rolls around, the Ford will continue to rake hay, pick up rocks, mend fences and probably pull a parade float or two. And I imagine many more generations of the Cook family will learn to drive on this wonderful and durable old tractor.

**BRYAN COOK**
**INDEPENDENCE, IA**

### ◀ THE FAMILY BAND

"We went by the name the Red Hats, and starting in 1949, we were on the air live for six years," says Jeanette Goebel of Stryker, Ohio. "Farm folks listened to the Red Hats show as they milked their cows, got their kids off to school or did other morning chores. Mom always said the years she played with us were the best ones of her life." The Ohio quartet consisted of (from left) mom Florence and her daughters Donna, Rosella and Jeanette.

**MULE-DRAWN SLED** "You don't see tobacco sleds like this around anymore," writes Barbara Hudson of Cape Coral, Florida. "This picture of (from left) my Aunt Burma, sister Vicki, me and Uncle Farrell is from 1955. The mule, Nellie, pulled our plow and tobacco sled, which was made from wood and burlap bags. I was 5 years old that summer, getting paid 15 cents an hour to work in the fields with the rest of the family."

**CHAPTER 2**

# FARM-RAISED KIDS

*Growing up on a farm gives a child an education like no other. From raising animals and growing crops to making ends meet and tinkering with tractors, these kids have a lot of respect for the country way of life—and some funny stories to boot!*

# RECOLLECTIONS OF YOUTH

## The good ol' days on the farm spark vivid memories

### THANK GOD FOR COUNTRY LIFE

Sitting in my grandparents' yard in the middle of August, I gain a new appreciation for the joy of growing up in the country.

As my grandma and I watch the clouds cruise by, she seems to be looking past them and back into her childhood. "It reminds me of a summer day out in the hay field when I was a little girl," she says. I smile and think what a blessing it is to enjoy the same pleasures she experienced nearly 80 years earlier.

Whether it's the sound of rain falling on the roof on a cold winter night or the smell of Mother's cooking drifting through the valley as my sister Maggie and I do evening chores, my memories of growing up in the country will last a lifetime. Though these things seem commonplace, I am beginning to realize that the little moments truly matter the most.

My parents run a small family farm on our grandparents' 5 acres. Maggie and I have been involved in 4-H, showing dairy cows and pygmy goats, since I was 8 and she was 6. We are country girls through and through and have spent countless hours playing in the dirt, making paths through tall grass, cuddling with barn kittens and lying in the pasture with one of our sweet Jersey calves.

Caring for our animals and doing other chores have taught me the value of hard work. There is no better way to start your morning than milking a cow and then coming inside for a home-cooked breakfast.

Being raised with strong family values, I learned that you may not always get what you want and must live without things you might like to have. Instead of watching movies and playing video games, I found things to do outdoors that were always more rewarding.

I am now 19 and off to college, but fortunately school is close enough so I can get back to the country on weekends. I realize how much I miss the simplicity every time I come home. Mother will have a big dinner cooking; Maggie and Dad will be telling me about how much the grass has grown, what pasture the cows are turned out on and how much milk Mabel is producing. I soak it all in and enjoy our family's way of being entertained by the littlest happenings and mishaps.

"And I would love to watch Daddy work," Grandma continues. "He always whistled when he worked, you know." Then I hear my sister calling me, saying it's time to do chores and go in for dinner.

I check on Jack, my big steer, and the heifers to make sure they have water. Maggie and I walk back to the house. Before going in, I pause to get one last glimpse of the day.

It's still warm out, frogs are starting to croak and a few of the brightest stars are visible in the new night sky. I thank God for this beautiful world and for country life.

**ALEAH BRIGHT**
**MONROE, WA**

When Aleah comes home, she catches up on the barnyard news and visits her favorite cows.

## AN EARLY RISER RECALLS GOOD TIMES

From 1950, when I was 11, until 1955, I worked alongside my parents, three sisters and three brothers on our 200-acre dairy farm in Walden, New York. My parents came from Holland, and owning the farm helped them realize their dream.

We all had before- and after-school chores. Mine involved working in the barn and caring for our 50 Holsteins.

Typically, I got up at 5 a.m. and helped with the milking and barn chores. Then I went home to eat breakfast, wash up and change for school. After school I changed again, grabbed a snack—some cookies or a slice of applesauce or molasses cake that Mom had baked—and went out to clean the stalls. (There were 25 down each side of the barn.) At 6:30 p.m. I'd go back for dinner and do my homework until bedtime.

Though we worked hard every day, we saved Sundays for church and visiting relatives. The cousins would play while the adults talked. Looking back, I realize that I got my work ethic from my growing-up days. I think of them as the good times. It's fun to reminisce.

**DANIEL VAN DAM**
**SOUTH KORTRIGHT, NY**

Daniel, right, and his younger brother Paul lean against a silo where the family stored corn silage in the 1950s.

## SLEDDING TO SCHOOL

Snow days? Never had a snow day when I was in school! Back in the mid-1940s, after a snowstorm and on extremely cold days, I remember our neighbor would come with a sled drawn by a team of horses and pick up all the kids from farms around us. I was 5 or 6, and my mom had bundled me up in a coat, scarves and mittens so that only my eyes showed. We all snuggled down in the straw-lined sled and off we went.

The neighbor drove back to his farm over roads no car could get through, up through his grove and over the fields and fences—that's how deep the snow was! A half-mile later, he brought the sled to a stop right across the road from our country schoolhouse. Classes went on as always, and it was fun.

Years later, at New Hampton High School, even though we all rode a school bus, we never had a snow day, either. We might have been an hour late after a storm, but we were there!

**DIANE BURCH**
**SOLON, IA**

## COLD DAYS, WARM THOUGHTS

I was born and raised on a farm near a little Nebraska town called Glenville. When we had a big snowstorm and the temperature dropped below zero, we would put all the livestock in the barn. This meant we had to get up at 4 a.m. to get our chores done and get to school on time.

The first thing to do was to chop blocks of ice out of the tank so the animals could get drinking water. Then we'd clean out the cows' stalls, put fresh hay down and put feed in their bins. Finally it was time for milking. Milk was squirted into the cat's mouth, as well as our own. It sure did warm us up! Farm life was hard work, but I wouldn't trade those days for the world.

**LAURA OCKER MILSTER**
**LOVELAND, CO**

A blizzard dropped nearly 20 inches of snow in some parts of Indiana (left). The snow made for a great playground (below).

## 31 HOURS OF SNOW

Ask my family about Indiana's infamous blizzard of 1978 and you'll hear about the fight to keep ourselves and our animals warm through three days and three nights of howling winds and extreme cold that included 31 hours of snow.

I was 10 years old then, and my memories of that time are different. We didn't have school for days and days! It was cozy and safe in the house. I was too little to do any outside chores. "The wind would blow you away!" I was told. "We'll gather all the eggs and get the firewood. You stay inside."

So we kids stayed inside, played games and drank hot chocolate. Between chores, Dad played with us. Mom told stories and cooked hot, delicious meals. What good times we had! We went to the windows and peered out at the swirling snow. We couldn't see the barn, the chicken house or even the garage, which was only about 20 feet from the window. Then we cheerfully went back to our games.

At night, my older brothers brought mattresses downstairs for us little ones. The upstairs was too cold for us, they said. Then they trekked bravely back upstairs to sleep where water in a glass froze overnight. We romped and played on the mattresses beside the warm stove before curling up, cozy and contented.

Finally the wind stopped howling. When we woke that morning, something didn't seem right. After so much noise from the blowing wind and snow, the quiet was too loud. Mom assured us the blizzard was over. We looked out the windows and saw snow piled higher than we'd ever seen. The highway was closed because of the deep drifts. Not even the plows could get through.

After a warm breakfast, we bundled up and went outside to explore. A big drift stretched from our porch roof to the highway. Snow was piled up over our clothesline! We pounded "steps" into the drifted snow and took turns sledding down our improvised mountain. We made snow tunnels, snowmen and snow angels to our hearts' content.

Then all the neighbor children came over! A snowbank was almost to the peak of the chicken house, so we slid down the roof, flying into the hay field that was now a winter wonderland.

Tracks were everywhere—big feet and little feet, trails of sleds crisscrossed with trails of toboggans and inner tubes. The frozen snow crunched under our boots and the sled runners sang as they whisked away loads of screaming, laughing children. It was the biggest and best playground in the world.

All too soon we tromped back to the house with rosy cheeks and wet mittens, stomping snow from our boots onto Mom's clean floors and sending coats and scarves flying in every direction—everywhere except where they belonged. Mom greeted us with hot chocolate, chocolate chip cookies fresh from the oven and a warm smile.

Finally, the country roads were open again. We went back to school the next day. Yes, the blizzard of '78 was a bad one—unless you happened to be 10 years old.

**BERTHA SCHWARTZ**
**ETNA GREEN, IN**

## SMALL ROOM, BIG MEMORIES

I grew up on a farm in the early '50s in Trough Creek Valley, Pennsylvania. At both ends of the valley were one-room schoolhouses. The one in Calvin taught first through third grades. This was where I was trained in the three R's by a teacher named Evadean Miller. Her sister Rachel taught at the other school, in Pine Grove.

Both schools had outhouses for boys and girls and a small shed for wood and coal. Boys had to bring in the supplies. There was no running water, so we had to carry it in with a bucket and dump it into a cooler at the back of the room so we could all have a drink. I carried water many times. One good thing about the trip to get it was that I passed my great-grandfather's house. He filled the bucket for me, and I was on my way back.

The photo below shows half of the room at the Pine Grove School. During lessons, the students were seated in the front of the room by class. When not being taught, you were given subjects to study until your time came. If you listened carefully, you might pick up something from another class that you needed.

The two schools stand to this day but are used for something else. Oh, the good old days!

**GARY L. STEEL**
**EVERETT, PA**

The Pine Grove School, 1949, with Ms. Rachel Miller and her class of fourth- through sixth-graders.

## TINKER, TEACHER, SANTA, DAD

When I was a boy, you could say, I was home-schooled both at home and at school. My father, who taught for 14 years at the one-room schoolhouse in Hornsby, Illinois, was my teacher for first through fifth grades.

The school was the center of our small farming and coal-mining community, and the teacher, with just two years of college, was supposed to be able to do almost anything. In my father's case, that included vehicle repairs and haircuts.

The tractor on our farm was a Farmall 10-20, and my dad, out of necessity, had learned to work on them. He'd fix a neighbor's carburetor and magneto and charge only for parts.

Lots of farmers soon found that this was cheaper and faster than hiring a professional. They must have figured the repairs were included in the $75 a month Dad was paid for teaching.

We boys didn't get haircuts very often, so when Dad did his amateur barbering, he'd wait until some kid got a professional haircut in town. Then he'd sit that boy down next to a shaggy-haired one and try to make the haircuts match. I guess Dad did a pretty good job, because no one ever complained. Plus, of course, it was free!

The high point of the school year was the Christmas program, which played to a crowd that was always standing room only.

Dad's Santa act was the best part. First you'd hear bells jingling outside. Then someone would raise a window, and Santa would stick his head in, along with his reindeer reins.

A lucky first-grader would get to hold the reins while Santa came in with candy and oranges. Then an eighth-grade boy would slip out, get below the window and pull on the reins. The little fellow holding the reins would almost skid across the floor to shouts of "Hold 'em!" and "Don't let Dasher run away!"

The school typically had about 25 students distributed among eight grades, with the older girls becoming teachers for the first- and second-graders. When I was in first grade, I much preferred reading with Betty, Dorothy or Wilma to my more-demanding father. Dad expected me to sound out every word I didn't know. I liked it better just to be told the word by Betty or Dorothy and move on!

Despite sometimes unorthodox methods, we did learn. I later became a principal for an elementary school and a middle school. The schoolhouse has been used as a horse barn for the past 50 years but it holds many memories.

**WILLIAM SIELSCHOTT**
**LITCHFIELD, IL**

## WHISTLE AT THE MIMOSAS

Whenever I see a mimosa tree, I whistle. With its feathery fernlike branches and bright pink blossoms, this tree conjures up memories of my childhood on the farm and especially of my Grandpa Bill.

As I became a teenager in the boondocks of southern Illinois with the Shawnee National Forest in my backyard, being far away from shopping malls and restaurants often bored me. But the many fun times with Grandpa Bill made up for the isolation and daily chores in the pig farrowing house.

Days with Grandpa were always filled with laughs and lessons.

Grandma and Grandpa lived just a few miles down the gravel road from our house. Grandpa would often visit us and help Dad in the fields. Between chores and feeding the sows, we'd play checkers and put together puzzles.

Grandpa gave us whole packs of Juicy Fruit gum, saying, "Life's too short for just one stick at a time." My sisters and I happily agreed.

His shiny bald head and goofy sense of humor reminded us of Redd Foxx, the comedian and actor on *Sanford and Son*. He sang silly songs, crunched giant ice cubes in his mouth and spoke to us often about geography and science, which he mastered from reading his set of the *Encyclopædia Britannica*.

Grandpa's Chevy truck suited his personality, too. It was sky blue with an attached white cab, and he drove it slowly, with his arm hanging out of the open window. The truck bounced over potholes, leaving a cloud of dust behind it as he slowed to look at deer or wait for turtles to cross in front of him.

The interior of the truck was filled with folded maps and notebooks, where he wrote what he paid for gasoline each time he filled up the tank. A plastic figurine of Jesus mounted on the dashboard bounced along with every pothole.

Whenever I rode with him, I lifted the figurine off its tiny suction cup and gently held it as Grandpa sang, "I don't care if it rains or freezes as long as I have my plastic Jesus glued to the dashboard of my car." That silly song started deep conversations about faith.

Grandpa also kept a worn silver whistle on a string inside his truck. The first time I asked him about it, we were driving past fences overgrown with tall weeds and clover. I picked up the whistle, and he slowed the truck and pointed to the roadside.

"See that tree over there? Do you know what it's called?" I shook my head as I gazed at a tree covered in pink petals.

"It's called a mimosa," he said, "and I think it's special enough that I toot on that whistle every time I see one." I didn't need any more encouragement as I placed the whistle to my lips and let out a long, loud whistle. That day began an endless search for mimosa trees every time I climbed into his truck.

Grandpa Bill passed away my freshman year of high school. I live closer to a city now, so spotting a mimosa tree doesn't happen as frequently. However, I still stop and think about Grandpa Bill every time. And, of course, I whistle.

**KATHY KAVELMAN MARTIN
COLLIERVILLE, TN**

## THE MISSING MILKMAID

One evening, as my older sister rushed to milk the cow before her fiancé arrived, I realized that Emma would be married in two weeks and that I was next in line to be the milker. Dread took over my 13-year-old life.

Milking wasn't a job you accomplished at your convenience. You did it every morning and evening, seven days a week, before school, church, parties, dates, you name it. No matter how cold it was outside, no matter how hot.

Then there was the scent. Emma didn't always smell good after leaning her head against the cow's hindquarters, getting switched with a tail that had been who knows where, or even stepping in a fresh cow pie.

The barn fragrance was bad enough, but we had no running water for cleanup. In summer, we donned swimming suits and took soap to the irrigation pond; in winter, we heated water on the kitchen range and chased everyone else out of our one-room shack. Then we'd fill a metal washtub and scrunch down into it.

The days counted down quickly. Each time Emma headed to the barn, I felt sick to my stomach. The closer the wedding date, the sicker I felt. Then I came up with a plan.

The morning after the wedding, as soon as I finished my last bite of breakfast, I jumped up from the table and started cleaning the kitchen.

After Dad finished eating, he went outside. Minutes later he came through the back door, milk pail in hand. "Helen," he called, then spotted me in the kitchen enthusiastically assisting Mom. "Oh, you're busy," he muttered. He stood there for what seemed like an eternity. From the corner of my eye, I saw him thinking. My heart pounded.

Then, without a word, Dad turned, pulled the door closed behind him and disappeared. A little later he was back with a full pail of milk.

That afternoon, I made it a point to help Mom can peaches. Somewhere in the middle of 50 quarts, Dad arrived with the milk bucket. He took in the collection of processed jars, the six waiting boxes of fresh peaches, the rows of full jars ready to be processed, and the steam rising from the canner on the stove. He stood there for another eternal moment, then turned to go milk the cow.

Over and over, Dad came looking for me at milking time. Though I was always a good worker, Mom had probably never had such eager help. Each time, Dad walked away and did the job.

In time, Dad quit looking for me. For as long as we owned a milk cow, Dad did the milking.

Decades later, Dad was in an assisted living facility. We visited as best we could, given his

Front: sister Hazel; back (from left): brother Frank, Dad, Mom, Emma and Helen

advanced Parkinson's. One summer afternoon in the backyard gazebo, we talked about farm memories. Dad grinned; his heart still lived on the land. Then I finally confessed that my over-the-top helpfulness after Emma's wedding had been a ploy to get out of milking. He chuckled. His eyes sparkled. He patted my knee and said, "But you did everything else."

**HELEN HEAVIRLAND**
**COLLEGE PLACE, WA**

## JUST PARK BETWEEN THE HAY BALES

When I was 13, my older brother gave me my first driving lesson in an alfalfa field. When on my own, I set up hay bales to practice parallel parking. But I knew I wasn't doing it well.

In 1956, after I turned 15—the magic number to take a driver's test—I passed the written exam.

In fall, I took my behind-the-wheel test. Parallel parking didn't go well; there were stakes to designate the parking space, not hay bales! But the real challenge was a traffic signal that turned yellow as I was halfway across an intersection.

Our town had only two traffic lights, so I didn't face this situation very often. I stopped in the middle and asked the examiner, "What do I do?"

"It's your test," he replied curtly.

So I shifted into reverse and backed up, then proceeded with the test when the light turned green. I received a score of 70 points—the minimum required to pass. Still, the examiner told me to never again back up in an intersection!

**PRISCILLA JACKSON**
**VIROQUA, WI**

Amanda (facing camera above and on the cart at left) learned about life on her family's Montana sheep ranch.

## GET THOSE HANDS DIRTY

When I see my 10-year-old squeamishly avoiding food on dirty plates in the sink or my 8-year-old cringing at the wet sand clinging to her hands, I'm reminded of a time when I was reluctant to get my hands a little dirty.

My parents owned a 500-acre ranch in Montana when I was young. I fondly recall summers running free across the expansive pastures on foot or atop my bony old gelding, and wildly sledding down the hills in winter.

It wasn't all fun and games, of course. We had the usual menagerie of ranch animals to tend: cows, sheep, horses, chickens, dogs and barn cats. There were always fences to fix and things to plow, scoop or burn. I probably didn't help as much as I should have, could have or would have if I'd been a little older.

Lambing and calving season was especially hard. Montana's wintry spring weather kept my parents watching expectant mamas at all hours of the day and night. I'd often come home from school to find a newborn lamb warming up on the opened oven door, or a calf being bottle-fed in the basement.

It was during this time of new life that my favorite childhood memory took place. One exceptionally cold day, I was checking on the sheep with my mother in the lower pasture when she spied a ewe in trouble. The poor thing was trying to deliver her breech lamb and needed

> **MY HEART POUNDED IN FEAR AND EXCITEMENT AS I PULLED WITH ALL MY ADOLESCENT MIGHT.**

our help. My mother calmly held the ewe's head and instructed me to grab hold of two spindly, protruding legs.

I hesitated, and I must have had quite a look of panic on my young face. The slimy little things were definitely not something I wanted to touch. But I worked up my courage and wrapped my fingers around them. I can still recall the feel of the unexpectedly delicate legs and their sharp little hooves as if it happened yesterday.

My heart pounded in fear and excitement as I pulled with all my adolescent might. The lamb was delivered with a gush, and I'd never seen anything so beautiful.

I was no stranger to seeing ranch animals being born, but to have a literal hand in it was something I cherished then and will cherish forever. I remember feeling giddy with delight to see "my lamb" being licked clean by her mother, and I'm sure everyone got very tired of hearing me tell and retell my heroic story.

Looking back, I'm so glad I didn't refuse to get my hands a little dirty. If I had, a miraculous moment and endearing memory would have been lost.

These days, I try to instill that life lesson into my own children. Sometimes you need to get your hands a little dirty to experience something amazing and pure.

**AMANDA RUSH
SALEM, OR**

## RUMORS FOR RENT

My parents lived on a farm 20 miles from my high school, farther out than any bus would go. So like many rural students, I rented a room in town during the week, then went home on Friday night. A boy in my grade was in the same situation, so our parents took turns driving us to town.

One Sunday, my parents were going to take us into town when a bad storm hit. It was raining extremely hard, and lightning knocked out our telephone. Dad said he would not drive in that storm but would take us to town the next day.

Monday morning, I was anxious to get to school, as I had a leading part in a play. School was almost out when we finally got to town. I rushed to the teacher in charge of the play to let her know I could go on. She was relieved, she said; she had been told that the neighbor boy and I eloped! Just then, the principal walked in, shocked to see me. He, too, had heard I eloped.

In one day, the rumor had spread through the whole school. I have never forgotten it!

**MILDRED MYHRE**
**SPRING GROVE, MN**

## ONE SOAP DID IT ALL

Growing up on a farm in Mississippi during the Great Depression, we made many of our necessities, including lye soap, which we used to clean everything. No coloring, no flowery scent—one plain soap did it all.

We started with a large wooden barrel full of fireplace ashes. Someone placed the barrel under the edge of our galvanized tin roof, where rain ran off into the ashes. As water drained through the ashes, lye was formed. It drained out through a spout near the base of the barrel.

The other ingredient was lard, which was rendered from the hogs we butchered for food. The lard was warmed in an enameled pan until it liquefied. Then the lye was poured slowly into the lard, and the very hot mixture was stirred until it became thick. If we stirred enough air into it, we would joke about it being Ivory soap. Then we poured the thick mixture into a shallow pan and let it cool before cutting it into bars.

Today, as I use my face and hand soap, shower gel, dishwasher soap, laundry detergent and other cleaning agents, I think how complicated life has become. Maybe we should still have just lye soap.

**DORIS DOLPH**
**PEWAUKEE, WI**

## A GOOD WORK ETHIC

### LITTLE ENTREPRENEURS

"We ordered this wagon (above) from Montgomery Ward in 1932 for $15.50," writes Robert Wilcox of Moberly, Missouri. "That was a lot of money during the Great Depression. It took us two years of odd jobs to make enough to pay for it. My sister Ginia and I asked neighbors to give us all the old prescription bottles they had. We then cleaned them and sold them to the drugstore for a penny each. We grew popcorn and sold it, charging a dime for a 2-pound bag and a quarter for a 6-pound bag. (Mother made the bags from old flour sacks.) I set traps and sold opossums for a quarter each and skunks for a dollar each, and I carried water to threshing machine crews for 25 cents a day. In the photo, Ginia is standing next to the wagon, and Dorothy Roberts, 2, is sitting in it."

### APPLES TO APPLES

"When I was growing up on a farm with my brothers in the '50s, one of our chores was selling apple cider from a bench at the end of our yard," says Susan Massi of Saylorsburg, Pennsylvania. "When a car stopped, the first one to the bench had the thrill of trying to make a sale. One sale failed miserably when a woman asked my little brother what kind of apples we used. His salesman's reply? 'Rotten ones!'"

Myrlen in 1947

## WHEN THE RAIN CROW CALLS

I'm enjoying my daily walk in the quiet solitude of the early morning. My meandering has taken me to the lake. The air is still cool and pleasant to the skin, belying the fact that we're headed for temperatures in the high 90s.

Across the lake, the sad call of a rain crow comes from deep within a stand of hardwood trees. Suddenly time stands still and then shifts into reverse.

I'm no longer a 66-year-old out for a morning stroll. I'm a 10-year-old boy standing on the front porch that runs the length of our unpainted tenant house in west Tennessee. It's not yet 6 a.m. in early June, and I watch in wonder as the sun rises. Although it's summer, I'm chilly in my short-sleeved shirt.

I hear a rain crow call from deep in the woods—a sure sign of rain, my dad always said. I've never seen a rain crow, and I've never known anyone who has. I read recently that they're cuckoo birds, and very shy. They live high in the treetops. Many people swear they're nothing more than mourning doves cooing, but if you've ever heard a rain crow you know the difference.

Hoe on my shoulder, my 10-year-old self tags along behind my brother and sister as we go to work in the cotton patch. My brother carries a gallon jug wrapped in burlap and filled with water drawn from our well and ice that we bought from the iceman.

My sister has a paper sack filled with crackers and cans of pork and beans. I walk as slowly as possible until my brother yells at me to keep up. I always go barefoot in the summer. Sometimes I catch saw briars between my toes; then the dew makes the cuts burn like the dickens.

Along about 10 o'clock I get tired, and we sit in the shade of a huge sweet gum tree. It's fine if there's a breeze blowing, but more often than not the air is perfectly still except for an occasional whirlwind.

At the end of a long day, after the cows are milked and the livestock watered and fed, we sit down to supper. Most of the time it's hot corn bread and fresh vegetables from Momma's garden. After supper we all gather on the front porch and enjoy one another's company. Sometimes my dad brings out an old guitar and plays "Wildwood Rose" for us.

The hot sun interrupts my thoughts and I return to reality. As I continue my stroll, I think about the unwavering sense of right and wrong my parents passed on to me and my siblings.

Life was hard and making a living from the soil was difficult, but we shared a sense of togetherness and knew the meaning of sacrifice and commitment. When I remember my childhood, I thank God for my parents and the lessons I learned from them.

**MYRLEN BRITT**
**HENDERSONVILLE, TN**

## THE HAND-ME-DOWN BLUES

Our family, like most, couldn't afford much during the Great Depression. Living on a farm near Benton, Arkansas, we had plenty of food, but clothing was hard to come by.

Each member of the family got a new pair of shoes in the fall from Sears, Roebuck or a local dry goods store. The boys' shoes were usually the brogan type that had to last until spring, when it became warm enough to go barefoot. Sometimes Dad had to repair the shoes with hay wire when the sole came loose. Then it was barefoot until fall again.

Aunt Golda, Mom's sister, was a live-in housekeeper and nanny for the Robert Mathis family in St. Louis. Mr. Mathis owned a shoe company, so the family lived very well. Their two sons were about the same age as my brother Fayne and me, and when the Mathis boys got new clothes, Mrs. Mathis would clean out their closets and tell my aunt to throw the older clothes in the garbage.

Aunt Golda, who couldn't imagine such waste, would save the clothes until she could get a box to mail them to us poor folks on the farm. Mom and Dad appreciated this greatly, but sometimes it caused problems for Fayne and me.

Think about it: The style of rich kids in the city was hardly the same as that of poor kids in Saline County, Arkansas. Our friends and neighbors had never seen clothes like that except in the moving picture shows.

To some people, Fayne and I were the best-dressed kids in Arkansas, but boys our age—who looked fine in their patched Big Smith overalls—jeered at us. Nevertheless, Mom said we were going to wear those nice clothes, and that was final.

Still, we looked forward to getting a package from Aunt Golda, because she would also send toys and ball gloves that the boys had ditched.

One day, however, we got a package with several pairs of brown corduroy knickers. Fayne and I had never seen a pair of those things except in *Our Gang* movies! To our horror, they were a perfect fit for both of us. We begged Mom not to make us wear those knickers; we considered running away from home.

Those awful short pants proved to be the most rugged clothes we ever had. I thought they would never wear out—and I had to suffer longer than Fayne, who was bigger, because when I grew out of mine I had to wear the larger pairs that he'd discarded.

We definitely felt like oddballs. Maybe if we'd moved to St. Louis, we'd have been right in style.

**ART WILSON
LITTLE ROCK, AR**

Short pants brought endless teasing to Art and his brother, Fayne, pictured on his first bicycle.

## FARM LIVIN' IS THE LIFE

Sometime in the early 1940s, my dad settled the family on a 160-acre farm about 10 miles west of Indianapolis, Indiana. My brother and I spent most of our childhood growing up there. The experiences of grinding feed, planting acres of tomatoes and driving away the corncrib rats in that rural environment prepared us for the rest of our lives.

Things changed in the 1960s when Dad developed the farmland into housing. Buildings were razed and the only original structures left standing were the farmhouse and the old shed, or garage as we sometimes called it.

Built in the 1940s for utilitarian purposes, the shed was a tin-covered structure with a dirt floor and an open concrete foundation. The only modern convenience it boasted was electricity.

The house was updated over the years, but the shed has remained essentially unchanged from when it was built.

My wife and I live on the site of the old barn. Our granddaughter lives in the old farmhouse and owns the old shed, which still functions, after all these years, as a two-car garage and storage place for tools and toys. And maybe it's the starting place for another generation's fond memories of old buildings.

**GEOFF BRADLEY**
**INDIANAPOLIS, IN**

Clockwise from top left: Mrs. Timberlake, mother of several of the farmhands, wraps her arms around brothers Geoff and Harry. Geoff's granddaughter Whitney, her husband, Cory, and their children Wyatt and Audrey still use the old shed. In 1948, Glenn Bradley, Geoff's dad, waves from in front of the shed. An aerial view of the farm buildings in 1950 shows the shed at lower right.

The working heart of the farm, the shed housed Glenn's workbench.

# LAUGHING ABOUT IT NOW

### A sense of humor never hurt anyone

## IT WAS A LONG WALK TO SCHOOL...OR WAS IT?

Douglas Beery, my father, grew up on a farm with corn, wheat, pigs, cows and chickens near Westfield, Indiana. They pulled the farm equipment with mules, and Dad claimed that one of those mules, named Rastus, was the meanest mule in the world. If he couldn't kick you, he'd bite you.

Dad had two sisters, and all three of the kids worked hard helping their folks. But I learned to take his stories about getting to school with a grain of salt.

My family lived in Santa Fe, New Mexico, during my elementary school and junior high years. And anytime I'd complain about having to ride my Cushman Road King scooter to school in bad weather, Dad reminded me about how he had to walk 5 miles uphill through 3 feet of snow in the winter—and 2 feet of mud the rest of the year.

Years later, Aunt Eloise told me that Dad actually had to walk only from the house to the barn, where he harnessed the horse to the buggy. Then he and Eloise would drive to the neighbors' house, put the horse in their corral and catch the bus to school. After school they'd take the bus back to the neighbors' house, hitch up the horse and ride back home.

My wife says she heard similar stories from her dad, Lee Stilphen, about his school days in Maine. He told her he had to walk 10 miles each way through mud and snow. She later learned that he had to walk only about a quarter mile to the end of their road, where he caught a bus. If he missed the bus, he rode his horse to school bareback. Then the horse grazed in the school yard until it was time to ride home.

Both of our fathers regarded farming as a tough way of life, and they respected it greatly. In the end, however, they realized that farming just wasn't for them.

**BILL BEERY**
**AZTEC, NM**

Douglas and Eloise (right) took the family buggy to a neighbor's house, where they caught a school bus like the one pictured below.

## COMPOST ROULETTE

There's a funny story behind my mother's pickled cherry tomatoes. Our soil in Virginia was very poor—all red clay—so when a local farmer with cows offered my father all the composted manure he could haul away, Dad jumped at the chance. He took the backseats out of the car, lined everything with plastic, and came home with three big trash cans full of manure, which he spread on the vegetable garden.

Turns out, it wasn't very well-composted. Oh, how the yard stank! We were so glad when winter set in and froze the ground hard. The next spring, we turned the soil and planted a typical suburban vegetable garden: corn, squash, tomatoes and peas. That summer, an astonishing number of cherry tomatoes popped up everywhere in the garden. But we hadn't planted them; it seems our free compost came with bonus seeds. Those cows must have gotten into someone's tomato patch.

We ate tomatoes all summer. And then, we pickled tomatoes for the rest of the year.

**HELEN NELANDER**
**BOULDER CREEK, CA**

## MOTHER HUBBARD'S PARADE

My mother remembers a funny incident from a day back in 1936, when Grandmother broke up the monotony of farm chores by announcing a drive to town. Four kids piled into the old Model T, and, since they were allowed to take friends along, their pals squeezed in, too. Kids sat on laps and rode on running boards. The car was brimming with children.

As Grandmother turned onto Main Street, she quickly noticed that hers was the only vehicle there. Suddenly, it dawned on her— it was Founders' Day! She had driven onto the parade route.

From the sidewalk, someone shouted, "Here comes the parade! There's Old Mother Hubbard!"

"No," someone else called out, "it's the Old Lady in the Shoe!" The crowd roared with laughter. Mortified, Grandmother frantically looked for a way out, but the side streets were barricaded. All she could do was drive down Main Street as spectators hollered, cheered and waved flags.

**JOYCE NEELEY**
**PUYALLUP, WA**

## PLANE OLD SILLY

I was 12, my parents were out, and I had just done my chores on our North Dakota farm. I went out to shake the dust mop, and I saw a plane overhead. I shook the mop in a circle, and the pilot must have noticed; he started circling and began to land!

I ran into the house, scared to death. "I just flagged down a plane!" I told our sitter. Thinking quickly, she ran out and asked the pilot how much it would cost to fly her home, as we had snowbanks 15 feet high. He said $20.

I was terrified my dad would be upset by the events, but all he said was, "*Hmm.* I wondered what those tracks in the snow were from."

**MARGARET SEHN**
**COTTONWOOD, CA**

## THE STENCH OF PRIDE

When he was 12 years old in rural South Dakota in the 1950s, my father, Gary, took up trapping for fun and profit. One day, he came upon his trap and saw not a standard raccoon but what looked to be an angry, overfed farm cat. Dad placed the caged critter in his bike basket and rode to school to show off his trophy.

He pulled up to the steps with a grin, raising the cage for rival trappers and gawking girls to behold.

"Gary, do you know what that is?" squealed a younger classmate. My father looked again at the surly creature.

"Yes, I do," he said, horror dawning. It was no farm cat—it was a common skunk! The creature sprayed a potent dose of anger all over my father in front of the entire school.

Dad attests he missed only a few days of school, but my aunt confirms it was a full week—and not for the smell but for his bruised pride.

**CARMEN VANDE STROET**
**HULL, IA**

## THE CAR DIDN'T RESPOND TO "WHOA!"

When I was a young girl, I often spent time on Grandma and Grandpa McFarland's ranch. Their place was only 5 miles from our house. The first 2 miles of pasture between us belonged to my parents, the rest to my grandparents. Six barbed wire gates separated the pastures, and red and white Hereford cattle grazed the rolling hills.

To take me home, Grandpa would hitch his bay team to the surrey, and we'd take the pasture trail instead of the main road, which shaved about 7 miles off the trip. When we came to a gate, Grandpa would say whoa, the horses would stop, and I'd jump out and open it. Grandpa would click his tongue, the signal for the team to pull the surrey through. Then they'd wait while I shut the gate and jumped back in. It was easy: The team was well-trained from many years of work.

I was 11 the summer of 1940, when Grandpa's youngest son, whom we all called Doc, decided it was time his father learned to drive a car. Doc bought him a used late-model Ford. I don't remember any formal driving lessons, but I'm sure Doc showed Grandpa what to do. Grandpa was in his late 60s by then, but aside from maybe a handful of car rides, he'd always traveled by horseback, team and buggy, or train.

So the next time Grandpa took me home, we got in the car. It started out with a little jerk, but we soon picked up speed as we rumbled across the bridge over the slough.

Grandpa turned off onto the pasture trail. We bounced over a ditch and across a cow trail. All was fine until we came to the first gate. I waited for Grandpa to brake. Instead, he said, "Whoa!"

Before we knew it, the gate made its way over the hood, up the windshield and clear into the air before crashing to the ground behind us. Grandpa was the kind of man who kept his tongue, but I could guess what he thought as he climbed out of the car and proceeded to wire the fence shut to keep the cattle in.

Five more gates to go. I wondered if we would make it home.

At the next gate, Grandpa actually applied the brake, though not with real conviction. By the one after that, he stopped almost in time, breaking only the bales that held the gate shut. Gate by gate he slowly got better, and by the time we got to the last one, he had actually learned how to slow down and stop.

I was happy to be home. My guess is that Grandpa felt the same, since, for the best I can recollect, that was the last time he drove a car.

**GENEVIEVE BRECHTEL**
**VALE, SD**

## DAY OF THE FULL MOON

When I was 7 years old, in 1941, my dad worked on a cotton farm near Newlin, Texas.

One day I was swimming with my sister, wearing only an old pair of blue jeans. Dad came and told me to get the owner's horse and go after the cows, which had escaped the pasture and were headed toward town.

Being as small as I was, it was hard for me to get onto the horse without a saddle, so I'd use a wooden fence to get aboard. Wouldn't you know, as I swung my leg over the horse, the seam in my old jeans split wide open. I didn't have time to put on another pair of pants, so off I went, ripped pants and all.

I chased the cows and calves down a country road until they ran into the yard of a neighbor lady's house. I got off the horse, and the lady and I turned the cows back toward our place.

Now it was time for me to get back onto the horse. The lady said, "Come here, son, and I'll give you a leg up." I knew that would never work, because she would see all my business. I begged off, but she wouldn't hear of it.

So I led the horse over to her and, as I threw my leg over its back, I unwillingly showed her the full moon. As I rode off, I thought I heard her laugh.

It was a long time before I saw the lady again, and I'm sure it was a long time before someone mooned her the way I did!

**FERRELL JONES**
**PARIS, AR**

By the time this photo was taken, Ferrell "Bud" Jones was 11 years old and riding his very own horse.

## HEADING FOR THE CREEK

It was 1951, and I was 9 years old on my parents' homestead in Loveland, Colorado. My Aunt Peggy and Uncle Harley had a new Studebaker Champion, and I couldn't take my hands off that jet plane on wheels. It looked as if it was going 90 miles an hour standing still.

I wheedled and wheedled to drive it until my aunt relented. Once I was placed behind the wheel on 160 acres of farmland and let loose, I promptly drove into a creek. The car had to be pulled out with the family tractor. I was wet and embarrassed, and my mom banned me from driving until I was 15. I loved that car.

Then, at age 71, I saw one at the Portland Swap Meet in Oregon and knew that I had to have it. I love my Studebaker Champion Starlight Coupe—people yell and scream when they see it. The only thing better than having a classic car is having a story to go along with it!

**JONATHAN COX**
**OCEAN PARK, WA**

## PANTS ON FIRE

As a boy, my grandpa Wytte Wilson was often given responsibility over his two younger brothers. One day, he was supervising as they picked corn in the field. The two brothers started intentionally throwing corn over the wagon, then going over to the other side to take breaks in the shade.

After this occurred several times, Grandpa told his brothers that if they continued, he'd set their behinds on fire. Both brothers looked at each other and, in an act of defiance, threw their corn over the wagon.

Grandpa grabbed one of them and started whipping him with a belt, only to jump back in bewilderment as his brother's behind literally caught on fire! Come to find out, both boys were carrying strike-anywhere matches in their back pockets.

Grandpa kept his word.

**DAVID WILSON**
**REDONDO BEACH, CA**

Alan Carnes, preparing a pig for county fair judging in 1952, says, "This pig kept me in school clothes for a couple of years with my winnings."

## SOME SMALL LESSONS IN BIG-CITY TABLE MANNERS

When I was 14, in 1951, I was chosen to represent Washington County, Oklahoma, on a 4-H livestock judging team. Living on 18 acres and raising livestock just to survive doesn't make you an expert, but I guess I qualified after entering some sort of farm animal in the county fair for five straight years.

I was the youngest of the group that set out for Oklahoma City with the county agent. We went out for dinner that evening—the first time I'd ever eaten in a restaurant. The wait staff brought each of us silverware and water, accompanied by a towel. I drank the water and put the towel in my lap.

At that point, the county agent leaned over and explained that I'd just gulped down the water from the finger bowl. Everyone laughed, and I didn't think it could get worse—but I was wrong.

After a wonderful chicken dinner, the county agent paid the bill, and I noticed he had forgotten some money on the table. Wanting to be helpful, I picked up the cash and followed the others out the door. After I gave the agent back his money, he explained what a tip was.

To make matters worse, as I was bringing back the money, some of the restaurant workers were clearing our table. I confessed what I'd done, and there was more laughter. I've eaten at many restaurants since then, but I'll always remember the first.

**ALAN CARNES**
**SPRINGFIELD, MO**

## UNUSUAL ORDERS

I grew up on a farm in North Dakota. We were tough people who grew our own food, milked our own cows and preserved every bit of food we could. Waste was just not a word in our vocabulary.

When I walked into the kitchen one day, Mom told me to take a pail of cream that was sitting on the floor and pour it into the can. I asked her to repeat what she'd said. She did, but in a sterner voice. I was bewildered and asked her why she wanted me to pour cream into the can.

"Just do it, and don't ask again," she said sternly. "But make sure you leave the pail over there."

I thought Mom was losing her mind, but I walked to the outhouse with the pail of cream anyway. Once inside, I took the cover off the toilet and poured sweet cream into the hole. Shaking my head, I set the empty pail in the nearest corner.

Later that afternoon, Mom and I were putting the separator together. My brother entered the separator shed swinging the empty cream pail.

"Why was this in the outhouse?" he said.

Mom started laughing and asked me, "Why did you leave the pail in there?"

"You told me to!"

**GREER GLANZER
CHAMBERLAIN, SD**

## A LICK OF TROUBLE

In 1939, my folks lived and worked on a large farm that my uncle owned in Yakima County, Washington. On one cold morning, my cousin Jim and I were outdoors with a friend whose father also worked on the farm. There was frost on everything.

An unused woodstove made of steel was next to the barn. It, too, was covered in frost, and for some reason I had the urge to lick off the frost. Before anyone could say anything, I licked that very cold stove with my warm, wet tongue.

My tongue stuck to the stove! It wouldn't come off and it hurt very much. The hired hand heard me yelling and came to see what was wrong. He blew his warm breath on the stove and my poor tongue was set free. Then do you know what he did? He spanked me! After some 75 years, my cousin still thinks it's funny.

**ELSIE STARKEL
SPANAWAY, WA**

## ROLL OUT THE PANIC

Growing up on the old family farm in northeast Pennsylvania, I woke to find my mother out of the house one spring morning in 1951, when I was 4. Standing next to the heating stove in our living room was a roll of new linoleum about 6 feet tall.

I heard Mom coming down the path and decided to hide from her and surprise her. I clambered onto a chair, then onto the top of the stove and, without giving it a thought, climbed on top of the roll of linoleum and lowered myself down into it. I soon found that I couldn't move.

Hearing that Mom had made it into the house, I began to yell for help. She could hear me, but she couldn't find me. When she finally figured out what I had done, she began to laugh, but all I wanted was to get out of that roll of linoleum.

Mom started to unwind the roll, but that didn't work; there was too much furniture in the room to unroll enough linoleum to get me out.

After some time, Mom decided that maybe laying the roll on the floor was the best way to get me out, and it worked perfectly.

Was I embarrassed! I also learned that day what the word "claustrophobic" meant.

**ROBERT WANDEL
LAWRENCE, KS**

## TAKING THE DIVE

In 1937, when I was 3 years old, I marched bravely toward the outhouse on our farm outside Sturgeon Bay, Wisconsin, very proud that I could now get there on my own.

With me was our spaniel Goldie, my constant companion and protector from the fearsome spiders living in the privy. As I got myself situated, Goldie leaped up to sit beside me and promptly disappeared down the other hole. She was not amused and made a great commotion.

Now, no boy worth his salt could fail to help his companion in time of need, so I reached down to pull her out. Her weight and frantic struggling all but assured that I would join her; now both of us were in the muck and in big trouble.

Our combined howling led my dear mother, bless her soul, to our rescue. I can only imagine what went through her mind, but mothers are resourceful, and she was soon guiding us to the outdoor pump. I still remember that water as the coldest I've ever felt on my skin. The next job was to heat up bathwater to finish the job.

I believe that when you fall headfirst down a privy early in life, you have nowhere to go but up.

**EARL GIGSTEAD
CRYSTAL FALLS, MI**

# TRACTORS, TRACTORS, TRACTORS

Childhood reflections on a farm necessity and a companion to all

## STICKING WITH IT

Almost everyone in my family will tell you that Daddy's 1953 Allis-Chalmers CA was the star workhorse on our small farm in south-central Texas. But I still have mixed feelings about it.

When I think back to the heyday of the Allis-Chalmers, I also think of stifling hot, dusty, itchy corn patches. I remember my daddy putting me in the tractor seat and telling me to keep pace while the rest of the family harvested our corn crop by hand and tossed the ears onto the trailer I was towing.

And at 10 or 11, I remember, I could not seem to get a handle on staying in the right place. I can still hear Daddy's loud voice over the noisy engine: "Too fast! Too slow! Easy on the clutch!" I vowed to vacate my seat for good the first chance I got.

But I also have good memories. I remember my grandmother telling me that Daddy sounded mean only because he had to holler to be heard over the tractor. She promised me that she'd buy me a pencil box if I finished the job. In today's technical world, a pencil box is probably not at the top of any kid's wish list. But on that day many years ago, it was the light at the end of the tunnel—or corn row—for me.

I stayed, and Grandma kept her promise. She allowed me to choose a lovely yellow-gold pencil box at the Perry Brothers Five and Dime in downtown Brenham. The box sported a built-in pencil sharpener, and the sliding lid doubled as a ruler. I was in heaven!

Interestingly, I was the daughter who ended up inheriting Daddy's tractor, and my husband, Robert, spent many hours restoring it. As the process neared the finish line, our yard looked like a holiday tractor wonderland, with shiny, freshly painted ornaments hanging from trees to dry. He gave me the job of painting the wheels. They were on the ground, and I had to keep getting up and down, which wasn't easy for me. My dear husband told me I looked "older than the tractor" as I shuffled back and forth.

So the Allis-Chalmers CA is now Robert's favorite toy. And I guess I'd have to say it's my favorite tractor. It does bring back many fond memories—especially of Daddy and Grandma. But the sight of it sometimes still makes me wince.

**MARILYN BORCHGARDT**
**WACO, TX**

Grandson Ben (above) adored the Allis-Chalmers tractor even before it was restored, says Marilyn (at left with Robert). Ben is now 13, and all four of Marilyn and Robert's grandchildren enjoy driving or riding on the tractor.

## LIKE A WHOLE NEW TRACTOR

Dad bought a new H tractor in 1942. Rubber and electronics were being diverted to the war effort, so it didn't have lights or tires. That's my sister and me in the wagon behind Dad. The H also didn't have an electric starter, which almost got it drowned.

One evening Dad left the tractor parked by the creek and a big storm hit that night. With the creek about to overflow its banks the next morning, he couldn't get the H started. By the time our neighbor got there with his horse team, the water was several feet deep, but they managed to pull the H to higher ground.

When World War II ended, we bought rubber tires, which was like getting a new tractor. After Dad got a full-time job, I did most of the farming until I went into the Army. While I was away, Dad traded the H for a Ford 8N, but the H will always be my favorite.

**RONALD REED
WICHITA, KS**

## HAND-ME-DOWN TRACTOR ▶

"My brothers and I grew up in western Pennsylvania on a small farm," writes Sandy Martin of Houston, Texas. "For Christmas 1953, we received a John Deere 60 pedal tractor. We rode that thing all over, pretending to farm. When we grew up and had kids of our own, they rode it, too. Not long ago, I decided to give it to one of my grandsons for Christmas. It was in terrible shape, so I restored it. I found rubber wheels, decals and even a new pedal sprocket online. I stripped it down to bare aluminum and repainted everything. The tractor looked brand-new when my 6-year-old grandson received it."

Terry Smith drives the Ford 861 tractor during hay season.

# FORDS FOREVER!

I grew up on a farm adjoining my grandfather's, which has been in the family since before the Civil War. My dad, Charles Smith, and his dad, Craig Smith, each milked about 20 cows, and they worked together farming the 100 tillable acres on our 466-acre hilly, stony farm. They always had Ford tractors.

In 1958 they traded in two Ford 8Ns, nicknamed Roy and Dale, for brand-new tractors. Grandpa got a Ford 861 Powermaster and Dad got a 661 Workmaster. I was 9 years old the day we gathered to watch the dealer unload them off the truck. I grew up with those two tractors—they were the only tractors on the farm from 1958 to 1970, when we bought a 1968 Ford 4000. But even after we started adding larger tractors, the 861 was the only one that could pull a chopper wagon up our steep hill in high gear. The 172-cubic-inch Red Tiger engine had plenty of torque, and the 861 didn't lug down like some of our newer tractors.

After Grandpa retired, I farmed with my parents for five years before moving on to a new career. But my four siblings and I still own most of the family farm. My wife and I built our home on one corner, and we raised our four kids here. My years growing up on the farm were so nearly perfect that I can't help feeling nostalgic for the tractors.

The 661's motor blew up in the 1990s, and Dad sold it for parts—which he later regretted. But when my folks died, the 861 came to me. I spent 10 years happily restoring Grandpa's tractor, overhauling the motor and installing a new clutch, brakes and fenders. During the years between getting it running and getting it painted, I used it without a hood and fenders to plow snow, haul firewood and take the kids on hayrides.

I jokingly tell people that my wife knows not to come between my tractor and me, but I'm not sure she knows I'm joking. With so many good memories of the 861 and the time when it was so important to our lives and our livelihood, it's heartwarming to see it finally restored to its former red and gray glory.

**TERRY SMITH**
**REXVILLE, NY**

Family members surround the newly refurbished Ford 861.

Terry's cousin and brother sit atop the new tractors in 1958.

The Super A has been the
family workhorse since 1952, and
it deserved a beautiful restoration.

## IN DAD'S HONOR

My father bought this Farmall Super A new in 1952. I was really proud of the tractor and claimed it as my own. All through high school, I ran it more than anyone else on the farm and always kept it in good shape. After I graduated in 1958, I joined the U.S. Marine Corps and left the farm. But I never lost my affection for that little tractor.

Dad gave me the Super A in 1998, and I happily left it at his house so he could continue to use it in his large garden and for other chores. When he passed away 10 years later, I restored the Farmall in his honor. Driving it reminds me of the good times I had as a boy farming with my dad. I will always cherish these memories.

**WAYNE GILBERT**
**VALE, NC**

# TRACTORS 1920-1960

Driven by successive generations of visionary engineers, farmers and marketers, the tractor evolved from a lumbering curiosity into its current versatile, comfortable, indispensable form in four decades of innovation unmatched in the history of agriculture.

**HARRY FERGUSON** patents the three-point hitch with draft control, a major breakthrough in practical hydraulics.

1926

1927

1928

1929

**ALLIS-CHALMERS** equips its Model U with rubber tires and sets off on a crusade to replace steel wheels.

**MASSEY-HARRIS** introduces the four-wheel drive Model GP—decades ahead of its time.

1925

1930

**INTERNATIONAL HARVESTER** debuts the Farmall, the first row-crop tractor.

1924

1933

1932

1931

**CATERPILLAR TRACTOR CO.** markets the first tractor with a diesel engine, the Model 65 crawler.

**JOHN DEERE** replaces the Waterloo Boy with the Model D, which remains in continuous production through 1953.

1923

1934

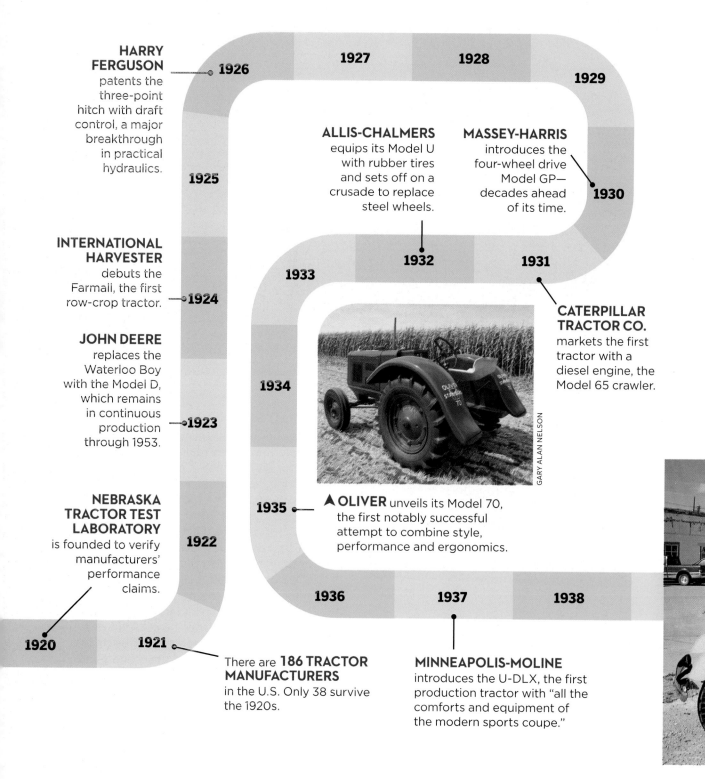

GARY ALAN NELSON

**NEBRASKA TRACTOR TEST LABORATORY** is founded to verify manufacturers' performance claims.

1922

1935

▲ **OLIVER** unveils its Model 70, the first notably successful attempt to combine style, performance and ergonomics.

1936

1937

1938

1920

1921

There are **186 TRACTOR MANUFACTURERS** in the U.S. Only 38 survive the 1920s.

**MINNEAPOLIS-MOLINE** introduces the U-DLX, the first production tractor with "all the comforts and equipment of the modern sports coupe."

**1957**

**1956**          **1958**

**WAGNER** sends the first
articulated four-wheel
drive, the TR-9, to the
Nebraska Tractor Tests.

**1959**

▼ **THE JOHN DEERE 4010**
launches the modern era
of farm tractors.

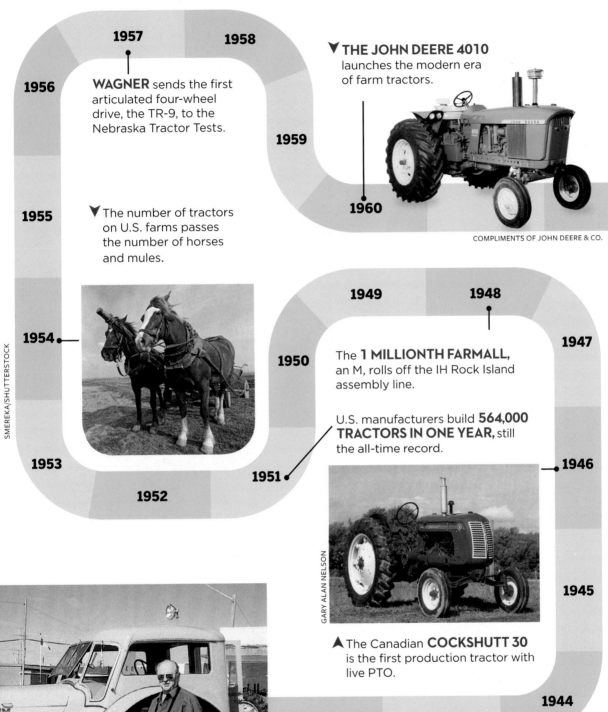

**1960**

COMPLIMENTS OF JOHN DEERE & CO.

**1955**

▼ The number of tractors
on U.S. farms passes
the number of horses
and mules.

**1954** ●

SMEREKA/SHUTTERSTOCK

**1949**          **1948**

**1950**

The **1 MILLIONTH FARMALL,**
an M, rolls off the IH Rock Island
assembly line.

**1947**

U.S. manufacturers build **564,000
TRACTORS IN ONE YEAR,** still
the all-time record.

**1953**

**1952**

**1951** ●

● **1946**

GARY ALAN NELSON

**1945**

▲ The Canadian **COCKSHUTT 30**
is the first production tractor with
live PTO.

**1944**

**1942**          **1943**

◄ This **MINNEAPOLIS-MOLINE U-DLX**
was restored by Glen Mason
of Davidson, Saskatchewan.

# LEAVING THE COUNTRY BEHIND

No matter where you are, farm life sticks with you

### RAISED A FARM GIRL

Christine Farr tells her daughter Adrienne Farr about the days before the civil rights movement.

**Adrienne Farr:** *Where were you born?*

**Christine Farr:** Kinston, North Carolina.

**Adrienne:** *What year?*

**Christine:** [Grudgingly] 1939.

**Adrienne:** *[Laughs] You look beautiful, Mom! Can you tell me one of your earliest memories?*

**Christine:** Living with my aunt and uncle, who I always called Mommy and Daddy. I was about 3 years old when I was taken there.

**Adrienne:** *Why?*

**Christine:** At a young age, my mother had a nervous breakdown. I understand that she was unable to care for me properly, so I was taken to my aunt, who raised me as if I were her own. It never really bothered me much. I would tell people, "I have two mothers and two fathers."

**Adrienne:** *What was the house like? Was it an old-time southern house with a front porch?*

**Christine:** Yes, it did have a front porch. It was in a rural neighborhood in the country, with dirt roads. Daddy—my uncle—had a car. It was an old model, but we got around in it. I was there with my cousins, who were raised as my sister and brother, and it was a very cheerful house.

**Adrienne:** *How many siblings did you have?*

**Christine:** At first it was just me and my older sister. As time progressed, Mama, my aunt, had maybe 10 children altogether.

**Adrienne:** *You worked on a farm?*

**Christine:** Yes, because that's how we were raised! Daddy was a farmer. He worked on different farms at different times. One was Mr. and Mrs. Hill's farm, outside Kinston. He had a garden there and at home. That's more or less how we ate. Daddy would grow collard greens, onions, cabbage...and tobacco. That's how he got paid. He would take the tobacco to town for them to weigh. I never knew how much he sold or what he made. But I know sometimes he'd say, "Well, we didn't get out of debt this year."

**Adrienne:** *Did you help on the Hills' farm?*

**Christine:** Oh, yes. At maybe 8 or 9 years of age,

Right: Mrs. Farr, pregnant with Adrienne, enjoys an office baby shower. Left: Mrs. Farr takes little Adrienne to a Harlem, New York, park.

I'd help pick tobacco or cotton after school.

**Adrienne:** *So after school, instead of doing homework, you'd have to go into the fields?*

**Christine:** Yes, maybe three times a week.

**Adrienne:** *And how was school for you?*

**Christine:** It was good. We had to walk there, but it was good. The teachers taught us well, considering the conditions at the time.

**Adrienne:** *How far away was the school?*

**Christine:** Oh, maybe 3 or 4 miles.

**Adrienne:** *You had to walk even in the snow?*

**Christine:** Yes.

**Adrienne:** *You've said that you would see other kids being bused?*

**Christine:** Oh, yes. The white kids were being bused. Seeing it didn't bother me, though, because I knew that was the only way we could get to school.

**Adrienne:** *Did you go to the same school?*

**Christine:** Oh, no. Different schools altogether. They went to brick schools; ours was just a plain white clapboard building. Two rooms for 40 kids.

**Adrienne:** *Did you ever feel that there were any major differences between the way you lived and the way other people lived?*

**Christine:** No. We were just programmed to live the way we were living. By high school, we rode buses to school; they had built new schools for us, and they were nice brick buildings.

**Adrienne:** *Do you remember how that felt, to ride on a bus to school for the first time?*

**Christine:** I know I felt better than I did doing all that walking! [Laughs]

**Adrienne:** *Didn't you have an accident, right before graduation?*

**Christine:** Yes. We had a kerosene wood heater in our house. I was sweeping, and I got too close to it. My skirt caught on fire. I ran to the kitchen while the fire was burning my skirt and coming up the back of my leg. My daddy snatched it off and got me to the hospital. It was a bad burn. I was out of school maybe two months but—I guess my grades were good enough—I managed to graduate. I moved to New York right after.

**Adrienne:** *Why'd you go there?*

**Christine:** That's mostly where all the other kids were going—they'd go north for a better job.

**Adrienne:** *Was this in the '50s or '60s?*

**Christine:** It was the '50s.

**Adrienne:** *Oh, gosh, so civil rights hadn't started yet! You guys didn't even have a television. Did you know what was going on in the world?*

**Christine:** We did have a radio, so we were able to listen. But I knew right away I wanted to go to New York. I felt that there were better opportunities for employment.

**Adrienne:** *What was it like telling Grandma and Grandpa?*

**Christine:** I think they were sort of expecting it. A lot of kids from that area were going to New York. My sister was already there.

**Adrienne:** *What was it like when you got there?*

**Christine:** The major difference was a better way of living. Finding a job wasn't as hard. I didn't have to work on the farm. I moved in with my Aunt Flora—we called her Aunt Pudding—and got a job at Lebanon Hospital in the Bronx. I worked from 4 p.m. to midnight.

**Adrienne:** *This was around the time of Martin Luther King Jr. and Malcolm X. Do you remember anything about that time?*

**Christine:** Well, I remember a lot of discussions about it. But we were still young and weren't living where this was going on. I didn't focus on it as much. Once I saw a small protest, but nothing big—people walking down the street. I think they just wanted to show people that they were serious about what they were doing.

**Adrienne:** *Did you ever feel any racial tension?*

**Christine:** No, I really didn't!

**Adrienne:** *So how did you meet Daddy?*

**Christine:** I met him through his sister at the hospital. She worked on the eighth floor, and I was on the seventh. I used to visit her house and your dad would be there, sitting there, staring at me. [Laughs] I wasn't sure that he was the one. But he was very nice and caring and polite.

**Adrienne:** *Do you remember your wedding?*

**Christine:** We got married at my friend Mary's house in Queens in 1967. It was exciting because I had to come from Manhattan out to Cambria Heights, and it wasn't easy. I got dressed at her house. I ordered the cake from Horn & Hardart, and a minister came from Harlem. My Aunt Pudding brought dinner: collard greens, chicken, you know, the usual. We got married in the living room, and the reception was in the basement.

**Adrienne:** *How long were you married?*

**Christine:** Forty-three years total.

**Adrienne:** *So Daddy was the love of your life?*

**Christine:** [Brief pause] Yes.

**Adrienne:** *Anything else you'd like to say, Mom?*

**Christine:** Ah...no. I'm just proud of my children.

**CHRISTINE FARR AS TOLD TO ADRIENNE FARR**

## IT MADE HER "MELT"

Moving our family from a small town to Boulder, Colorado, in 1964 was quite a culture shock. Our new local grocery store had a meat counter that stretched nearly the whole length of the store and sold many things I had never heard of. One day, as I was shopping there, a package labeled "melts" caught my eye. It looked like beef heart, which I had loved on the farm where I grew up, so I bought one.

I put the melts on to cook for a couple of hours, but strangely, the more it cooked, the worse it smelled. When we sat down to eat, my husband took one bite and said it was inedible. I took a bite and agreed. We threw it all away.

The next time I went to the grocery store, I pointed to a package of melts and got up the courage to ask the butcher what it was.

"Bull spleen," he said. "For fishing bait."

Needless to say, I did not tell him about my new recipe.

**BETTY HUBIN**
**SPOONER, WI**

The Hondls dressed in their best
to take Bernadette to school.

## COUNTRY ROOTS

How times have changed since September 1962, when my family joined me for a picture in the yard of our farm near Owatonna, Minnesota (above right). Just about to leave for the University of Minnesota in Minneapolis, I was the first in the family to attend college. The occasion called for proper clothing: my father, John F. Hondl, in his suit; me in a puffed-sleeve dress with my hair in rollers (to be styled later by my older sister, Nadine); my mother, Dorothy, in her Sunday best; and younger sister Colleen smiling in a full skirt.

Our family's '57 black-and-white DeSoto Fireflight had plenty of room for my three suitcases, a wicker wastebasket, my clothes and the portable manual typewriter I had received for high school graduation. I remember my dad giving me my gift early because he couldn't wait for me to open it.

Along with dorm essentials, I took some valuable lessons my parents taught me on the farm: Work hard, be responsible for yourself and don't give up. Because Mom and Dad did not have the opportunity for education, they stressed to their children the importance of schooling.

In 1962, with no computers, Facebook or cellphones, I kept in touch with my family through letters; long-distance phone calls were for emergencies only. My parents came to campus only to drop off in the fall and pick up in spring. There were few frills. No trips to Target to buy coordinated dorm room decor, and no expensive restaurant meals. The first summer after my freshman year, I returned home to help bale hay, repair fences and assist with the grain harvest.

My parents' expectations drove my success. After graduating, I earned a master's degree in journalism at the University of Michigan.

Much to my dad's dismay, the Chrysler Corp. stopped making his DeSoto in 1961. I fondly remember it as an elegant ride that took me from my rural beginnings to the big city, where a university education and a world of new experiences awaited.

**BERNADETTE THOMASY**
**SACRAMENTO, CA**

## PAINTED-ON NYLONS

I grew up on a small farm in central Michigan with no electricity or running water. This country girl moved to the city of Flint after college and got a job as secretary to the chief inspector of the Buick Motor Tank Division. Nylon stockings were unavailable at the time, as nylon was reserved to make parachutes for the war effort. So we working girls had to come up with a substitute: We bought tan-colored suntan lotion and painted our bare legs to look as if we were in stockings.

On a particularly hot day, working in a room with no air conditioning, I took off my shoes under my desk to cool my bare feet. I was concentrating on my typing, pounding the keys so the print would go through seven carbons. My boss interrupted and called me to his office to take dictation. Flustered, I got up and grabbed my pencil and pad and walked into his office barefoot. Soon, my suntan lotion secret was out.

This country girl never lived it down until the end of the war, when I quit my job to marry.

**GERTRUDE CHESS**
**HOUGHTON LAKE, MI**

**NEIGHBORHOOD SHOPPER** "When I was 12, Daddy bought a red International truck and developed a milk route," says Rilla Bellury of Eclectic, Alabama. "He'd go to farms and pick up milk in tin cans and take them to Southern Dairies. I'd often go with him. One day, a lady asked me if I ever stopped by any stores. My father said that I could if she needed me to pick something up for her, so she gave me money and a list. Daddy dropped me off at Newberry's store, delivered the milk, and then picked me up. Soon I had several people I was shopping for. The lists included things like a little girl's dress, socks, school supplies and even shoes!" Rilla is second from the right in the bottom row of this photo from 1928.

## CHAPTER 3

# FARMHOUSE FUN

*When you have a barn, animals and a creek nearby,
how could you ever be bored? From sledding behind
a tractor to making mud pies, simple pleasures
are embraced and celebrated on a farm.*

# NOW THAT'S ENTERTAINING!

### Country folks certainly don't lack for amusements

## NO HOT CHOCOLATE FOR WHINERS

Growing up, we lived where my friends all said you had to import sunlight. My parents are still there today, atop a hill with a drive that winds through sun-dappled woods and opens to a rich green pasture.

All that land was our playground when I was little, and it was a real treat when snow fell in this part of north Georgia. Then we'd go canoeing down the hill that had transformed overnight into the best slope in the South.

Yes, canoeing. My daddy would use the yellow nylon rope he usually reserved for camping and he'd tie our canoe to the tractor hitch. We were country kids, used to tractor fumes and problem-solving, but I don't think it occurred to us to use trash-can lids. Why would it? We had the canoe.

We'd bundle up in whatever we could find to stay warm and wrap our feet in Ziploc bags before shoving on our sneakers. Mama would tuck us into the canoe and cover us with quilts. My brother would scoop up snow and throw it at us girls—and everyone would wail and holler when that icy cold inevitably found the gap between collar and neck.

A few inches of snow was all it took to make this contraption work, and we'd be off flying down the hill or turning doughnuts.

Sometimes, though, we would get enough snow for things to get really exciting. One year there must have been more than 5 inches,

because pictures show the little ones sinking nearly to their knees.

That was the year Daddy made it his mission to show us what that old canoe could really do. He pulled us all over those 38 acres, the tractor chugging right along, while we skimmed our hands along the powdery surface. Then suddenly, he'd have us in a tailspin, going faster than we'd ever gone, and with one extra turn of the wheel, *whoosh!* We'd land on our faces in the drifts.

Everyone always got up laughing, especially when Mama said, "No hot chocolate for whiners."

Now we live in subdivisions and apartment complexes, and my kids go sledding on trash-can lids. My baby sister is the only one still at home. The tractor died long ago. I'm not sure she even remembers the rides, except for what we tell her.

But one of these days when the sky takes on that heavy cloud load and the flakes start to fall, we're going to gather back there around a roaring fire. We'll bundle up the nine grandkids and we're going to canoe that old hill, even if we have to pull the rope ourselves.

**LINDSEY BRACKETT**
**CLARKESVILLE, GA**

When snow fell on their farm, Lindsey and her siblings jumped into the canoe.

Before Welk hit it big, his first bands were the Hotsy Totsy Boys and the Honolulu Fruit Gum Orchestra.

## A-ONE AND A-TWO AND...

It was in 1922 at a barn dance in Danzig, North Dakota, when Lawrence Welk came into my mother's life. My mother, Pearl Johnson, was 11 at the time, and she tapped her foot and watched in awe as her older sisters danced the polka with their handsome cowboys.

When Lawrence took a break from the stage, a fiddler took over, playing a lively jig. As Lawrence walked through the crowd, he noticed Pearl and asked her to dance, spinning her around the floor just once. But that was enough time for Mom to become completely smitten.

Everyone from the southeast corner of North Dakota knew all about Lawrence Welk. He was a farm boy from nearby Strasburg who fell in love with music as a teenager. His father agreed to buy him his first accordion for $400 (today, that would be well over $4,000) on the condition that he would stay on the farm until he was 21 to pay off the debt. By the time Lawrence was playing barn dances in 1922, he was having such a good time making music, you could hardly tell he had already put in a hard day of work on the family farm.

**GLENDA BONIN**
**TUCSON, AZ**

Hank "The Yodeling Ranger" Snow

## NORTHERN STAR

In the 1940s, while spending summers on my uncle's farm in Canada, I used to tune in country radio stations out of the South, especially WSM in Nashville, Tennessee, for the Grand Ole Opry. I loved bluegrass and old-time fiddle music.

We also had some outstanding country artists in Canada, including Anne Murray and Ian Tyson. But my favorite was Hank "The Yodeling Ranger" Snow from Nova Scotia. Hank was similar to Johnny Cash in that all of his songs told a story.

Many years ago I sent Hank three songs I had written, and he picked one for one of his albums.

Hank's career lasted more than 50 years, and he performed at the Opry many times. I was fortunate to have seen one of his shows there shortly before he died.

Even today, in my 80s, I love to get out one of my guitars and rattle off one of Hank's old songs.

**GEORGE BOWSER**
**NORTH YORK, ON**

## ALL THE FUN THEY COULD PACK IN

In the '40s the highlight of the summer for my family was an annual trip to our grandparents' farm in Sorento, Illinois, in August. We fished, rode in the buggy, picked raspberries and swam in their farm pond. The most memorable event was sitting under the big box elder trees in their front yard and listening to our grandfather's stories.

The traditional reunion picnic on the last day of our visit was another favorite. Everyone played in the softball game, then dug in to the delicious food my grandmother and aunts had made: fried chicken, potato salad, baked beans, cakes and homemade ice cream. Then we took photographs. One of the pictures (below) was of our grandmother and her five grandchildren. When she positioned herself in the middle of the bumper of my uncle's car, I jumped onto her lap, thinking that, being the firstborn grandchild, I deserved it. But she asked me, "Do you want to let the littlest sit here?" I nodded yes and moved aside.

**ROBERT L. SULASKI**
**EDWARDS, IL**

Josephine Griffiths with a lapful of grandchildren. Robert, at age 6, is on the far left.

## A LESSON IN HOW (NOT) TO

I grew up in Fort Lupton, Colorado, on my parents' dairy farm. After returning home from the Army and finishing college, I was offered a coaching and teaching position at a rural school. Before I could decide what I wanted to do, my father died. I ended up selling our dairy cows and stayed on the land, farming hay and starting a commercial beef herd.

My neighbor Elmo managed a ranch. He was a real character. Rattlesnakes had bitten him more times than he could count. He took me under his wing, teaching me what he knew.

One afternoon I found him trying to start an old dirt bike. He was struggling and talked me into pulling him behind my pickup with a rope.

We tightly knotted one end of the rope to the fork of his bike and the other to my bumper, and down the driveway we went. Eventually, the bike fired up, but the throttle stuck wide open. When Elmo came racing up alongside my window, I couldn't decide whether to slow down or speed up. By then it was too late. The rope had reached its maximum length. The bike, at full steam ahead, hit the end of the rope and spun around in midair. Fortunately, Elmo missed that rollicking ride. Instead he simply took a heroic flight through the air and landed in a patch of wheat stubble. I slammed on the brakes, jumped out of the car and ran to him. Elmo was just fine, albeit a bit bruised and plenty creaky. He got up, limped over to his bike and kicked it.

Elmo sure taught me plenty of how-to over the years, but I think, in the end, his lessons in how-not-to were even more valuable!

**LEE AMATO**
**FORT LUPTON, CO**

## THIS LITTLE PIGGY

In 1938, when I was 8 years old, my parents took my older brother and me to a country picnic at a friend's farm in the southern New Jersey countryside, a drastic change from our urban life around Camden.

We started playing tag with the children. As my brother chased me, I sped across a large open area and sank up to my thighs in pig manure. This necessitated a quick trip home for a bath and a change out of my Sunday best.

I didn't realize what a hit I'd made until years later, at my mother's funeral. I introduced my wife to Mom's lifelong friend Sue, who proceeded to relate the entire episode to my wife in vivid detail!

**JOSEPH CORBETT**
**BANNING, CA**

## FARM-TO-ENGLISH DICTIONARY

After 30-plus years as a transplanted city girl, I have deciphered most "farmerisms" uttered by those working the land: folks like my husband, my father-in-law and our neighbors.

First, things have multiple names. The terms chopper wagon, forage wagon and green-feed wagon are all the same thing. The difference between a hay elevator and a conveyor? Not much. A dairy animal may have calved or freshened, but either way it has just given birth. And manure is the same as...you get the idea.

And then there's a whole list of terms that are often misused by nonfarmers. An udder is the whole bag hanging under the cow, not each little dangly, which is called a teat. Also, a heifer that has a "hot quarter" didn't just pull change out of the clothes dryer. That cow has an inflammation in one section of her udder.

Hay is feed, a mixture of grasses that have been cut, left to dry and baled. Straw is bedding, the stems of either oats or wheat that are left after the combine removes the grain. (And despite these definitions, cows sometimes nibble at straw and lie down on hay.)

Tractors are usually diesel-powered and capable of pulling large implements and wagons. A tractor is not used to mow the lawn. It is a workhorse of a machine that, in this part of the Midwest, is usually John Deere green or International Harvester red. A good-natured rivalry exists between the supporters of each.

Then there are commonly used phrases:

"Well, I s'pose..." This indicates the end of a meal, a conversation or a rest period. It means, "I suppose we ought to get back to work."

"Could you give me a hand a minute?" For this 60 seconds of assistance, turn off the stove, make sure the kids are safe, put on work boots and grab a jacket.

"Can I have a bandage?" Either the wound is still bleeding after being wiped on a pant leg, or there's no duct tape handy. Be prepared to call the paramedics.

"While you're in town, can you pick up a bolt?" The store clerk will ask if it's metric or standard, fine or reverse thread, hardened, lag or carriage. In other words, buy every type of bolt, have your farmer pick out the right one and return the rest later. This also applies to hoses, belts, tires and gaskets.

"Cows are out!" Generally shouted around midnight during a thunderstorm means it's time to get up from a dead sleep and herd cattle.

Now you'll be able to nod knowingly. Well, we've been talking awhile, so I s'pose...

**LINDA PERONA
BRIGHTON, WI**

# KIDS KNOW HOW TO HAVE FUN

### A big imagination plus a farm equals good times

## SIMPLE THINGS MAKE LASTING MEMORIES

In the '50s, my good friend Janet lived on a dairy farm in a two-story stone farmhouse with a large covered front porch in rural southeastern Pennsylvania.

The property had a wonderful stone barn with a hayloft where we would hang out often. One of our favorite activities was spying on Janet's father in the barn as he milked the Holsteins or mucked the stalls. It gave us great joy to think he didn't know we could hear him softly talking to the cows.

We enjoyed the fragrances as we shared stories, gazing out the large open doors that overlooked the driveway that seemed a mile long, winding past the corncrib, the silo, and fields of hay and corn. We had more fun those days, enjoying the simple things.

There was always something to do on the farm. We waded in the stream that flowed through the meadow, capturing tadpoles and box turtles to get a closer look. We learned to walk on stilts made by Forrest, Janet's older brother. It's a wonder none of us broke our bones as we hobbled around, laughing until our sides hurt! Sometimes we picked red clover to string wildflower necklaces or gathered English plantain weed for shooting the little flower tops at each other.

One of the many highlights of the farm was riding on the tractor. Sometimes Janet would beg her dad to let her drive the old Co-op, and her face would light up with delight as she hopped up on the worn seat and took the wheel! Chickens, cats and dogs would run for their lives as the big green "monster" loudly motored around the farmstead.

Then came winter and school, which meant snow days! Some days, I'd stay at Janet's when we heard a storm was coming, and we'd wake up to a winter wonderland. Instead of going out into the freezing cold, we would open the upstairs window and haul in snow off the roof, filling the old bathtub to the brim. We would build mini snowmen or artistically add food coloring until the warmth of the house left the tub empty, with various colorful stains.

Before we realized it, those magical times became memories— lasting moments that bring warm feelings to our hearts!

**KARIN RASMUSSEN
GRASS VALLEY, CA**

The beautiful stone-walled barn (above) held dairy cows; Janet (right) waves happily while riding the tractor on her family's farm.

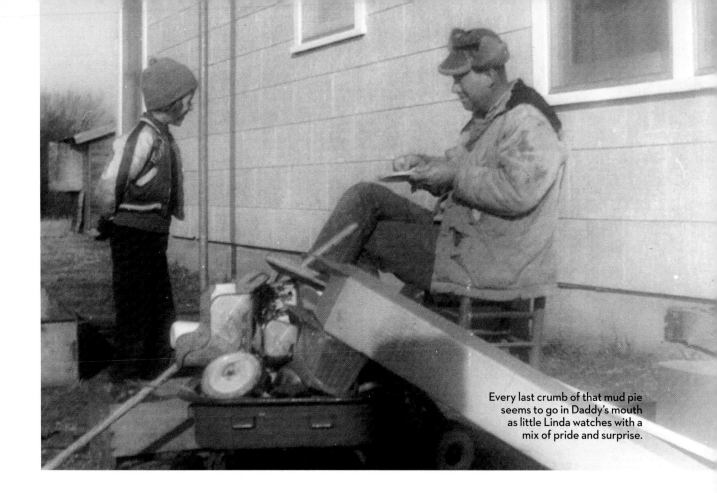

Every last crumb of that mud pie seems to go in Daddy's mouth as little Linda watches with a mix of pride and surprise.

## MUD PIE MAGIC

My daddy was a small-scale farmer and rancher. Despite his hard work and his farming know-how, his profits were low. This meant that we didn't have what most folks would call nice things. However, I was having too much fun as a kid to know that I was poor.

I spent many a day cooking outdoors. In the mornings, my portable kitchen would be on the back porch, where the concrete slab made a nice kitchen floor. When the noon sun appeared, I loaded my pots and pans into my little red wagon and hauled my kitchen to the front porch.

It was amazing what goodies I could prepare with such basic ingredients as dirt, water, grass, rocks and flowers. I could whip up anything from fried chicken to chocolate cake.

I never tired of my kitchen chores. No, I didn't have a microwave to speed up the meal preparation or an automatic dishwasher to do the dishes. I knew Mom and Dad would love me even with dishpan hands.

My "kids" loved me, too. I had six little charges in all: four cats, one dog and one rabbit. They were such good kids, always well-behaved and never complaining.

Of course I didn't spend all my waking hours in my play kitchen. There was also real work around the farm, and one of my favorite early chores was bottle-feeding three motherless Jersey calves. Daddy had bought them thinking one of our cows would adopt them, but our cow had different thoughts. That was OK. I had fun feeding them and naming them: Peanuts, Popcorn and Cracker Jacks.

And life on the farm could be dangerous. I found myself on many occasions fighting wild, bloodthirsty rustlers in the peach orchard. With my stick horse and six-shooter, I always saved the day.

But all my heroic moments couldn't compare to my special moments with Daddy. I remember one chilly day when I was 5 years old as if it were yesterday. I met my dad coming around the house. He was wearing his big, heavy Army coat he got while he was in the Korean War. He asked me if I would fix him something to eat.

I began preparing one of my famous mud pies and handed him a plate. Daddy placed each bite right up to his mouth, and I believed he'd eaten it all, because he returned a clean plate. I was so astonished that I raced into the house to tell Mom.

My daddy had a way of always making me feel very special. Even something as simple as a plate full of mud pies became magical.

LINDA MCDANIEL
HUNTSVILLE, TX

Pat's brother Walt shows off Elsie, the "big mean bull" that guarded the creek.

## THE HUMAN SALT BLOCK

It was an unbearably hot, humid day, and my brother Walt and I had decided that the only way to survive it would be to go swimming in the creek behind Mr. Blickez's barn. Across his pasture and through some woods was a deep swimming hole fed by several cold springs.

The only problem with our plan was that this pasture was guarded by a huge, mean Hereford bull. Mr. Blickez had told us that Elsie—yes, that was the animal's name—was the meanest bull in the township, maybe even the county, and we believed him.

But the hotter it got, the more we thought there was something fishy about his claim. For one thing, we remembered that Mr. Blickez liked telling tall tales; for another, Elsie seemed an odd name for a bull. Finally, I talked Mom into asking permission for us to walk through the pasture, but then another problem surfaced.

Mom said she would talk to Mr. Blickez if we would take our cousin Joanie along with us. At 10, Joanie was almost two years older than me and a head taller. She insisted on giving me knuckle rubs and calling me Pat the Rat. If her teasing ever got around my grade school, it would be all over for me. In fact, at the time I still had a vague headache from an altercation with her that very morning. "I'm not going swimming with that dumb cousin," I told my mom emphatically.

"Either Joanie goes with, or you stay home alone," Mom said in her no-nonsense tone. With sweat streaming down my face and back, I carefully weighed the advantages and disadvantages.

On our way across the pasture, we stopped at the fence to admire the swimming hole. The sun sparkled across the cool waters as the salty perspiration ran down our hot tanned backs. Suddenly Walt yelled. Elsie had snuck up on him and was licking his back.

Joanie and I dove under the barbed wire fence, but while I was on the ground I looked up and saw that Elsie wasn't a big mean bull after all. She was just a friendly calf, and she was going to keep licking my brother's back as long as he stood still.

Walt finally snapped back to reality and joined us at the creek's edge. "Betcha can't swim across the creek! Betcha can't hold your breath for a minute!" we whooped happily at each other, jumping in. The water was just as wonderful as we had dreamed.

We had many good days growing up and visiting our secret swimming hole guarded by the so-called "big mean bull." And as it turned out, for a cousin, Joanie hasn't been too bad. She's been one of my best friends over the years. As for Walt, he never did take up Mr. Blickez on his suggestion that Walt hang around the farm as a human salt block.

**PAT ARBEITER**
**GRAND JUNCTION, CO**

## GOING MOBILE

Growing up in rural Plymouth, Michigan, I used to visit a farm down the road that was run by two brothers, Bill and Rudy. The brothers didn't mind me wandering in the barns. They had a dusty old family buggy in the corner of one barn, and I would climb up and pretend I was driving a horse.

One threshing season when I was 10, I asked Bill if I could help. He told me to search the barns for all the empty burlap bags and carry them out to the thresher. I did what he asked and later got to eat dinner with the threshing crew under the big maples by the house. In those days, the noon meal was dinner; the evening meal was supper.

After the threshing was done, Bill called me over, thanked me and gave me a dollar bill. I gulped and asked if he would sell me the buggy. He thought for a minute and said with a twang in his voice, "How about three dollars?"

I ran home and dug a dollar out of my piggy bank and got my mom to advance me the rest. The next day Bill delivered the buggy, complete with a harness, to my front door. He winked at Mom and remarked that I drove a hard bargain.

When my dad got home that night, he asked the obvious question: "What are you going to use to pull the buggy?" I hadn't thought of that. But Dad had an idea and called an auctioneer friend, who sold him a skinny old nag that my brother and I named Tom. Dad stood me on a box and taught me how to put on the harness, and I was mobile.

Tom grew fat in my grandpa's pasture, and my brother and I traveled all over our backcountry roads having the time of our lives.

**JAMES G. BRAND**
**STANWOOD, MI**

James bought the buggy; his dad bought the horse. But brother Sandy took the reins when Aunt Margaret and Uncle Tyke came to visit.

Riders Linda (left) and Linnie saddle up Babe and Sunny and head off for adventure in Big Bear Valley. Linda takes Babe to a summer rodeo in 1954 (below).

## OPEN-AIR EXPLORATION

Some of my most treasured memories of summer were made in the San Bernardino Mountains of Southern California. In the summers of the early 1950s, my best friend, Linnie, would come to Big Bear Lake from Lucerne Valley. We lived on opposite sides of Big Bear Valley.

I'd call her, saddle up my horse, Babe, and ride like the wind through the ponderosa pine forests of Big Bear to our favorite rendezvous. I remember how much fun it was to gallop together, back through the forest, to my mother's fox farm to plan our day.

Linnie and I pretended that we had three horse ranches in Big Bear. We gathered up pine needles, carefully stacked them in squares and made corrals big enough to put our horses in. My mother would spread mayonnaise on slices of bread and pack them for a picnic for us. We then rode out toward the north end of Big Bear Lake off the main boulevard and into the woods,

making our way to the meadow on the Fawnskin side of the lake.

We got off our horses and sat in the soft meadow where leafy green watercress grew wild. Our horses grazed as we picked through the cloverlike plants, plucking out bugs and debris before stuffing the cress between the bread slices.

I can still remember the cool breeze, smell the pine trees and feel the intense sunshine on the meadow overlooking the lake. We gabbed and laughed and listened to the gentle sounds of our horses chomping and pulling at the vegetation nearby. After we stuffed ourselves, picking watercress out of our teeth, we mounted our horses and rode around the lake. Big Bear Lake was much lower in those years, and we found a favorite area where we trotted our horses into the water! They treaded water underneath us. It felt like floating on a magic carpet.

**LINDA MCDOUGALD WATSON**
**VALENCIA, CA**

## CAUTION: CRAZY CATTLE CROSSING

When I was around 10 years old, my best friend, Deb, her sister Julie and I went to the creek by their house one day to play. First we found a huge block of foam that we used for a raft, which we enjoyed falling off of for hours.

As we made our way down the creek, we came upon another treasure: a large triangular sign with the words "cattle crossing" and the image of a cow.

I can't remember which one of us came up with the master plan, but we all agreed it was brilliant. We went to the road, and when a car finally came, Julie stood at the side of the road, holding up the sign. An older couple, with curious expressions, slowly came to a stop. Julie proceeded to the middle of the road, holding the sign high in front of her with both hands. Then Deb and I came out of the ditch, hunched over with our fists on our heads with index fingers pointed for horns. We said *Moooo!* as loudly as we could. When we got to the other side of the road, all three of us ran into the woods and dropped to the ground, laughing so hard it hurt.

Now I'm nearly 60, and I still have those same two wonderful friends. We often laugh about our antics over the years and muse about what that couple in the car might have said to each other after the "cattle" ran away giggling!

**ROBYN HICKERSON**
**CLARE, MI**

## COUNTRY KICKS IN DAD'S TRUCK

In the '40s, when I was in high school in Battle Creek, Nebraska, we didn't have television to watch, so we found other ways to entertain ourselves. For instance, we would take a ride in our autos and "squirrel" around, driving loops in the snow. Or we would park by a farmhouse at night, blink our headlights on and off, and wait for some sign of life; then we'd spin our wheels in the gravel, taking off in hopes that the farmer would chase us. I had no car of my own, so when I went "squirreling," I would drive my dad's red truck.

One Sunday night, my girlfriend and I were parked about 2 miles from town, and we barreled away when we saw a farmer's yard lights come on. The chase was on! At the edge of town, I saw that the farmer—Mr. Sheve—was gaining on us. We made it into town, but he was right on our tail. I turned down an alley and turned my lights off. I shut the motor off, too, even though the temperature was a record low. Now, in those days, I was a bit shy, but I did get up the courage to hold my girlfriend's hand to help us keep warm. A few minutes later, I was brave enough to put my arm around her. Oh, what a thrill! After about 20 minutes, we figured we'd outsmarted Mr. Sheve, so we slowly drove to our church for the Sunday evening service. As we walked into the church, guess what they were singing: "Bringing in the sheaves, bringing in the sheaves, we shall come rejoicing, bringing in the sheaves."

**ROBERT RISOR SR.**
**VANCOUVER, WA**

## ONE-COW OPEN SLEIGH RIDE

When I was 6 or 7, Dad made a sled out of spare boards and Formica. It didn't look like much, but Formica is as slick as glass on snow. For a real sledding adventure, Dad might pull us behind the tractor, a Ford F-150 pickup, or even our horse. One day, he decided to try using cow power. With some difficulty, he roped a young calf that had grown up on the fat of the land and hooked him up to our homemade sled.

Now, when you think of a calf, you usually think of a somewhat docile creature that would be the bovine equivalent of a big kitten. But this animal, Bossy, was a most healthy, hearty, headstrong critter. He had grown big and bold after grazing free for months.

When my friend and I slapped the reins down on his rump, Bossy took off like the unbroken steer he was. We held on for dear life when he hit a terrace and launched the sled like something off the *Wide World of Sports,* promptly ejecting my friend. With the reduced weight, Bossy plowed ahead unencumbered. That cow dragged me all over that hill, through the pasture, the thickets and the woods, with me careening off pine trees. (Now I know why one of John Wayne's characters once described cows as trouble wrapped up in a leather bag.)

The calf reached the creek and plunged in, pulling me, the sled and my objections through the frigid waters. You've never seen anyone stand up so fast. I was soaked to the bone. My buddy, as it turned out, was the fortunate one—I had a long, cold, wet walk back up the hill.

When I reached Dad, he just had a big laugh and sent me in to change out of my wet clothes. (Mom found the whole situation a little less humorous.) Afterward, we looked for the calf to make sure he was OK. Sure enough, he was down in one corner of the pasture waiting patiently. When Dad took the harness off him, he just batted those big brown eyes and slowly trotted away. No livestock were harmed in the making of this story—just some boyish pride.

**RICK JACKSON**
**NEWTON, NC**

Kimberly Osborne Townsend (in gray jacket at right and below) tells of tubular travels down snowy slopes in her story, below left.

## SLEDDING FROM DAY TO DARK

On snow days, Mom would gather all the neighborhood kids and our friends in our station wagon and we'd head out to Grandma and Grandpa Hurst's farm with sleds and sometimes inner tubes.

Pictured with a tube (above right) are Amy Cee and me. The other photo shows me in front with Jennifer Davis Hayes. Jeff Osborne, Robin Sumner Aleman and Pete Ruby are behind us.

From the top of a hill, we'd slide all the way down to the church parking lot. We'd play for hours, sometimes daylight to dark, and when we were practically frozen stiff we'd have hot chocolate and marshmallows.

Some snow days we'd go to Grandma and Grandpa Osborne's place and ice-skate on their pond and have hot chocolate there, too. The best part was that snow days were spent with family and friends.

**KIMBERLY OSBORNE TOWNSEND**
**WHEELERSBURG, OH**

## LET IT SNOW

We kept a large sheep named Topsy as a pet. My brother and I would hitch her up to our sled, and she would pull us around. We had lots of snow in the '50s and '60s and no shortage of winter fun.

**BETH CHIPCHASE**
**VIA FACEBOOK**

## WHAT BIG TEETH YOU HAVE!

It was 1964, and we had just bought a small farm in Republic, Missouri. David, our 5-year-old son, loved to explore the farm while we built fences, repaired the barn and did other chores.

While making his bed one morning, I was shocked to find a pile of cow teeth beneath his pillow. Apparently, David had found a cow skull on a rock pile, knocked its teeth out with a hammer and hidden them under his pillow, hoping to hit the jackpot with the tooth fairy!

**JANELLE JONES KNOX**
**SPRINGFIELD, MO**

## CRUSHED BY A COW...OR WAS HE?

Showing our Brown Swiss dairy cattle at the Missouri State Fair was the highlight of my childhood in the '70s and '80s.

With nothing much to do for four days at the fair, other than keep our animals clean, we played a lot of pranks. The dressed-up townies weren't immune to them: One of our favorite tricks was to stuff a pair of jeans and a shirt and put them under each side of a resting cow. Then we'd just have to wait for the screams and a townie shouting, "Help! The cow killed him!"

**DENISE LEWIS**
**MARSHFIELD, MO**

## HOOKED ON FISHING

Our little brother, Matty, loved to go fishing. As the snow would start melting each spring, he'd check every day to see if the creek on the north side of our house in Marenisco, Michigan, had begun to flow.

He kept his waders—hand-me-downs from older brothers, and almost as big as he was—by the door. Mom found a big branch in the woods and trimmed it down to size to serve as his pole, which was his prize possession. With twine and a good, strong safety pin, he was in business.

And Matty was always digging in the garden for worms, which he kept in an old coffee can filled with dirt. He liked to be prepared.

He was determined to catch a big fish so Mama could fix it for supper. We knew there weren't any fish in the creek—just a lot of pollywogs. But Matty was certain a big fish was in there, waiting to be caught. Mom even made a little dock for him, and our sisters Frances and Rosalyn made sure he didn't fall into the water.

Nobody had the heart to tell him the truth. On the other hand, he was never sad when he didn't catch anything. He just stood there for hours, throwing his line into the water and hoping he'd catch a fish.

When I look at the photo below of him fishing, it reminds me of what a great life we had living in a small town in the 1950s.

**BETTY BIONDICH**
**MENOMONIE, WI**

Frances, Rosalyn and Matty posing at the creek in 1950.

## DOODLE-BUGGING ABOUT TOWN

In the '50s, when I was a teen in Holstein, Iowa, my father was a farmer, and it was a difficult way to make a living. When I'd visit my friend Virgie Prouty for a week in Worthington, Minnesota, it seemed that her family had everything—including a garbage disposal. It was the first time I'd heard of such a thing.

Virgie's father would give us 15 cents, and we'd put gas in the tank of the Hiawatha Doodle Bug that I'm sitting on in the photo (right) and we'd ride all over. The basket really came in handy.

I'd love to get on that Doodle Bug and ride again, but perhaps it wouldn't be quite as much fun as when Virgie and I rode together. Still, my memories of our times together are wonderful.

**DOROTHY CONOVER JOHNSTON**
**BAXTER, IA**

## ◄DAD'S GIFT

"In 1949, my cousins Jerry and Charles, who lived next door, received a new pedal car that looked like an International tractor. Since we lived on a farm, I wanted a pedal tractor just like it," says Dennis Schultz from Newfane, New York. "As my sixth birthday drew closer, I hoped for a new tractor of my own, but I knew that my mother and father couldn't afford such an expensive toy. Instead, my father, Carl Schultz, surprised me with a tractor he built himself from old tricycle parts, pipes and sheet metal. I rode that tractor for many years and will always cherish those special memories of it, knowing that my father made it with love for me."

**THE COOL KIDS** "This photo was taken in 1926 in Rochester, New York," writes Dolores Siebert of Saratoga, California. "The creek behind our farmhouse was the very best place to cool off on hot summer days. That's me, holding a bunch of flowers, with my brother and sister."

**CHAPTER 4**

# CULTIVATING ROMANCE

*The country can provide the perfect backdrop for young love. Maybe it's all that fresh air? Some of the couples here were lucky enough to fall head over heels, or at least have a cute tale to share about their down-home affair.*

# FATE STEPPED IN

## Cupid pays a visit to the farm

### HER SHY GUY

The summer before my senior year in high school, I spotted an evening dress in a store window. It was 1949, and I was visiting my Aunt Ruby in the small town of Lattimore, North Carolina. It was the most beautiful dress I had ever seen, and I wanted badly to wear it to my senior prom.

I was the eldest daughter of a struggling cotton farmer who couldn't spare his children to work for others. But I begged my parents to let me go to Lattimore to pick cotton for a week so I could buy that dress. Aunt Ruby had told me about a man and his nephew who farmed 40 acres of cotton and hired people to pick it.

My parents gave in, and I went to work on a Monday morning. "Do you see that young man across the railroad tracks?" Aunt Ruby said. "Ask him where he wants you to pick."

As I approached, the young man turned and walked to the other side of a car. I walked over to him and he moved again. It turned out he was very shy.

I had been studying about introverts and extroverts in school. I made up my mind that I would get that young fellow—whose name, I learned, was Howard—to talk to me.

That day I worked alongside Howard's cousin William, who was a talker, like me. The next day I took a row between William and Howard. I picked so fast I had to help with their rows, too.

William knew that Howard was interested but was too shy to say anything. This was the first time a girl had expressed interest in him, and he fell like a rock. Soon William was taking messages back and forth between us.

The entire neighborhood was abuzz with the news that shy 22-year-old Howard was interested in a girl, and everyone was rooting for us. I plotted with his Uncle Tom to have Howard take me home on Saturday afternoon, but I still doubted I'd see him again.

The following Tuesday, Howard drove up with William. Howard had lost his pick sack and asked if I had seen it. Of course, his pick sack wasn't missing at all: He'd made that up so he could visit me. Then, to my surprise, he asked me to go to a movie on Saturday.

Howard hid his face from the camera while on a double date with Rosita at the Broad River.

Even more amazingly, he brought William along for the first 20 or so dates! William and I talked while Howard held my hand. But despite his shyness, Howard seemed so content in my presence. One night I whispered to him, "Can you and I go to the movies alone?"

We were married 15 months later, proving that opposites really do attract. The marriage lasted 48 years, until his death. And in case you were wondering, I did make enough money picking cotton that week to get my evening dress.

**ROSITA JOLLEY JONES**
**DALLAS, NC**

### A REAL KEEPER

I took a horse to the Ross County Fair in Chillicothe, Ohio, in 1958. I was 13. A group of guys had horses down at the other end of the same tent. The blond, blue-eyed, 6-foot 16-year-old in the group offered to help me with my saddle. We dated 5½ years and then married on Dec. 25, 1963. Now, 53 years later, he's still helping me with whatever I need him to do. He's a keeper.

**BETSEY FARABEE**
**VIA FACEBOOK**

Betty Lou French and Jake Huffaker snuggled up close on the Ambassador Bridge in Detroit, Michigan, a day before they wed in 1950.

## POSTSCRIPT FOR A PEN PAL

During my senior year of high school, in 1945-'46, I discovered that popular magazines were printing the names and addresses of pen pals.

I began corresponding with a girl named Kathleen, who lived on a small farm with five sisters, five brothers and her widowed mother in the Clinch Mountains of southwest Virginia. She'd seen my name in a southern agriculture magazine, and we wrote for more than two years.

When I planned a trip to Georgia to visit another pen pal, Kathleen invited me to spend a weekend with her family in Virginia. By then, some of her siblings were married and had moved away, so only two brothers and two sisters remained at home.

After I got back from my trip, I noticed that Kathleen's letters weren't quite what they had been. Because her brothers liked me so much, I was still invited to spend Christmas with her family that year. Kathleen eventually quit writing to me when I moved to Pontiac, Michigan, to live with an aunt and uncle and get a job, but I still heard from her mother and one of her brothers occasionally.

One day in 1949, I got a letter from Betty Lou French, who lived in North Tazewell, Virginia. She was one of Kathleen's older sisters. She wrote, "I asked my mother if she thought it would be OK if I wrote to you."

We began corresponding and called each other for several months. When I planned to go home on vacation, I asked her to spend the weekend with my family. We were engaged that weekend, and have celebrated 62 wonderful years of marriage together.

**JAKE HUFFAKER**
**KNOXVILLE, TN**

## MEANT TO BE

In the mid-1950s, I was running the family farm at age 17 after my dad died. A few years later, a friend asked to keep his horse on the farm, and he let me ride it. One day, after milking the cows and finishing the chores, I rode several miles on a winding gravel road near East Troy, Wisconsin. Along the road I was riding, I saw a small barn on fire, so I had to stop. I met the family and a girl named Bonnie. We talked, and I asked her out for a date. She accepted. That fire forged our fate: We married in 1959 and celebrated our 55th wedding anniversary in 2014. If my friend had not kept his horse on my farm, and I had not ridden down the old gravel road by the farm with the burning barn that day, I never would have met the love of my life, Bonnie.

**HERBERT W. CROPP**
**ROCKFORD, IL**

When a fella needs a Life Saver

The candy with the hole

...still only 5¢

## KISS OF THE HOPS

Hops are a pioneer crop here in Oregon's Willamette Valley. My grandfather, who came here as a baby on the Oregon Trail in 1847, was growing hops before the turn of the century. My father told stories of harvesting hops with crews of Native Americans from the Warm Springs Reservation. They traveled more than 100 miles with ponies pulling travois (a type of sled).

During the Great Depression, my parents were barely making a living on their 80-acre farm. So when Prohibition ended in 1933, my father decided to start growing hops—one of the main ingredients in beer—again for more income. Unfortunately, growing hops is labor-intensive and expensive. His first crop sold for 7 cents a pound, while total production costs were probably around 20 to 25 cents a pound.

Still, we persevered. And for me, hops harvest became the most interesting time of the year. We paid pickers a penny a pound, which averaged about $2 a day. But it was the Depression, so people welcomed any opportunity to work harvesting farm crops. About 50 people usually showed up, including a large number of young girls and women. Many successful relationships, including my parents' marriage, were the result of couples meeting in a hop yard.

We built a structure in which pickers could camp, and we made available fresh straw to fill their mattress covers. We also provided potatoes, homegrown vegetables, and milk from our dairy cows. After an evening meal, campers would gather around a bonfire. If pickers had a musical instrument, they'd play it, much to everyone's delight. It was a happy time, and folks came back to pick year after year.

Hops were picked from the vines and put into tall baskets that held about 25 pounds. After emptying two baskets into a large sack, the picker would call, "Weigh me up," and the weigh man would come with his tripod and scales. Then he would give the picker a ticket.

Dad promoted me to wireman when I was 14. Whenever a picker called, "Wire down," I would take a long pole and let the wire holding the tall vines down to a suitable height for picking. The work sure was a lot better than picking hops, a job I was not too fond of doing. It was around that time that the girls became more interesting, too. Because my job gave me some free time and there always were attractive girls my age, I pondered a lot about how to approach them. I discovered that they never objected when I spent my spare time

Cloth sack barrels were used in the '30s to collect the harvest of the tall hops plants.

picking hops and filling their baskets. What a great way to get acquainted!

But after 10 days or so, all the hops were picked. The pickers took their tickets to my mother, who added them up and paid them in cash. And all too soon, everyone packed up and headed for home. After all the activity of hops harvest, going back to everyday farm life was a big letdown.

**BYRON GRIM AS TOLD TO RUSSELL BAGLIEN**
**WOODBURN, OR**

# FEELING TWITTERPATED

## They had butterflies in their stomachs

Wayne met Claudette when he bought supplies for his farm (above). The couple take a stroll on a date in 1953 (right).

## BEST REASON TO BUY A FARM

At 27, after serving in World War II, I dreamed of owning a piece of land. So I moved from central Illinois to Shelbina, Missouri, and bought 236 acres for $6,000. The plot of land was situated on a dirt road and was half farmland and half trees, with an old house that had no running water or electricity. Obviously, it was not what you'd call prime real estate. But it was mine.

I was alone for the first time in my life, and I found it liberating. My days were filled from dawn until dusk with plowing and planting corn. Dinnertime came and went, and I barely remembered to eat.

I wouldn't say I was a great success at farming in Missouri. However, when I went to the store to buy some plowshares, I met a nice woman named Claudette working behind the counter. I also ran into her at St. Mary's Catholic Church in Shelbina each week. I found out later that her manager had kept asking her about "that tall boy (and eligible bachelor) from Illinois living out in the country in an old house with no water, no electricity and no housekeeper."

Claudette and her sister soon visited my farm and put up some curtains. To show my appreciation, I took Claudette out for a ride in my Studebaker truck. We married in 1954 and have now been together for more than 62 years!

I later sold the Missouri farm for a $3,500 profit and bought 40 acres in Illinois. For many reasons, the Missouri farm was a good idea. I will cherish memories of the farm and meeting my beloved.

**WAYNE FORAN**
**BEMENT, IL**

## MY SECRET CRUSH

My younger sister Ann and I eagerly looked forward to *The Brady Bunch* every Friday night at 8 p.m. We thought their modern California house was so cool...and so very different from the potato farm where we lived. They even had a live-in housekeeper, which seemed foreign to us. Ann liked Bobby and Cindy, but I liked Jan and envied her long blond hair and, of course, I secretly thought Peter was very cute! The Brady adventures were a special treat for two young girls from Schnecksville, Pennsylvania.

**MARY ALICE WALTZ**
**READING, PA**

## CLEANUP IN AISLE ONE

I was a high school freshman in Dallas, riding my horse on a typical Saturday. I wanted to grab a Coke at this new store called 7-Eleven, but there was nothing to tie my horse to. So I decided to try a ground tie, in which the reins dangle to the ground and the horse is supposed to stay there. Supposed to.

I went inside and was immediately faced with the cutest boy from study hall. *Oh, golly,* I thought, *I sure hope I can impress him!* As I approached, he smiled, but his expression soon changed to horror. When I heard the clop, clop, clopping behind me, I knew why. My horse had followed me into 7-Eleven!

Mumbling apologies, I tried to back her up through the narrow aisles. Then, almost halfway out, she raised her tail. I soon found myself scooping up horse manure with two pieces of cardboard on the floor of the brand-new 7-Eleven. That cute boy never smiled at me again.

**MARGERY MCKNIGHT**
**EVERGREEN, CO**

## FIREBOX FUMBLE

To say that my mother was excited when my father asked her for their first date would be an understatement.

At the time, she was living with her grandmother on a farm in Iowa. For cooking, they used an old woodstove. My great-grandmother asked my mom to go out to the corncrib and bring back a bucket of cobs, which they burned as fuel in the stove. While she was doing this, my father was up on the roof of a nearby shed doing repair work. As Mom walked by, Dad yelled down—would she like to go roller-skating with him the following Saturday? Mom agreed happily and was so excited that when she got back to the kitchen, she dumped the bucket of corncobs into the stove's water reservoir instead of the firebox! (Remember how those woodstoves had a reservoir for heating water right next to the firebox?)

Great-Grandma came out and asked my mom what in the world she was doing. With a very red face and a sincere apology, Mom fished the cobs from the water reservoir and went back outside for another bucket of fresh, dry cobs.

They did go roller-skating the following Saturday night, which led to 60 happy years of married life.

**DARRELL TESDALL**
**FOUNTAIN VALLEY, CA**

## CLEAN PLATE CLUB

Coming from a long line of farmers, I grew up eating plain old homegrown and farm-raised foods. When a nice fellow asked me to lunch at a fancy restaurant, I took one look at the menu and started to sweat.

Pretending to be indecisive, I asked my date to order for me. He chose the shrimp dinner. At least I'd heard of shrimp. What the waiter brought over was a plateful of what looked like the biggest grubworms I'd ever seen. Still, I wasn't about to look uneducated. I'd just do what Mama said and clean my plate. Everything would be fine.

And the shrimp were delicious, though maybe a bit crunchy. My date was friendly and showed a good sense of humor, though it was odd that he seemed to laugh throughout the whole meal.

When the waiter brought the bill, he took one look at my plate and his eyes widened. He looked at me, then at my date, and then they both started laughing. My face flushed. I knew I'd done something funny, but what? Finally, they kindly explained that I wasn't supposed to eat the shrimp tails. Or the parsley, for that matter.

**JUDITH CARRIG**
**PALM COAST, FL**

## BLAZING SADDLES

In the '30s and '40s, I lived on a small farm on the outskirts of Salt Lake City, Utah. I took the school bus with the same 10 kids every day—until one fateful morning, when I saw a new student board.

Dorothy Miller was about my age and attractive to boot. Over the next few months, we became good friends. We both had horses, and we started riding them together for fun after school and on the weekends.

One warm early summer evening, we decided to ride together on her horse, she in the saddle and me behind her. At the end of the ride, just about dark, we stopped in front of her long driveway. She turned to me, and I could see in her beautiful blue eyes that it was time for our first kiss. It was fantastic—a kiss I will never forget, even though I'm now an 86-year-old man.

**RON ERICKSON**
**ORANGE, CA**

In 1912, Fred and Martha Vincent drove his horse and buggy (above) 16 miles to a Methodist parsonage to get married. In 1944, Bob and Kathleen, both 16, show off a cow (right) named after Kathleen. With four older brothers in the service, Bob became his dad's helper on the farm.

## WELCOMED INTO AN AMAZING FAMILY

My in-laws, Martha and Fred Vincent, lived with Fred's parents for four years after they married in 1912. Looking back on those early years, Martha referred to Fred and herself as "crazy kids." They later raised two girls and five boys, including my husband, Bob.

Fred and Martha's first major purchase was a $200 upright piano. They paid $6 a month for it—out of Fred's $37.50 monthly teacher's salary—but it got plenty of use. Martha played the piano for joy, and both adults and kids joined in on sing-alongs. She also traded raspberries and eggs for lessons for Bob and his two sisters. The entire family learned how to play musical instruments.

I met Bob in Homer, Michigan, when we were 14, and we dated through our school years. Fred had become a dairy farmer, and I loved spending time on the farm. When Bob and I married in 1947, I was instantly welcomed into his amazing family. Martha and Fred became Mom and Dad to me.

> EVENTUALLY, THE COUPLE HAD 38 GRAND-CHILDREN, WHO THOUGHT AS MUCH OF THEM AS I DID.

Back then, fun was simple and included the whole family. Mom and Dad always made time to mix fun with the work required around the farm. There were family reunions, car rides and picnics. We played board games and sometimes went down to the cellar to play Ping-Pong on a long, narrow table. During the winter, we used snow to freeze ice cream in the crank ice cream maker.

Mom and Dad embraced education and the changing world. They welcomed progress and its upgrades, like electricity and running water. The olden days, Mom admitted, were not as romantic as they seemed.

Eventually, the couple had 38 grandchildren, who thought as much of them as I did. The grandkids sent letters, visited, attended reunions and confided in their grandparents when they needed advice, which speaks volumes for the kind of people that Martha and Fred were. They sure were loved.

**KATHLEEN J. VINCENT**
**BATTLE CREEK, MI**

## THE BUCKSKIN BUCCANEER

"When I was growing up on a farm in the Midwest in the 1950s, one of my favorite things to play with my siblings was cowboys and cowgirls. We even tried to lasso our amiable dog Tippy," writes Rosemary Kuhn of Naperville, Illinois. "So when Walt Disney's five-part *Davy Crockett* serial came out in the mid-'50s, it was a must-see. I had all the Davy Crockett paraphernalia—lunch box, school bag, T-shirt, suede vest with silver buckles and classy fringe, and, of course, the famous coonskin cap. Although I was only 6, seeing Fess Parker on the screen playing Davy won over my heart. How I wished I were Polly—or at least the actress who played the role (Helene Stanley). I remember Davy returning home to her after a long absence fightin' for freedom. Lovely prairie Polly, dressed in her long calico dress and apron, was swept up in his arms. My heart did multiple flips for my handsome hero, Davy!"

CHAPTER 5

# ANIMAL TALES

*What would life on the farm be like without furry and feathered friends? Enjoy these stories of loyal horses, sassy cows, ornery birds and more. Whether raised as livestock or as pets, these animals surely contributed to the family farm.*

# A HORSE, OF COURSE!

### Hardworking companions and true friends

Left: New riding student Elise is eager to learn. Below: A child pats Vicki's team.

## SADDLE UP FOR VALUABLE LESSONS

I can't remember a time as a kid when I did not want a horse. I thought our cattle were just odd-shaped horses so I sat on their backs, saddled them with rugs and rope, and braided their short manes.

One morning, Dad was rototilling the garden and I was walking behind him picking up worms so we could go fishing later. When I asked if I could have a pony, he said, "Maybe someday."

I ran into the house and told Mom, "Dad's getting me a pony on Sunday!" I quickly learned my first lesson in disappointment: There is a big difference between "someday" and "Sunday."

Dad was known for his workingman's handshake and always kept his word. If he said he was going to do something, he did it. That week Dad traded some work toward an old saddle he'd found in a friend's barn and brought it home to me. I cleaned it up and thought I had struck gold.

On Sunday morning, the sound of a whinnying horse jolted me out of bed and brought me crashing down the stairs. Not one, but two of the most beautiful ponies in the world stood in the pasture.

For the next few days I brushed and braided, cleaned water buckets and stalls, saddled them, and struggled to bridle them.

Within a couple of weeks I could climb up onto the smaller pony, Dynamite, all by myself. I learned how to ride, fall off, land on my feet and get back on. And I gleaned a few other valuable lessons as well:

**Others will help you find your way.** Whenever I got lost on a trail, my pony found the way back to a place we knew. He also taught me that sometimes it's better to listen to his language and cross the brook downstream. The waters may look calm, but sometimes others know better what lies beneath the surface.

**Make sure everyone has a warm and safe place to rest.** Whether it's a high spot of dry ground, the shade under a big tree or a softly

Tillie the mule had an easy gait—"sure-footed for dodging rocks and rabbits," as Ben Rash put it.

bedded stall, both humans and horses do best with an occasional nap and a good night's sleep.

**Share drinks with friends whenever you can.** A morning coffee or afternoon iced tea always goes better with friends. And never ask your horse to drink out of a bucket or trough that you wouldn't use.

**You don't have to forget, but always forgive—and pay attention next time.** The way horses and people are raised sometimes makes them want to kick you. Don't take it personally. Learn to read the signs and dodge a bad situation. Above all else, never kick back.

**A pony is the best therapy for a kid.** If your child wants a pony and it's not an option, find one he or she can visit, brush and ride. For there is nothing like the nuzzle of a pony to warm a child's heart.

After Dad died, my co-worker Mark stopped by to talk and said, "Vicki, you were right. We bought our daughter a horse, and it's the best thing we ever did."

Someday when I can compose myself properly, Mark will know how much those words meant to me.

**VICKI SCHMIDT
HEBRON, ME**

## TILLIE, THE JUMPING MULE

Ben Rash had a mule, Tillie, who was his faithful hunting companion for more than 30 years. They both enjoyed matching wits with the wily raccoons in the woods around his New Providence, Iowa, farm. What's more, Tillie was a jumping mule. When the trail led to a fence, Ben dismounted so Tillie—carrying a bag of hunting gear—could jump over. She could clear a four-barb fence from a standing start.

"Tillie never met a fence she didn't like," Ben used to say. Tillie's ability to go airborne was attributed by longtime raccoon hunters to a "jumping gene" found in certain breeds of horses. Tillie also was tough and seldom spooked.

A compassionate owner and instructor, Ben improved Tillie's jumping. Over time, Ben literally raised the bar, in this case a 12-foot-long two-by-four, until Tillie was clearing a 4-foot-high bar.

Season after season, Tillie raised her head and cocked her ears when Ben opened the barn door for a night on the trail. Finally, the years slowed the gait of man and mule. Even today, neighbors say they can hear the best friends following their hounds across the timbered hills.

**REX GOGERTY
HUBBARD, IA**

## OUR SILVER DOLLAR "MUSTANG"

My daughter, Karen, first approached me about having a horse when she was 5 years old. We lived on the outskirts of Reno, with more than an acre and a small barn, so boarding a horse was no problem. But she wanted a mustang, which was not my idea of a good prospect.

I tried to explain that a mustang did not come "ready-made" and that it would be a long time before she could ever ride it. Karen refused to be discouraged. With adoption fliers readily available, she was on me often.

One day my husband, Tom, came home with a trailer behind his pickup. Karen was out the door in a flash as Tom and a friend unloaded a big red dun gelding. "My horse, my horse!" Karen chanted in delight.

"My horse," said Tom's friend, George. "His name is Idaho, but you can ride him as often as you want." Karen's face fell and huge tears filled her eyes. "But I wanted a horse all my own."

"How much money you got?" George asked, grinning. Karen ran into the house and returned with a shiny silver dollar her grandmother had sent her. "I got this," she offered.

"Then you just bought yourself a horse!" George replied, sneaking the coin back to Tom.

Idaho was 25, and George was looking for a place for the horse to retire in comfort. He stood 16 hands tall, had feet like dinner plates and was as gentle as a stuffed teddy bear.

Idaho's years as a packhorse had exposed him to so many unexpected situations that nothing startled him. He had one pace: the breakneck speed of a garden snail. He would walk placidly around the pasture as Karen sat tall in the saddle and lived out her dream.

He cared about the precious cargo on his back, and that was even more apparent when she was on the ground. He would follow Karen with his nose resting on her hip or her shoulder. Eventually we realized that Idaho's hearing and vision were going. But he made sure he knew where she was so he didn't hurt her by accident.

As the years went by, he grew a little more doddering and would go to sleep while "galloping" across the plains of a little girl's imagination. When I heard an exasperated "Mom! He's doing it again!" I'd run to give his bridle a shake to wake him up.

Idaho gave rides to all the kids in the neighborhood, endured having his mane and tail plaited in braids and ribbons, wore hats with holes cut out for his ears and even walked around with one hoof painted with bright pink nail polish. But my favorite role was his first: a "mustang" purchased for one silver dollar.

He was easily worth a million.

He lived a good, long life and passed on quietly at age 32. Now when Karen's 6-year-old daughter, Kaely, sees a photograph of Idaho, she perks up and asks, "Can I have a horse, too, Grandma?" I just smile knowingly and hope her mama has put aside another silver dollar.

**LINDA SCHWARZ
RENO, NV**

Gentle Idaho was the perfect horse to fulfill young Karen's cowgirl dreams.

## DASHING THROUGH THE SNOW

Dad grew up on a small farm in northern Vermont during the Great Depression, which meant that he was comfortable working with horses and that he was deeply frugal.

To give you an idea how far Dad would go to get a good deal, consider that he once sawed an old barn in half, dragged it home with a bulldozer and pieced it back together. That was 50 years ago, and it's still there, chain saw scars and all.

One autumn, Dad got the idea to spread manure in the winter to save time in the spring. However, he needed a free horse to pull the spreader through the snow. This led him to a big, strong stallion that belonged to summer people in a nearby town. They said Dad could use him over the winter in return for boarding him.

His name was Smokey, although he wouldn't listen to us no matter what we called him—and Dad called him a lot of things. Smokey had run wild and free all summer over a 40-acre pasture with no one paying him any attention, as near as I could tell.

That didn't deter Dad. He came up with a harness and built a manure sled out of planks. As he planned and prepared, I could see Dad being transported back to his glory days of kinship between man and horse. It was too bad Smokey came from a completely different generation.

Finally the big day arrived, and both Dad and Smokey were excited, although for different reasons. Dad parked the sled in the north end of the barn, facing the big open door. Then he filled it with the first load of manure.

He got Smokey out of his stall and with quiet confidence harnessed him and hitched him to the sled. Smokey seemed raring to go, which Dad took as the beginning of a great working relationship. Then he turned his back for a second, and Smokey was gone.

With the big door open and the winter wind beckoning, Smokey took off. Dad was right; the stallion was very strong—and fast. The loaded sled barely slowed him down. Luckily it wasn't hard to follow him. His tracks in the snow ran through the field into a grove of maples, where the sled jammed between two trees.

Smokey stood quietly, energy spent and perplexed about why he'd suddenly stopped. The sled was smashed. On the bright side, the manure had all been spread. Dad put Smokey back in his stall, where he spent a quiet, uneventful winter.

The next spring, Smokey headed back to his carefree life, and I helped spread the manure.

**NATHAN STRONG**
**IRASBURG, VT**

## WHERE DO PONIES COME FROM?

One summer, when I was about 6 years old, my folks took me on a trip to my great-aunt and great-uncle's farm in Wonewoc, Wisconsin. Besides their milk cows, they had chickens, hogs, horses and two beautiful pinto ponies.

It was love at first sight.

I played with Hazel, the younger pony, all day. That night, I couldn't think of anything but her. I finally asked my mom where she'd come from. Mom hesitated, then told me that Hazel "came from a seed."

The next day, I was in the orchard with some other kids, gathering windfalls. I bit into a seed and remarked that maybe I should have saved it because it might grow into a pony someday.

I don't think I've ever been laughed at so hard in my life.

**CHARLES W. LEMKE**
**FORT ATKINSON, WI**

## THANK GOODNESS FOR EASTER

My grandfather Cal West was a horse trader in the Great Depression. At wheat harvest, the family would head up to Kansas with horses and mules to sell. Grandma drove a cook wagon filled with supplies, and she and their daughters cooked and washed for the threshing crews.

After the wheat harvest, Grandfather bought horses and mules in Kansas to sell to the coal miners back home in the mountains of southeast Oklahoma. One year, my Aunt Bernice, who was 7, fell in love with a Paint mare in the trade herd and offered all her harvest earnings for the horse.

It was a deal Grandfather couldn't refuse, and Bernice got her mare. She named the new horse Easter because she was as colorful as an Easter egg, and they became inseparable.

In those days ranchers didn't have fenced pastures, so the livestock ran loose in mountain valleys that offered grass, water and protection from the winter winds. Each spring, family and neighbors got together to round up the animals.

The spring Bernice turned 12, she and Easter were riding flank when some horses took off in the wrong direction. They were chasing them through tall grass near a burned-out shack when the ground suddenly fell out from under them. Easter's back feet had broken through the boards covering an old dug well, and she and Bernice both tumbled in.

Bernice slid off and ended up trapped between Easter's rump and the side of the well. They were standing in 2 feet of numbingly cold water, but Bernice realized that there was another reason her foot hurt: The horse was standing on it.

Easter and Bernice (at left with her father) fell into danger on an abandoned farmstead.

Amazingly, Easter stayed perfectly calm. If she'd panicked, who knows what would've happened? As it was, though, Bernice patted Easter on the rump and asked her to move her foot, and the horse obeyed.

But they were still trapped, and no one had seen them fall into the well. Bernice yelled and yelled and cried a little before her family finally found them at dusk.

They lifted Bernice out with a rope but decided they'd have to come back the next morning for Easter. Well, Bernice threw a fit and refused to leave, so Grandfather sent home for shovels and lanterns. They dug a ramp down into the well, but Easter wouldn't climb up. So Bernice suggested harnessing her to Tarzan and Duke, their two big work mules. Sure enough, they pulled Easter up the ramp until she went the rest of the way.

Easter went on to enjoy a long, happy life helping Bernice raise her family. That mare took the kids everywhere. I'm sure all the wonderful Easter stories inspired my love of Paints. In fact, I've been raising registered Paints for 25 years now, and each spring at foaling time I can't wait to see if I'm about to meet my own Easter.

**SANDRA MANTOOTH**
**ADA, OK**

## CAUGHT IN A WHIRLWIND

In the spring of '58 I was in need of a broke saddle horse to use for calf roping on the amateur rodeo circuit, as well as for regular cow work.

I had a good friend whose father, Wilf Little, ran a ranch near Vermilion, Alberta. They called Wilf "Big" Little because he was big. He was also a good wrestler, a nearly unbeatable boxer and one of the craftiest horse swappers in the business. One of Wilf's four sons, Herb, took after his dad and said he had a big buckskin stallion that might suit me. He'd named the horse Hornet, which fit him well, according to the fellow who broke him.

So one day I went over to give Hornet a try. Herb was breaking a mare at the time, so we took a good long ride through their pasture. The family had 30 or 40 head of horses running out there, and as we approached the herd, Hornet started getting riled up. I should've suspected there was a good reason.

We were about 50 yards from the herd when a young, unbroken black stallion came flying out of the bunch with crazy eyes and ears pinned straight back. Before I could blink, the stallion slammed into us and sank his teeth into Hornet's withers, barely missing my right leg.

Herb had given me a heavy steel bit with a chain curb and thick reins, like lines on a driving team. I managed to keep Hornet's head turned away, which wasn't easy since he was spoiling

for a fight. He reared and bucked, but I stayed on, stood up in the saddle and smacked the black stallion's head with the reins doubled up in my fist.

I was a lot younger and stronger then, but I don't know that the blow hurt the stallion so much as startled him. He jumped back with a look that said, *Where did you come from?* Then he wheeled and hightailed it back to the herd.

Hornet, however, was still as mad as his namesake, wheeling and bucking and bawling ferociously. Herb finally got his green mare going and we put some distance between us and the other horses. Old Hornet, though, kept sliding sideways and trying to go back to teach that young upstart a lesson.

I did end up trading for Hornet, and I put a lot of miles on him. He wasn't fast enough for a rodeo roper, but he turned out to be a pretty good ranch horse. As for the stallion fight, I never made much of it. But Herb spread the word and one day a guy said, "Are you nuts? Why didn't you jump clear?"

"I've been thrown from falling horses and I had one do a complete cartwheel on me," I told him. "I've been bucked off more horses and bulls than I can count, but quit a horse? Never even thought of it."

**CHARLES YOUNG**
**VIKING, AB**

**While trying a horse, Charles found himself smack in the middle of a stallion fight.**

Malcolm and his sister Beth ride Roxy and Judy while Dad drives the wagon (left). The horses could guide him back to the barn (above) as well as any GPS.

## WE MADE A GREAT TEAM

Farming with horses was already in sharp decline in 1945, the year I was born. But it was a thrilling time to live on our farm because Dad had both a John Deere B tractor and a team of workhorses named Roxy and Judy. They were my buddies and a wonderful part of my young life.

Roxy loved attention. He would often come up near the fence hoping to get his nose or ears scratched. Judy the mare also loved an occasional pat on the nose, and she would nicker when I was close by.

Dad would drive the team to do farm chores or haul hay in from the meadow, or hitch them to the manure spreader to clean out the barn. Sometimes he would let me take the lines to guide them.

When not working, Roxy and Judy spent time in the pasture or the barn. As I wandered by I heard their nickers, which meant, "Are you going to get us a handful of oats?" and I often did. I'm not sure if Dad knew about the snacks; Roxy and Judy never told.

At age 10 I learned how to drive the tractor. My first love was plowing the stubble fields in the fall after the grain had been harvested. I felt like a real farmer.

We still used Roxy and Judy, though, and I got better at driving them. "Don't want them to get rusty," Dad would say, but he was always careful not to overwork them.

Dad always took Sundays off from work, other than doing the necessary livestock chores. He left the house early one Sunday evening to start them but came back and told my mother that Roxy had gone to sleep. She told me Dad meant Roxy had died.

I ran to the barn, hoping Dad was wrong. I gently gave Roxy's nose a rub, but there was no movement. Dad sold Judy soon after. My buddies were gone.

I grew up, finished high school and got a job with a dairy association. I continued to help Dad on the farm until a heart attack took his life on Christmas Day in 1973. Farms were continuing to get larger and I decided to quit farming five years later.

Today I keep my farming blood happy by climbing into the neighbors' big fancy tractors. You just drive them to the field and set the computer, and the machinery turns over acres and acres in a few hours.

But in my mind I can still see my father hitching the team up to the wagon. When the sun would start to set, Dad would yell out, "OK, let's go home." Roxy and Judy looked at each other and almost smiled. Dad would relax the lines and the horses knew right where to go. Maybe GPS isn't that new after all.

> I'M NOT SURE IF DAD KNEW ABOUT THE SNACKS; ROXY AND JUDY NEVER TOLD.

**MALCOLM DIRKSEN**
**TWIN BROOKS, SD**

## STUBBORN WHITE MULE

I was born in 1921 on a farm near Oberlin, Kansas, and Pete was an unpredictable, lovable and exasperating white mule that lived with us.

At the age of 6, I would ride Pete (right) unattended around the farm. Dad would bridle him, and then I was on my own. Mounting him was a challenge. To prove my independence after Dad left for work in the field, I'd lead Pete alongside a rack on the side of a shed, climb the rack and mount up.

One fall day, I rode out to the field, a mile away, where Dad was racking cane hay. I was feeling very grown-up, bouncing along the way, when Pete came to a sudden halt to satisfy his appetite for the fallen hay.

Yelling "Giddyap!" and kicking Pete in the ribs didn't have any effect, but suddenly he took off at a dead run. It was the wildest ride I've ever had. We stopped less than 6 feet from Dad, and by then I had bounced up onto Pete's neck, clutching his mane for dear life. It was as if Pete were saying to Dad, "Here's your little brat."

Dad lifted me back into position. He told me I had had enough riding for a while and should go back home and put the mule in the barn.

Later, Pete was sold to a neighbor 4 miles away from us. One day we looked in our corral, and there stood Pete. Dad called the neighbor, who came and got him. In a week's time, the mule got away again and returned to our place. The men talked it over and decided to trade back.

It remained a mystery how Pete got out of the neighbor's corral. The neighbor never saw Pete leave and we never saw him return; Pete traveled at night, apparently. We assume he lifted the wooden latch on our corral gate, pushed it forward and walked in, or else he jumped the fence.

Pete lived out his natural life happily in the pasture.

**VIOLA VANDERWEGE**
**NORTON, KS**

Pete was a pistol. Viola is seen riding Pete solo and at the front of siblings (from left) Ila, Ruby, Mildred and Lavina.

# THAT DARN COW

## A most amusing and stubborn creature

### A BARGAIN COW

My family lived on a chicken farm in the foothills of the Blue Ridge Mountains when I was a child. My father often took a job in the Virginia shipyards to make ends meet. Times were hard for us, so everyone was expected to pitch in and pull his or her load.

My family bought a cow, supposedly a good buy, from a Mr. Absher, who said she gave the sweetest milk in the county. We couldn't swear to that because so far we had not been able to milk her. Dad said she would calm down once she got used to us. I think he forgot to mention that to the cow.

My older brother went out to milk her. Luckily, she was tied to a cinder block to hold her in place. As he sat down, she knocked him sideways and lit out as if her tail was on fire.

She was a Guernsey all right, but she pulled that cinder block straight up the sloping road like a mountain goat. My brother ran with all his might and grabbed the cinder block in an effort to stop her, but the cow had other plans. My brother held on tight—a cow was a valuable commodity in those days.

The cow decided to run through an old-fashioned tent revival. As the preacher saw the cow coming through the tent flaps, right up the center aisle, he dived out of the way.

The cow continued out the back of the tent while the congregation scattered. We heard later that we became part of the sermon.

Onward up the mountain went cow and boy, fighting each other every step of the way. Soon my mother was right behind them in the old pickup with us kids hanging out the windows. We all arrived at the top of the mountain, where the cow had roamed freely before being sold to us lowland farmers.

Our mother tied the cow's rope to the bumper and helped my wheezing brother into the truck bed. We came down the mountain slowly, everyone the worse for wear except the cow, who pulled at the truck as if she could change its direction.

When Dad got home, the story was told with all the exciting details. He realized the only one who had gotten a bargain was old Mr. Absher, who had received hard-earned money for a cow that was related to a jackrabbit.

The cow was again tied to the old truck's bumper. Up the mountain we went, with our bargain cow that was anything but a bargain pulling and jumping the whole way.

Mr. Absher hemmed and hawed but finally gave back our money. Once untied, the Guernsey took off for her mountaintop—at least until someone else from the foothills needed a deal on a milk cow.

**DRUSCILLA PYLES**
**MILLERS CREEK, NC**

This Guernsey looks a bit more peaceful than Druscilla's family milk cow.

### TAIL TRAPPING

I was my dad's helper for years on our South Dakota farm. Many times, especially in the winter, the cows' tails were wet and very unpleasant. This was especially true if one hit you in the face!

Dad had a remedy, and I wonder if it was a common one. He strung a wire 15 inches above the backs of the cows along the length of the barn. Then he attached gopher traps to the wire.

Before you sat to milk the cow, you put the tail hair into the trap, which didn't hurt the cow but kept you safe from being slapped by a wet tail.

**LOIS LAFERRIERE**
**ELK POINT, SD**

Tubby (above) was like a pet to Mae, whose photo shoot with the calf didn't quite go as planned (near right).

## TEARS FOR TUBBY

My folks bought their first house in the early '40s after Dad got a better job with the Duluth, South Shore & Atlantic Railway in Marquette, Michigan. We lived just inside the city limits in what was still a rural area.

Mom was raised on a farm, so she was pleased that our new place included a small barn with two stalls and a chicken house.

In the spring of 1948, when I was 6 years old, my parents bought a calf to replace our cow, which had been butchered the year before. So one day we drove to a local farm and returned with a white and brown calf we named Tubby.

We didn't own a truck, so Tubby rode home in the backseat of Dad's car with my 9-year-old brother, Steve, and me. As you can imagine, the trip was a lot of fun for us kids.

Later that summer, Mom thought it would be cute to take a picture of me sitting on Tubby's back. All went well until the snap of the camera shutter sent Tubby charging off on a run, with me holding on for dear life.

I lasted for about 30 feet before I hit the ground. Mom was quick enough to shoot a follow-up picture, so we had photos of me both on and off Tubby!

When summer had passed, the day arrived for poor Tubby to be butchered. I must have been somewhere else with my mom on the fateful day because I have no recollection of how it happened. All I knew was that the barn was empty and that we had plenty of meat for dinners.

I hadn't lived on a farm like my mother, so I didn't understand that what happened to Tubby was not unusual. Livestock aren't meant to be pets, and most farm kids know and accept that truth.

Whenever we had beef for dinner, I would tearfully ask, "Is this Tubby?" This went on for a couple of weeks until Dad had finally had enough and declared, "No more cows!" That made me feel a little better about poor Tubby.

**MAE TROTOCHAUD**
**BRUCE CROSSING, MI**

## Bringing in the HARVEST

### ...SO VITAL TO VICTORY!

NEVER before in history has food figured so much in American calculations.

Today we are a rationed nation, sharing our food with our boys abroad and their comrades-in-arms.

In order that there may be food for all, the railroads not only are moving great quantities from canneries, packing plants, fruit and vegetable areas but are sending thousands of cars into the harvest fields to haul millions of bushels of grain — your daily bread.

You may wonder how the railroads can take on so big a job as the harvest these days and still keep the war effort rolling. Here is the answer in one word — *cooperation.*

The railroads work together. While crops are still ripening in the fields, their plans are already laid. When harvesting starts, Pennsylvania Railroad contributes a share of its freight cars, along with other railroads, to

the great American car "pool"...and there's a reserve army of cars all mobilized to move the crops to elevators and ship sidings.

Result: Plenty of cars for agriculture, the load evenly distributed among many railroads.

It is this sort of teamwork, going on every day, that is enabling the railroads to do for their country what United States Senator Clyde M. Reed of Kansas described as "the most phenomenal job in their history."

★ *50,299 in the Armed Forces*
★ *28 have given their lives for their country*

**PENNSYLVANIA RAILROAD**

## Avoid Losses from BACTERIAL DISEASES with

**1951**

Fast Acting, All-Purpose

# SULMET*

SULFAMETHAZINE *Lederle*

Easy-to-give, Time-proved, Low-cost
Effective with Once-A-Day Treatment

against

**FOOT ROT • SHIPPING FEVER • CALF DIPHTHERIA
METRITIS • CALF SCOURS • BACILLARY ENTERITIS
AND OTHER COSTLY BACTERIAL DISEASES
OF ALL FARM ANIMALS**

• Available in six dosage forms: POWDER, TABLETS, OBLETS*, TINTED EMULSION (for pink eye bacterial infections), SOLUTION 12.5% (may be used as a drench), and INJECTABLE SOLUTION (by or on veterinarian's prescription).

• Your veterinarian is your dependable ally in the constant war against disease. Consult him for the most effective management practices and disease-control procedures to meet your individual needs.

Free literature gladly sent upon request. *Reg. U.S. Pat. Off.

**LEDERLE LABORATORIES DIVISION**
*AMERICAN Cyanamid COMPANY*
30 Rockefeller Plaza       New York 20, N. Y.

*Lederle*

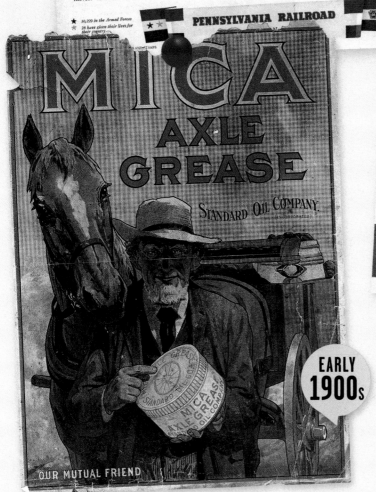

**EARLY 1900s**

## HANG ON TO YOUR HAT!

In the '60s, before livestock trailers were common, most farmers in the Kansas Flint Hills put homemade wooden stock racks on their pickup trucks and used them to haul hogs, cattle, sheep and whatnot to market or from one pasture to another.

One day our neighbor Jim was going to pick up a new bull about 15 miles from home, and he asked my cousin to ride along. My cousin was 10 or 12 years old and always up for an adventure, so naturally he said yes. He had no idea just how much of an adventure he was getting himself into.

They loaded the 2,000-pound bull into the bed of Jim's ancient pickup with no problems and headed back. Jim wasn't one to hurry without a very good reason, so he was tooling along at his usual 25 mph pace when one of the side racks fell off and bounced into the ditch.

They were only about halfway home, and Jim didn't want to stop and try to put the missing rack back on because he was afraid the bull would jump out and they'd never get him loaded again. The best course of action, he decided, was to floor it and hope the bull would be too scared to jump out of the speeding truck.

"Hang on to your hat!" he said. The old truck's speedometer only went up to 80, and Jim put it to the test—probably for the first time in the truck's long and poorly maintained history. My cousin says his life flashed before his eyes on every curve and corner of the rough gravel road. Adding to the tension, the brakes weren't working particularly well that day.

Somehow, though, they managed to get back to the farm in one piece, and Jim hopped out to open the pasture gate. That's when the bull decided he'd had enough of this wild ride. Instead of jumping out of the side of the pickup bed, the bull bolted straight over the roof of the cab and right down the hood. He hit the ground at a dead run and then disappeared into the pasture.

So that's how you get a bull home when part of the stock rack falls off.

The next morning, Jim found the bull happily grazing alongside his new lady friends. No one ever again managed to get him loaded into a pickup truck, though. And my cousin? He thanked Jim for the ride but said he'd just as soon walk next time.

**KATHRYN I. WOODEN**
**AGENCY, MO**

## DOWN AND OUT-HOUSE

Visiting Uncle Johnny was an adventure with one drawback: His facilities consisted of an outhouse in the pasture. The field was fenced to keep the cows inside. A hefty bull lived with them, and he had an equally large complex about people visiting his domain.

On one visit, I had to go to the bathroom, so I went to the fence and surveyed the area. The bull and the cows were off in another corner, so I scampered through the gate and sprinted to the outhouse. After taking care of business, I tried to open the wooden door, but it wouldn't budge more than a few inches. All I could see through the small opening was a side of beef.

A cow had come to stand in the shade the structure provided and was barricading me inside! I screamed and pushed with all the might my 9-year-old muscles could summon, but to no avail. After about 15 minutes, I heard the squeaky back door of Uncle Johnny's house, so I shouted.

I knew rescue was on the way when I heard my father's deep laugh as he realized a cow had locked his daughter in the outhouse.

**AMY L. TREECE**
**SHERMAN, TX**

## BLUE SUEDE MOOS

Gramps had a radio in the barn for listening to the daily milk prices and the market report. One morning in the '50s, he went off to deliver eggs and left me in charge of milking the cows. Milk prices didn't interest this 12-year-old kid, so I switched on Carl Perkins' "Blue Suede Shoes."

The normally placid cows heard this racket and went ballistic, pulling at their stanchions and mooing. The bull, hearing this manic mooing, kicked open the gate of his stall and came in search of the noise. At first he thought it was me and started chasing me around the barn, with Perkins still in full cry. Finally he figured out the source of the sound and wasted no time butting the radio into the hayloft.

Unsatisfied, however, he turned his attention back to me. I'd retreated to his stall and closed the gate. Wanting in, he attacked the gate with his horns. That's what my grandfather saw as he walked into the barn. To this day, I can't imagine what he must have thought.

Gramps opened the barn door and the bull abandoned me for the pasture. In absolute silence, we milked the cows. It was a long time before my grandfather trusted me alone with the cows again—or the new radio.

**JIM WEST**
**MARSTONS MILLS, MA**

# BIRDS OF A FEATHER

### Chickens and roosters and ducks, oh my!

## THE MIRACLE ROOSTER

I was 10 years old when I got my chickens, back in spring 1981. With my parents' permission, I ordered a regular United Nations of chickens, including Blue Andalusian, Araucana, Silver Spangled Hamburg and Buff Minorca breeds. When 40 fuzzy chicks arrived, I nurtured the tiny puffs as they grew into a rainbow assortment of hens and roosters.

An Araucana rooster named Chanticleer, Chant for short, became my favorite. He was not as large, lean or regal as the other males, but he won me over with his pluck and perseverance. Chant and the rest of the flock soothed me after a hard day at school.

On Christmas Eve 1985, my mind was less on my chickens than on the anticipation of opening presents the next morning. But when I went to their pen to feed them, I got a shock I'll never forget. Chickens were scattered everywhere. Many were dead. Something had gotten into the coop. I knew that animal death was part of farm life, but why on Christmas Eve?

We corralled the surviving chickens back inside the pen. Noting that some were missing, I checked their outdoor run, where I found Chant lying on the ground. Dad tenderly picked up my motionless prize rooster, checking for signs of life. I didn't know why he bothered.

"He's alive," Dad said.

How was that possible? I followed Dad's direction to fetch my 4-H display cage. He put the rooster inside and we went straight into the house, placing the cage on an ancient wicker rocker by the warm stove.

"What do we do now?" I asked.

"We wait," he said. I was touched that Dad gave Chant a place of honor next to the stove, especially because farm animals were not usually allowed in the house.

I said a quiet prayer. We had done what we could; the rest was up to Chant. My parents urged me to go to bed before Santa came. With a final glance toward my motionless feathered friend, I headed up to put the day's events behind me. Sleep came reluctantly, but it came.

*Cock-a-doodle-doo!* The familiar cry woke me from a sound sleep, but it sounded different than

Matthew's flock of chickens was most important, even on Christmas Eve when other kids his age focused on the next day's presents.

usual. Instead of a distant cry from the barn, it was as loud as if it was coming from right inside the house. Then it came to me—Chant!

I ran down the steps and into the kitchen, never glancing at the gifts under the tree. Standing among the sunbeams that streamed in through the window, Chant proudly stretched his neck and burst forth with another grand crow.

It was Christmas morning—and Chant wouldn't be caught dead missing it!

**MATTHEW LIPTAK**
**BALDWINSVILLE, NY**

## THE PEACEABLE KINGDOM

We adopted our calico cat, Cally, from close friends. She was quite elderly and fading fast. When she first arrived on our farm, our aging dog Tango initially approached her somewhat warily, given the reaction Tango elicited from our other cats (typically a hiss, scratch and spit). Instead, Cally marched right up and rubbed noses with Tango, and they became fast friends, cuddling together whenever it was time to take a nap. Tango loved anyone who would snuggle up to her, and Cally was the perfect belly warmer.

In no time, Cally became the leader of the farm, with great nobility and elegance. But our free-range Araucana rooster seriously questioned this dog/cat relationship.

He was a bit indignant about the communal nap time and would strut up the sidewalk, walk up and down the porch and perch on the railing, muttering about how improper it was, and at times getting quite loud. They ignored him, which really bugged him, proud bird that he was.

One fall morning, as I opened the front door to get the newspaper, I was astonished to see not just a cat and dog snuggled together on the porch, but the rooster as well, tucked up next to Tango's tail. As usual, Tango and Cally didn't move a muscle when I appeared.

The rooster, however, was startled, almost embarrassed, to see me. He stood up quickly, flapped his wings and swaggered off crowing. No, I didn't have my camera, and I never found them all together ever again.

I figure a dog, a cat and a rooster sleeping together was our farm's version of the lion and lamb lying down together. The peaceable kingdom was right outside our door, a harbinger of what is promised someday for the rest of us. Despite claws, teeth and talons, it will be possible to snuggle in harmony.

Our special Cally made it happen on earth. I suspect she's met up with Tango, and possibly one rooster, for a nice nap on the other side.

**EMILY GIBSON**
**EVERSON, WA**

Partners in hijinks, Glenn, left, and Irvin found a rooster more than a match.

## TROUBLEMAKERS

In 1938, I was 6 and my friend Glenn was 7. He lived in Rocklin, California, and he had a large chicken pen in the backyard.

One day when his parents were gone and his two older sisters were watching us, Glenn thought it would be fun to torment the chickens by throwing tin cans at them. We couldn't throw the cans through the wire fence, so Glenn opened the gate and let the chickens out. They scattered in all directions. Glenn threw only one can before the big old red rooster came after us. We started running around yelling, "Help! Help!" The rooster was right behind us. Suddenly, the back door opened and one of Glenn's sisters reached out and pulled me inside. Glenn fell down and the rooster jumped onto his back. While Glenn yelled, his sister chased off the rooster with a broom. She dragged Glenn inside and cleaned up his scratches and peck marks.

We were trapped inside the rest of the day. Red walked up and down the yard. Every time we peeked out, there he was. We didn't dare go out until Glenn's folks came home. They were upset with Glenn for letting the chickens out, but by then it was dark and the chickens had all gone into their coop to roost.

**IRVIN POOL**
**CARMICHAEL, CA**

Barn cat Cally was the queen of the farm.

Sarah lovingly cared for her pet ducks, Lucky and Honey, for 14 years.

## A TALE OF TWO DUCKS

One fall afternoon when I was about 6 years old, my parents loaded my sister and me into the car and told me I was going to get an early birthday gift.

My head started spinning with the possibilities. All along the way my parents gave me clues.

"Is it a miniature pony?" I asked excitedly. "No," my mother replied, "it's much, much smaller." I was mystified as we reached the small farm where we bought animal feed.

When we got out of the car, the nice lady who owned the feed store greeted us with a knowing smile. "Hi, Sarah," she said. "A couple of little guys want to say happy birthday to you." She took us behind their big white farmhouse. I could hear a range of noises, from quacks to gobbles and clucks.

As she swung open the gate, it was as if all the poultry in Noah's ark had been let loose— birds were everywhere. Loud birds, speckled birds, bright birds, fluffy birds, birds in a pond, birds in tall grass.

The lady introduced me to a honey-colored duck with a brown speckled breast. Any hopes of getting a pony melted away as I stared into those deep brown eyes. She told me they were called call ducks, and that they never grew much bigger than the 1½-pound feathered friend I was holding.

She said this little duck would be mine on one very strict condition: that I take very good care of her and love her all of her life. I was almost too excited to hear her say that call ducks mate for life and that I had to pick out a companion for Honey, the name I quickly gave my small duck.

I selected a young male with an emerald green head, grayish brown body and purplish wings— the picture of a handsome duck if I'd ever seen one. I named him Lucky, because Honey was lucky to have him.

Lucky and Honey led a life of luxury on our farm. Honey sat on a couple of nests, but she and Lucky weren't the best parents, so no eggs ever hatched. Instead, the two lived out their days basking in the sun by their water bowl, getting little scraps of goodies and occasionally bickering with each other; it was an arranged marriage, after all.

I kept my promise and took very good care of those ducks, loving them until the day they died at age 14.

SARAH SUBIK
FONDA, NY

## DON'T MESS WITH MAMA!

More than half a century has slipped by since I lived on a farm in East Texas, but the memories are as sharp as if it were yesterday. The daily wonders of the natural world—whether it was a summer breeze that made the heat bearable or the gentle pitter-patter of raindrops—touched my heart.

Most endearing was watching brood hens hatch and raise their families. We had two high-strung white leghorns, three Plymouth Rocks and a Dominique named Mrs. Penny.

Mrs. Penny had two personalities. When she was between families, she was timid and indecisive. Each afternoon at feeding time she remained on the outer fringe of the flock, dodging every threat. That's when we called her by her first name, Henny.

But when she had a brood of little yellow biddies following her, she became confident and aggressive, attacking anything that appeared to be a threat. Even Red Man, our big Rhode Island Red rooster with 2-inch spurs, gave her the right of way. That's when we called her Mrs. Penny.

Hours after her last egg had hatched, Mrs. Penny was out in the yard with a blanket of yellow puff balls clustered about her feet.

Mrs. Penny was a disciplinarian who taught each new brood how to search for food and fend for themselves. Strolling along looking at the ground, first with her left eye and then with her right, she'd cluck between each tilt of her head. Then, suddenly, she'd stop, rip up the ground with sharp scratches, step back and release a brace of short clucks. Then her youngsters converged, pecking at anything that looked like nourishment.

As a mother, she moved among the farm animals with an air of supremacy, demonstrating an uncanny ability to sense danger. If she encountered a bluffing situation, she ruffled her feathers, lowered her head and dashed forward in mock attack. When the danger was real, she reacted with loud, sharp commands, spreading her wings to the ground and ruffling her feathers. Sadly, she lost her life defending her biddies when a red hawk attacked. Afterward, her brood scurried about under the care of Red Man.

Motherhood turned that hen into a Sherman tank. The perseverance of Mrs. Penny was awe-inspiring!

**HARRY P. NOBLE
IOLA, TX**

## THE FAMILY OWL

One summer day, my husband came home to our western Minnesota farm with a little fur ball the size of an apple. It was a young owl. My two young sons, Charles and Clem, and I fell in love. We named the owl Rosco Lonnie.

We wanted to do our best to take care of him. I was worried because he wouldn't eat. Finally, I thought, *What do I like to eat when nothing else tastes good? Bread and warm milk.* So I put a little in a teaspoon, and he happily ate it.

Our back porch became the little fur ball's home. We kept his food there, and that's where he learned to fly. He flapped his wings and went from one step to the next. Little by little, he flew farther and farther, but he always came back.

Rosco was very fussy about whom he let hold him. He liked me, my mother, and his favorite, Charles. He didn't like Clem too much because he would squeeze Rosco too hard.

People didn't believe that he would come to me when I called him. One morning, Paul, the man we were working for, wanted to show Rosco off to some friends. So I called for Rosco and opened the front door, and he came flying in and skidded across the linoleum floor in the living room. We were very proud!

After having so much fun that summer, we had to move and could not take Rosco with us. We shed many tears for our family owl. But anytime I look at this picture, I'm reminded of the many happy memories we had with our Rosco Lonnie.

**MELVA LARSON
RICHFIELD, MN**

Charles (left) and Clem Larson and their feathered friend.

# LITTLE MISCHIEF MAKERS

## The antics of these rascals left heartwarming memories

Edward and his trusty companion prepare for the adventures that a day on the farm brings.

### BING, THE COUNTRY DOG

It was rare in the '50s that a farm in northern Idaho didn't have at least one dog. Ours was Bing, a mixed breed with a helping of Australian shepherd, border collie and even some coyote. As is fairly common in Aussie breeds, Bing had one white eye. Dad thought Bing was a good name, since the sire was called Bob, and Bing Crosby and Bob Hope were at their peak.

Bing and I were inseparable. He would run alongside my bike, swim during our daily summer treks to the farm pond, stay low and close when I went squirrel hunting, lope right beside our sleds on snowy days, and snuggle up to my sleeping bag on warm summer nights outside. When I got older, he'd follow the tractor I was driving or ride on the seat with me when he got tired. He had a distinctive sound—definitely a happy bark—when he heard one

of our vehicles coming up the hill. He knew it was us long before he could see us.

Bing loved to chase birds. He would lie motionless, waiting for sparrows or robins to come down and peck in the lawn for bugs. Then he bounded after them and watched as they took flight, chasing them until they landed on a fence or telephone line. Once, he made a mad dash straight for a lone robin that was too busy foraging to notice him. About 3 feet away, Bing stopped abruptly. We laughed and decided he didn't know what to do if a bird didn't fly away!

This country dog had a big influence on my lifelong affection for canines. He taught me everything I know about companionship, loyalty, affection and devotion.

**EDWARD J. MCBRIDE**
**COLFAX, WA**

## THE DAY THE RUNTS ESCAPED

In the '50s, in western Massachusetts, my parents had a small farm. The best time of year was spring, when the piglets were born. I would rush to the pen to give each one a name and begin our new friendship.

Early one summer morning, the piglets managed to sneak out of their pen. When the little band of escapees was discovered, the whole family frantically tried to round them up. Everyone was dashing here and there, trying to grab the pink, slippery critters as they squealed with excitement. This spectacle made me laugh and laugh so hard, my side ached.

After many hectic hours, we rounded up the fugitives and placed them back with their mother, where they began nursing, no worse for wear!

I learned an important lesson from those piglets: Friendship comes in many forms.

**FRANK BLANCHETTE**
**HENDERSON, NV**

## GRANNY'S SHEER TERROR

One of my childhood delights was visiting Granny at her home in rural Georgia. She was a long-legged Irish woman who loved everything about the country—the land, her chickens, the cows, you name it. There was one thing, though, that she could not abide, and that was a spider. Years earlier, a family member had been bitten by a black widow, and the panic that ensued left its mark in her mind.

My grandmother was, as they say, getting along in years, so when I was there, I helped out by fetching the mail. One day she was relaxing, rocking in her chair on the porch, when I plopped an abnormally large pile of mail in her lap.

As Granny began sorting through the mail, I sat down in another rocking chair. I had barely gotten comfortable before a sizable spider crawled out from between the letters and made contact with Granny's hand. Granny squealed so loudly that I thought I had rocked on a cat's tail.

I can hardly describe the whirl of activity that happened next. When she saw the spider, she tried to sling it from her hand. Unfortunately, it landed back in the mail pile, which was still in her lap. She jumped up with the energy of a woman half her age, letting all the letters drop to the porch. I was transfixed, watching every move. Her fear was infectious. I yelled, "It's on your skirt!"

Granny always wore a long skirt, a matching top and an apron. She quickly untied the apron and began flapping at the unwanted creature. When she realized it was still on her skirt, she flashed me a sympathetic look and said, "I'm sorry, baby." It took a split second to realize why she had apologized. Only moments ago, we had been sitting quietly. Now, with the speed of an Olympic athlete, Granny shimmied out of her skirt and sprinted into the house. I watched the bewildered spider run for its life, also making an Olympic jump off the porch to the ground.

While I was picking up the mail, Granny reappeared at the screen door, again fully dressed in a long skirt and clean apron. We glanced at the pile of clothes. Not realizing the spider had taken the perfect opportunity to flee, Granny said in a firm voice, "Burn everything!"

And I think she meant it.

**JO UPTON**
**FAYETTEVILLE, GA**

## THUNDERATION!

In the '30s, my granddad's family had a picnic in the front yard of his farm near Goshen, Ohio.

My mother's brother Galen had brought his big dog, Judge, who was terrified of thunderstorms. Of course, a storm hit and everyone ran inside.

When it was over, my mother, Lida, went to the privy and came back screaming about an animal. It turns out Judge had dived down the privy hole.

Galen pulled Judge out and scrubbed him, but the dog smelled so bad he rode home in the trunk.

**JOHN MORRIS**
**WARREN, MI**

## BUTCH'S BAD HABIT

On our family's Ohio farm in the '50s, our pet lamb, Butch, would follow us everywhere we went.

Butch had one bad habit. He loved to come up behind you and, when you least expected it, butt you with his woolly head.

One day some businessmen came to see my father, and my mother told them that they could find Dad working in the field. I happened to look out the window and saw the men walking down the lane, but they were not alone. Butch was following them, getting closer all the time.

It was too late to warn them, and I saw Butch come up behind one man, lower his head and—well, you know what happened next. That man went flying through the air and wound up in a mud puddle.

Before Butch could take aim again, the men ran to their car, and I doubt they ever returned.

**FRANCES JOHNS**
**HOUSTON, TX**

## MILKY WAY

One of the childhood memories I reflect on the most is of my sweet barn cat. I never got to hold her or pet her—she would skitter away whenever anyone approached. But she was so pretty, all white and fluffy. Whenever I sat down on the three-legged stool to milk a cow, she would suddenly appear, a few feet away, with a cute *meow* to announce her presence. I would squirt milk to her and laugh as she stood on her back legs and lapped it up in midair. To this day, I still smile at the memories of that special barn cat—whom I called Milky Way.

**DOT SAURER**
**SANTEE, CA**

## SNOW ANGEL

I inherited two farm dogs from Dad. One, a collie mix aptly named Happy, was delighted by snow. Her winter coat made her comfortable in the cold, like a sled dog.

When she got cabin fever during the winter, it was obvious from her melodramatic sighs. So I'd open the doors and she'd rush outside and immediately drop to make snow angels. She would roll on her sides, digging into the snow with her feet, grinning the whole time.

Sometimes she'd pause for a minute to take it all in, as if she couldn't believe what a lucky dog she was. Then she'd take a bite of snow and get back to her angels with a new burst of energy.

One wintery day, a couple of feet of new snow accumulated over a base that was already at least 3 feet deep. The wind was whipping so much that it felt as if we were in the Arctic.

I looked up and spotted Happy carefully and quickly making her way toward me, trying to skip across the top of the crusty snow without sinking into the deeper stuff. The strong wind was sometimes blowing her off course, and her line was a little zigzagged. But she was unconcerned, smiling as she made her way to me. I don't think I ever saw a snowy day that she didn't love.

With Happy, you couldn't walk out into snow and grumble and scowl. Her delight was infectious, and her ability to entertain herself meant I could go about my chores and enjoy the companionship that made time seem to fly by.

I decided last summer what my New Year's resolution would be. This winter, when the snow gets deep enough, I'll make some snow angels and a snowman. When you walk outside and expect snow angels, life is good.

**MARLENE SMITH**
**HOMER, NY**

Happy loved snow days.

**HUNGRY COW**
"That's my brother, Joe Hohler, riding our milk cow, Betsy, while I lead them around the backyard in 1934," writes Jean Doyle of Boardman, Ohio. "Betsy loved to eat the clothes off my mother's clothesline on our farm near Monroeville. It was my job to keep her away when the line was full."

**CHAPTER 6**

# HARD, HONEST WORK

*No one ever said farm life was easy. Read about the dedication and perseverance of those making a life off the land and those that did so through some of the toughest times in history.*

# UNTIL THE COWS COME HOME

## A farmer's work is never really done

Left: Lyle's family and their Oliver 70 harvest wind-flattened oats in 1937. Above: The vaunted IH seeder.

## FEELING HIS OATS

March was always the time to grease up the oat seeder. Dad raised about 220 acres of oats every year on our 640-acre farm near Churdan, Iowa. International Harvester manufactured our seeder of choice. It was simple and could be kept in good running condition with a little lubrication, a pair of pliers and a screwdriver.

But first we had to clean the seed with a Clipper fanning mill. I cannot remember that my dad ever bought seed oats; he always planted oats he'd grown the previous year. We turned the mill by hand, and it had two screens that we constantly had to remove and clean. It was a formidable, time-consuming job.

To seed 220 acres of oats at 4 bushels per acre required 880 bushels of seed weighing 32 pounds per bushel. Using an iron shovel—lightweight aluminum shovels weren't available until years later—we shoveled oats from one side of the granary to the mill. Then we shoveled them from the mill into an empty bin. From the bin, we shoveled them into a large wagon. From the big wagon we shoveled into the seeder wagon and then finally into the oat seeder. I once asked my dad if all this shoveling had a wearing effect on the seed. He offered no comment.

A team of home-raised horses weighing about a ton each pulled the seeder wagon, which was a 36-inch-wide wagon box mounted on high-wheeled wooden running gear. Soft ground and even ponds with standing water posed no problem. Seeding a combination of alfalfa, sweet clover, red clover and timothy along with the oats, we could easily plant 70 acres a day.

Once the oats were seeded and the soil was suitable for tillage, a converted 14-foot single straight disk worked the seed into the ground. The disk had been built to be pulled by six horses, but in 1937 Dad bought a new skeleton-wheeled Oliver 70 tractor to pull it and a 30-foot straight-toothed harrow.

He'd also use a heavy roller to flatten old cornstalks, which plugged up the sickle bar of the oat binder come harvesttime.

With all the work of seeding oats completed, the new oat crop was on its own. The only thing to worry about was the weather, especially wind and hail. In the summer of 1937, wind flattened Dad's oats, and he could cut from only three directions—against the grain and from each side.

Don't you miss those days?

**LYLE SPENCER
GOLDFIELD, IA**

## 1,000 MILES AT 28 MPH

In 1957, my boss, Leo, came down to my place by Ulysses, Nebraska, and asked me to go to Shreveport, Louisiana, with his brother to buy a four-wheel scraper at a sale. After that, I was to drive the scraper back home.

We were in Shreveport the morning of the sale, in time for Bob, Leo's brother, to buy a LeTourneau D Pull scraper for around $7,000. It was electric, with switches about 2 inches long: one for steering left-handed and three for the right hand. It also had air brakes, plus a crash bar to hold on to and run the switches. The top speed was 28 miles per hour.

I drove it around until noon to get used to it, since I had never even sat on a scraper before. Because it had no rearview mirror, I stopped at a filling station to get one. Bob gave me $200 cash and then I was on my own. Of course, I couldn't travel at night because the scraper had no lights at all—no headlights, brake lights or turn signals! And this was February, so the nights were long.

On a Sunday morning I stopped for Mass and then started back down the road. Monday was a good run, but Tuesday was cold and rainy, so I stopped at a junkyard, where the owners cut the windshield and roof off an old Ford truck and welded pipes to it. We attached the new roof to the LeTourneau, and I finally had some protection from the rain.

Every day as I headed north, I had to put on more clothes to stay warm. On Wednesday night I stopped in El Dorado, Kansas, and stayed in an unfinished motel for $3.75. The clerk told me to park the scraper right in front of my room.

Thursday I had breakfast early and filled up with diesel before heading for Nebraska. At the state line the Nebraska highway people delayed me two hours because I was 8 inches over the width limit. When I walked into the weigh station, they asked where I'd come from and where I was going. When I said I had started in Shreveport and was heading northwest of Lincoln to Ulysses, one of them replied, "I never would have thought anyone would drive a scraper that far!"

I passed through Beatrice at 4 p.m., and, boy, was that nerve-racking! School had just let out. The next morning I stopped at the station outside Milford for coffee and a doughnut. Someone said there was freezing sleet south of Columbus, so I got moving again, but the sleet became so bad that it caked on the windshield, and I had to look out the side of the scraper for 15 miles. I finally made it to the Ulysses corner, where the highway meets the country road leading home.

The trip cost $120 for fuel, meals and motels, and the tires lost about an eighth of an inch of rubber over six days and more than 1,000 miles. It was so great to be home!

**GENE E. NOVAK**
**RISING CITY, NE**

Gene's father, Emil, operates the scraper shortly after its epic 1,000-mile trip.

## BETTER THAN BABY-SITTING

Below the home I grew up in, a series of sloping fields surrounded three sides of our neighbor's active farm. Dairy cows grazed in the pasture directly across the road from us, while the other farm fields produced hay.

During the summer when I was 14, my sister, Sabrina, then 11, and I worked haying those fields. Perfect weather meant Mr. Webster could not wait for his regular seasonal help, and so he approached my parents, asking if we might work for him. What began as a favor to our neighbor rapidly became one of the most memorable and satisfying experiences of my life.

We were responsible for following the baler, moving the bales into groups for easy pickup and then helping to load them onto the trailer that would transport them to the barn. Then it was our responsibility to stack the bales in the barn for winter storage.

Summer's cooling breezes and warm sunbeams lifted shimmering clouds of hay dust into the country air, filling it with the sweet smell of freshly cut dried grasses.

I will always remember the pleasure and delight of watching the barn gradually fill as we moved each load into place, climbing up and over bales to build the stacks as high as Mr. Webster directed.

We walked countless miles behind the tractor that summer, lifted and placed countless bales of hay. Each Friday after work, we went into the farmhouse's cool kitchen, where Mrs. Webster paid us our wages and, on occasion, had cookies and cold lemonade waiting.

Time will never dull the sense of pride and amazement I felt in receiving those checks. Though my parents said we needed no payment, Mr. Webster insisted on paying us the wages of a farmhand, which were significantly more than the dollar-an-hour baby-sitting rate!

Mr. Webster privately reported to my parents that he felt guilty for working us too hard and insisted that we had been the best workers he had ever had. As the years went by, he hired young men and then stopped active farming. For years after his passing, we grieved the loss of that idyllic scene around my parents' home.

Today the farm is active once again, though with beef cattle rather than dairy. Hay wrapped in white plastic is piled like so many giant marshmallows outside, not inside a dimly lit barn crisscrossed by sunbeams and floating dust stars. Despite the changes, there is a peace in the air again, a calm that comes from watching cattle graze and grasses blow.

Seeing these pastoral images, I'm reminded of that special summer and that life's simplest and most precious gifts derive from a hard day's work caring for the land and its creatures.

**LAUREL RICHIE MERTENS
MANCHESTER, CT**

Laurel and her sister, Sabrina, learned to love the land by working on Mr. Webster's farm.

## DADDY'S LITTLE FARMHAND

The door creaked as I opened it, the chill of the night softening as I stepped over the threshold and into the dimly lit barn on our Michigan farm. Through another door I heard the sound of milk hitting the bottom of the metal bucket that my father was using to milk Bossy.

I walked through the door, sat on a stool near my dad and began to do what I did best.

"Why do they call it 'the winter wonderland,' anyway?" I asked. I rambled on with other musings, never stopping to hear a reply. As I talked, I watched the cats gathering. The liquid made a rhythmic sound as Daddy's skillful milking quickly filled the bucket. Like many farmers, my father had much more to do than to say, so he continued to milk the cow while listening to his second-youngest daughter chatter away.

"We sure get a lot of milk from Old Bossy, don't we, Daddy?" and "Those cats sure like it when you're milking!

"If it keeps snowing like this, we might not have school tomorrow, huh, Daddy?" and "Why didn't you ever sing with us, Daddy?"

My father turned the milkers toward the cats with a smile on his face. I watched as the cats licked the freshly squirted milk off their fur. This was a rare playful act from my father. When the pail was full, Daddy got off the old milkin' stool. Because there was more to do, he ordered me back to the house with the bucket.

"Oh, no! I'm supposed to help you with the chores, Daddy! Ma says to help you in the barn."

In such a moment, the heart of a young child cannot possibly understand what goes through the mind of a father. He had already worked a full day and just needed to get through the rigors of the after-supper chores. I knew nothing of my parents' financial pressures as Daddy waited to hear if he'd ever be called back to work. I didn't understand all that a day required of a mother and father of eight. I knew only that my mother had called on me to help in the barn.

Daddy led me through the routine of scooping the corn feed and pulling apart another bale and distributing it to each of the cattle. He showed me how to collect the eggs so I didn't startle the chickens. With eggs and milk in tow, I was sent through heavily falling snow toward the house.

Just inside I put the pail on the top step and shouted, "Milk!" I directed my musings toward my sisters. I listened as they told me that Winter Wonderland was a state motto and that Daddy was much too busy to sing in our singing group.

**JOANN WEGERT**
**ELMORE, OH**

## THE FROZEN MILK RUN

When I was growing up on our family farm in western Pennsylvania, our local dairy didn't come out to pick up milk. We had to take it to them every day in 5- and 10-gallon cans.

Besides our own milk, my grandfather also hauled milk for four or five neighboring farms. I often helped him pick up the full cans from the neighbors, deliver them to the dairy and bring back the clean, empty cans after the dairy ran them through a washer. It was a time-consuming job in the best of times, but winter turned it into a real test of endurance.

We didn't have today's big snow-removal equipment. The secondary roads could drift shut for days, and we couldn't get through with the truck. The only way we could get the milk to the dairy was to hitch our farm's team of Belgian horses to a sled and haul it 5 miles across the fields to the highway, where a truck from Vale Wood Farms would meet us and take it the rest of the way.

The milk truck brought extra washed cans that we took back to the farms. Each of us ended up with someone else's cans for a few days, but it all got sorted out later.

At times, we were out there in near-blizzard conditions. Sometimes the snow was so deep that the horses got stuck and we'd have to shovel a path for them. Sometimes it got so cold that the milk froze, and the dairy would have to wait until it thawed before emptying the cans. It could take us all day to deliver the milk.

I'll never forget how the wind whipped the snow around our sled and how cold it was. But those were very special times. Living on the farm taught me the value of hard work, and I wouldn't trade my days there for anything.

**TERRY MAKIN**
**SUMMERHILL, PA**

Regina's mother, Dimple, shows off one of the family's prize melons.

## PICKING IN THE STORM

My family grew the best watermelons in the county when I was a child, and I'm not talking about just a few in the garden. We usually planted a thousand hills, all by hand. Then we'd water each hill and cover it with a page from a mail-order catalog to keep the sun from drying it out.

To keep the pages from blowing away, we placed soil around the edge of each one, which was slow, hard work. But many days could go by without rain, and the seeds needed every bit of moisture. It was Dad's idea, and it was a good one—until a thunderstorm rolled in late one night.

The slick paper that had shielded the tiny plants from the scorching sun would now block them from much-needed rain. I'm not sure how I got chosen to go with Dad to remove the pages; maybe it was because I was the oldest and the other kids were asleep. For whatever reason, only my dad and I went to the watermelon patch that night.

We each took a row and went as fast as we could, carefully removing the pages so as not to damage the tiny plants. The night was pitch-black, so we relied on flashes of lightning to find the next two or three hills.

Soon big drops of rain began to fall. It felt cool at first, and then icy cold as the wind picked up. Sometimes my dad got ahead of me and I felt all alone until the next flash revealed where he was. It gave me courage to keep moving.

When we finished, we ran to the house, drenched by the downpour. I don't recall Dad thanking me, though he may have. But those were our watermelons. We all shared in the satisfaction of eating them and in the financial rewards. I felt good about finishing the job. And I got the feeling that Dad thought I was a good worker, whether he said so or not.

Ever since, whenever I earn compliments or promotions for sticking with a hard job until it's done, I think about the night I picked Sears, Roebuck pages in a thunderstorm.

**REGINA GOLDEN**
**CORINTH, TX**

## HEY, WATER BOY!

My fascination with threshing began when I was 4 years old. I remember sitting on the front porch on a hot July morning, listening for the distant rumbling of a steam engine pulling a threshing machine. My dad said he'd arranged for me to ride on it as they set up on our farm. I was so excited.

The year I turned 10, the man who owned the threshing machine offered me a job as water boy at 25 cents a day. I accepted on the spot; it never crossed my mind that I'd have to ask my mother for permission. When I worked up the courage, she said she did not want me around those men, who were mostly our neighboring farmers. They would smoke, chew and use language a 10-year-old should not hear.

So next I tried Dad. I explained how I planned to use our old vinegar jugs. I would wrap them in burlap and attach a string so I could hang them on my pony Fanny's saddle horn. I added that he wouldn't have to buy me clothes or firecrackers because I'd have my own money. This seemed sensible to him, so we both approached Mom. After I agreed that I would keep moving and not hang around listening to the men, she finally said yes.

On my first day, I worked the hand pump on the well until the water was cold, then filled the jugs and wet the burlap tied around the jugs. That helped keep them cool. Then off I went to the field. The pitchers were throwing the bundles of wheat onto a wagon, where other men loaded them just so, with the grain heads facing the middle of the wagon. This was so interesting to me that I lingered long enough to hear some of the language my mother was worried about.

But as I stood there absorbing all the stories, I began to hear men calling, "Hey, water boy!" from the other wagons. So I made my rounds to the other wagons, stopped at the threshing machine and returned to the pump for more water.

Before long it was time for the big dinner meal. Everyone tied the horses in the shade and fed and watered them, so I did the same for Fanny. Then we all washed at a big washtub. If you've never eaten a harvest dinner, you've really missed something. There were piles of mashed potatoes, fried chicken, tomatoes, fruit and lots of pies. The men ate in two shifts—the first for the machine crew so they could eat and go grease up the machinery, and a second shift for the pitchers and wagon men. I ate with the cooks, which wasn't bad because some good-looking girls were helping the cooks.

By the time harvest ended several weeks later, I was older, richer and better educated. My fingers were burned from firecrackers, and Mom had washed out my mouth with soap. To this day, I can still hear that far-off yell, "Hey, water boy!"

**BILL MENTZER**
**IOLA, KS**

Threshing wheat was hot, hard work that brought the whole community together.

## WHEN THE COWS LEFT HOME

I grew up with six siblings on a farm in northern Illinois where our 12 heifers and 37 homegrown Holsteins were the envy of local cow buyers. For years, Daddy refused offers to buy the entire herd. It wasn't until a wild blizzard hit that he finally began to reconsider.

Farming was challenging enough, but in the fall of 1968, Daddy took a job operating a sign truck for the Illinois State Highway Department. It was a good job, with plenty of exercise and good pay. He planned to sell the cows after he got settled in his new job, but he always found an excuse to delay the sale—with a barn full of new hay, the fall wasn't the right time, and in the spring the milk price would usually drop, so that wouldn't work either. Daddy kept on in this vicious cycle for more than nine years.

By the winter of 1977, Daddy was 80 years old and still putting up signs for the state. He credited the rigors of farm life with keeping him in top physical condition, but his schedule had no wiggle room. Up at 4 a.m., he would milk, eat breakfast and be on the sign truck by 7 a.m. He was home by 4 p.m. to do chores and the evening milking. Ma helped him morning and night because it was just the two of them left on the farm—I was the youngest child and the last one to leave home, attending seminary four hours away. Ma did the chores, handling 125 bales of hay each day, seven days a week. These were the old rectangular bales that were as long and as heavy as a bale dared to be.

During winter break of 1977-'78 when I was home from the seminary, the temperature had dropped below zero, and heavy snow driven by angry winds made visibility negligible. Once the milking was done, it was time to run the barn cleaner. A spreader full of manure would freeze up quickly in this weather, so I was eager to finish cleaning the barn and get back inside. It was one of those times I wished Daddy had sold the cows.

The manure spreader was positioned under the barn cleaner chute. When the cleaner was turned on, the electric motor responded slowly in the extreme cold, struggling to overcome inertia. The chain started to move and within a few seconds—weakened by age, rust and stress—it broke, just outside the barn door.

We walked into the storm to make the repair, the snow preventing us from seeing our task. We'd made these repairs often, but never under these circumstances. Driven by an unforgiving wind, pellets of icy snow pecked at our faces and backs. The cold penetrated deep into our bones.

Just then, the barn radio inside played the song "Take This Job and Shove It."

Daddy stopped and stood upright. The frustration in his voice was tinged with humor as he pointed toward the radio with his wrench.

"He's got a point there," he said.

Daddy had had enough. Two months later, he came in from the barn and went straight to the phone. The cows and heifers were sold and gone by noon.

Never make a big decision without sleeping on it first, Daddy said. Well, he slept on this one for nearly 10 years!

**RICHARD R. SUNDERLAGE**
**ADAMS, WI**

The family loved their cows, but a cosmic signal told them enough was enough.

Heidi's photo of her dad's hand tells the story of his life. Right: Heidi with her dad, Donald Glamann.

## FATHER'S HANDS

I took a photo of my father's hand. People say a picture is worth a thousand words, so look closely. That hand will tell you a story.

In 1950, those steady and courageous hands held a rifle in the Korean War. After the war, they proudly placed a wedding band on my mother's finger.

I was not a stranger to the power of those hands. Whether fixing scraped knees or bicycle chains, they were miraculous to a child of 4.

I saw them work with precision, maneuvering the intricate tubing of a dialysis machine, so that his wife, ailing with kidney disease, could stay at home with her children.

Those hands were comforting as they held my brothers and me close at our mother's graveside.

His hand felt nervous on mine as we walked down the aisle on my wedding day. It clung tight to my fingers, not wanting to let go.

Those hands were joyful and loving as he held his grandchildren and great-grandchildren.

There was desperation in those hands, folded in prayer, at his dying son's bedside.

Dad's hands are wrinkled now. They bruise easily and ache when the weather changes. Yet they are great storytellers, and they have a few more stories left to tell.

**HEIDI STRAUSS**
**WAUTOMA, WI**

## PICKING VEGETABLES LEFT HER ALL WET

The work opportunities for a 12-year-old on Long Island, New York, in the '50s were a bit limited. But one local farm was paying 25 cents a bushel for picking tomatoes and 50 cents a bushel for green beans. I was excited. Not only would I have spending money, I could provide my own transportation—on bicycle, of course.

After picking the tomatoes, discarding the unacceptable ones, and chasing away bugs and squishing spiders, that quarter was one hard-earned piece of money. When I got promoted to picking green beans, the farmer turned a hose on the three bushels of mounded beans I'd packed. The weight made the beans sink, so I had to take from one basket to make proper mounds on the other two. Then I had to pick more beans to mound up the third.

I was much happier in my next job, selling Christmas cards door-to-door. The next time I picked tomatoes was 40 years later—in my own garden.

**JANET BURR**
**CALVERTON, NY**

## GRANDPA'S GINSENG GARDEN

Ginseng may sound like some trendy New Age herb, but I remember walking through my grandfather's ginseng garden when I was just a little girl. My mother's parents, William and Emma Berger, lived on a large farm in Marathon County, Wisconsin, which has been the ginseng capital of the U.S. for more than a century.

According to agronomists at the University of Wisconsin, ginseng once thrived as a wild forest plant along America's Eastern seaboard, stretching all the way from Maine to Alabama, and west to Michigan, Wisconsin and Minnesota. Ginseng was one of the country's earliest marketable herbs.

But wild ginseng was severely overharvested; it's now an endangered species. In Wisconsin, you can't harvest ginseng on state land; you need a permit to harvest it on private land, and then only between Sept. 1 and Nov. 1.

Early attempts to domesticate ginseng failed until the Fromm brothers carefully duplicated the plant's natural forest conditions on their

> **GRANDPA'S GINSENG GARDEN WAS ABOUT HALF THE SIZE OF A FOOTBALL FIELD.**

Marathon County farm in 1904. Thanks to the Fromms and the area's ideal growing conditions, Wisconsin produces more than 90 percent of the U.S. ginseng crop, and Marathon County accounts for up to 95 percent of that.

Grandpa's ginseng garden was about half the size of a football field. Ginseng grows best in a cool forest environment, so Grandpa covered the entire crop with a shed made of hand-hewn slats that provided shade while maintaining air circulation. He sold his ginseng crop to China, where the root has been used for thousands of years to treat various ailments, promote relaxation and enhance strength.

Growing ginseng was a big risk and a lot of work, but it helped my grandparents send my mother to Lawrence College (now Lawrence University)—and it was very unusual for women to go to college then. When I drive past ginseng gardens along the roads of Marathon County today, I always wonder what Grandpa Berger would think of them.

**JEAN SEPSTEAD**
**RANDOM LAKE, WI**

Above: Jean's grandparents weed young ginseng. Right: the plants grow under handmade shade.

Harry "Pat" Hess (above) continued a long tradition of high-quality postal service begun by New Lothrop's first two mail carriers (left, from left), Venus Wilson and Cyrus Judd, seen when the routes were first established sometime in 1905.

## PRIORITY MAIL

Every Christmas, Harry "Pat" Hess' family would become unpaid post office employees.

Postage at the time was 2 cents an ounce, but farm families around New Lothrop and Maple Grove, Michigan, often couldn't get to town to buy stamps. When Pat, our mailman, collected hundreds of unstamped Christmas cards from the boxes on his rural route—along with piles of pennies for postage—it became a tremendous job to stamp everything. So each night his kids sat around the kitchen table licking stamps.

Pat, like fellow carrier Hiram Walter, went above and beyond for his customers. In response to many a note left in mailboxes, he often delivered groceries, drugs and other emergency supplies—even harness parts—when a busy farmer couldn't take time for a trip to town. He'd pick up what was needed and then drop off the parcels on the next day's rounds.

Such tasks were a challenge in the early years of his route, which began in 1910 when Pat covered 12 miles with a pack on his back. In time he went to a horse and buggy, and there were days when farmers had to use a team of horses to pull him over muddy roads.

Each day he started with one horse, covered half his route, stopped at home for dinner and changed horses. Then, as he finished his rounds, he got out of the buggy and walked the last 2 miles so the tired horse wouldn't have to pull him.

He kept lanterns beneath blankets in the buggy to keep his feet from freezing in the months when he started out before daylight and came home by moonlight. Then he warmed up by doing a couple of hours of chores on his farm.

When I was growing up in the '40s, I also entrusted my two pennies for postage to our mail carrier. Usually it was for letters responding to offers of free merchandise that I'd clip from newspapers, magazines or cereal boxes. It brought excitement to a farm girl's day to wait for something like the greeting card samples I once received. With my trusty bicycle I earned enough money selling boxes of cards to buy my mom—and myself, too—our first electric mixer.

For all 41 years of Pat's rural route, postage for a first-class stamp was 2 or 3 cents an ounce. It wasn't till six years after his 1952 retirement that the rate went up to 4 cents. We all agreed Pat wouldn't have stood for such a thing!

JANET RUDDY
NEW LOTHROP, MI

Here's how the Ford looked hauling hay in 1968 (above) and all spiffed up in 2008 (left).

## THE '41 FORD BOOMERANG

Work was thin and money thinner in southern Missouri after the Depression. So my future father-in-law, Allison Norton Sr., sold his shack and acreage and bought a new 1941 1½-ton Ford truck. He and his wife, Verna, packed their belongings and their small daughter and drove to Idaho, where forests were full of first-growth timber. After turning the Ford into a real logging truck (removing the fenders, making reinforcements, etc.), Allison often made as much as $100 a week.

Two years later, he and Verna had enough money to buy 123 acres of prime bottomland with an old house, barn and sheds. Allison continued logging for a few more years, so between that and the farm, the truck saw plenty of work.

Years went by and the old truck came to sit behind a shed, watching times change around it. Allison Jr. and I married in 1954, and a decade later, when his father decided to retire, we bought the ranch, machinery, cattle and the truck.

Junior brought the Ford out of mothballs and made the necessary repairs. Soon it was hauling a ton of trash to the dump and bringing home all the lumber we could afford from the mill.

At planting time, it carried oat seed and supplies. My husband extended the bed for haying season and hauled more than 100 tons of hay into the barn. After that, Junior gave the truck side boards, since it was time to combine oats and drive the crops to granaries miles away.

After a time, the old Ford began spending more time parked than anything else, but someone always brought it back to life for one more big job. One spring Junior was using it to haul orchard and garden debris to a burn pile. It wasn't long before a passing neighbor stopped to see if he needed help. "No, thanks. I'm OK," my husband said.

"What about your truck?" the neighbor asked. The blaze had traveled some 50 feet and set the wooden floorboards afire! Junior and the neighbor soon had it out.

Not much later, Junior and I set out to retire and move. We sold the ranch and equipment three times. Yes, three times. And each time we sold it, for some reason or another, it came back to us—along with the truck. Then one day a new neighbor mentioned he might like to buy the old truck and restore it. He paid us what Allison Sr. had paid for it brand-new some 50 years earlier: $800. Time went by with no word back, so we assumed the truck was gone for good.

Then, in 2008, our oldest, Clay, got a strange phone call. The man said his father had bought an old truck to restore, but he got sick and had given up on it. The caller had heard that Clay was good with cars, and would he want a job finishing the restoration? It didn't take too many more questions before both Clay and the caller were laughing. It was our old '41 Ford, of course.

**SHARON NORTON**
**HARRISON, ID**

## WELCOME TO MANHOOD

In the late '40s I spent my summers working on a neighbor's dairy farm in New York. Mr. Tomkins farmed with horses, so I handled a team of them.

And I earned his trust, because one day he told me to take the black mare and gray gelding to the Martin place to help thresh oats while he attended a funeral. Talk about excitement!

Next morning I woke up before the rooster. It was time to set off into a man's world! I arrived early before most of the other help but found a member of the ground crew, and we headed to the first field of shocked oats.

With only one man pitching, it was easy to build a balanced load with tight, tied-in corners. This is important because the slippery bundles can slide off. By the time I finished unloading that first wagon at the threshing machine, three more teams and half a dozen other men had arrived. When I pulled back into the field, three pitchers were waiting to ambush me. Since I was a rookie, I expected the worst.

They pitched bundles at me three at a time from both sides. They laughed and hollered, "Can't you keep up?"

I didn't have the sense to keep my mouth shut and hollered back, "Can't you guys work any faster?" The bundles really came at me, and I lost all hope of building a load that would stay on.

I drove to the separator slowly, but the wagon hit a hole. The bundles on the right front corner slid off and took half the load with them. I stayed on by grabbing the standard, but the horses took off running. I was able to stop them before I lost more. I delivered my half-load to the threshing machine. Then I went back and picked up the bundles.

Everyone laughed about it, and I was very happy to hear the dinner bell. After dinner, I couldn't find my hat—until I spotted it nailed above the barn door. After prying it loose, I discovered my horses were missing, too. I found them munching hay in the machine shed.

I'd learned a useful lesson about working in a man's world: Don't let your mouth overload your wagon!

**CHARLES BROOKS**
**SCOTTSDALE, AZ**

## "JUST" A FARMER?

My dad said he was "just a farmer," but I don't believe that. Anyone who was raised on a farm or ranch knows that a farmer is a jack-of-all-trades—including obvious roles such as mechanic, veterinarian, businessman and carpenter. But farmers also have talents that often go overlooked.

### FARMERS AND RANCHERS ARE...

- ▸ **ARTISTS** Most farmers would scoff at the idea, but what's more scenic than a herd of cattle grazing on rolling pasture, military-straight rows of corn or waving seas of small grain? Farmers truly are artists who work on vast, living canvases. And their art ends up as a meal on people's plates.

- ▸ **TEACHERS** Their classrooms are tractor cabs, box stalls and hay fields. Farmers do most of their teaching by example, and students need only to keep their eyes and ears open to learn. They offer lots of practical, hands-on lab experience. And you can't beat their teaching credentials, including their hard-won YOE (Years of Experience) degree.

- ▸ **GAMBLERS** Despite personal or religious beliefs, farmers are the original high rollers. Every time they open a corral gate or pull the planter out of the shed, they are betting the farm against countless disasters that can strike at any time.

- ▸ **THEOLOGIANS** Farmers have a down-to-earth understanding of where they and God fit into the universe. God provides sun, soil and rain. But no farmer would expect to find Him digging postholes or greasing the combine.

- ▸ **WILDLIFE MANAGERS** Intentionally or not, farmers and ranchers provide room and board for much of this country's wildlife. Many farmers are also hunters, but that's almost beside the point. Their fields and pastures provide food and habitat for a host of game and nongame animals. And everyone benefits.

- ▸ **HISTORIANS** Sit down at a kitchen table with an old farmer and a pot of coffee, and you'll hear enough stories to write a book. They will tell you about horse lore, epic storms, kids' mischief, threshing, shredding, logging and the best tractor ever made. And don't forget the hands-on historians who pull that rusty old tractor or manure spreader out and rebuild it to preserve family memories for generations to come.

- ▸ **HUMORISTS** You may not see farmers onstage doing stand-up, but they are masters of the understated, deadpan delivery. Dad once pointed out crooked soybean rows and explained that the field was too wet when he planted it, so that when it dried out, the rows must have warped. I'll also never forget the compliments I received on my dancing after a rat ran up my pant leg. Humor makes it easier to get through the long days of being "just a farmer."

**RICHARD WENKEL**
**ST. PAUL, MN**

Sisters Shirley and Cathy saw more than their fair share of dirty plates and silverware as kids.

## WASHING DISHES WASN'T FOR SISSIES

When I was a girl in the '30s and '40s, washing dishes for our family of 12 was no easy job.

First we had to bring in water from an old pump in the backyard, then heat it up on a stove in two white galvanized dishpans. With no sink or indoor plumbing, we set the dishpans on an old wooden worktable.

Then my sister Shirley and I began this tedious chore, which fell to us by virtue of being the eldest daughters. How we hated washing all the silverware and those mismatched, chipped, cracked dishes!

On the plus side, the dishes rarely required scraping or pre-rinsing because not a speck of food remained on anyone's plate. And we didn't use glasses or side dishes, so there were fewer items to wash.

We made suds with Mom's homemade soap, which we also used for bathing, laundry and housecleaning. The washer knew she'd better get the plates completely clean, because the best part of the dryer's job was the devious pleasure of putting them back in the dishpan if they weren't!

To dry the dishes, we shook off as much water as possible, since we had no dish-draining racks back then. As it was, we went through several cotton drying cloths every time we did dishes.

The hardest part was washing our thin, dented aluminum pans, to which everything stuck. A wiry scouring pad came in handy, but it was still slow going. In fact, when it came time to wash those pans, the dish dryer usually caught up—much to the dismay of the washer, who had put much effort into keeping the dryer behind!

When we were done, we carried potato peels and other scraps out to our animals. One of the older boys carried the dishpans to the garden and dumped them; Mom said the soapy water kept away bugs. Then one of the boys would mop the floor, while the person who had dried dishes hung the towels to dry.

Things sure are different these days. I store leftovers in aluminum foil, plastic wrap or airtight containers. When I rinse dishes, food residue goes into a garbage disposal. Then I load all the dishes into a dishwasher.

The last step: I push a button and walk away, knowing that the dishes will soon be clean, sanitized and dry. We've come a long way since I was a little girl!

**CATHY REITS**
**BYRON CENTER, MI**

## MOM'S THERMODYNAMICS

I have pictures in my mind's eye of my mother, most of them with her bent over some household task that kept our farm north of Saranac Lake, New York—and all of us—going in the '40s. The most memorable images are those of her dealing with our stove and furnace.

Some of my friends' parents had gas or even electric stoves. In the midst of cleaning our kerosene model, I timidly suggested such a change. My mother actually stopped scrubbing for a moment and fixed me with her glare.

"That would be nice," she said. "We'll buy it with your next paycheck."

I was only 10 at the time, and my next paycheck was what my mother liked to call pie in the sky. I once broached the subject of an allowance, a heresy I'd learned from a rich classmate.

"Absolutely," she said. "Would a dollar a week be enough?"

For the briefest moment my heart leaped, until I recognized the tone of her voice. "Pie in the sky," she said, shaking her head. "Where do you get these notions?"

When it was time to light the furnace each fall, she became the keeper of the sacred flame, and she tended it with formality and expertise. Not even my father could be trusted to make the proper foundation of paper, kindling and scrap wood. If it went out, the water pipes could burst.

The goal was to keep the house bearably cool during the day and just above freezing at night. My parents calculated the amount of coal necessary to make it through the winter, counting it a triumph when the last shovelful in the cellar was used on the first unfrozen spring day.

I remember with pride when I was first trusted to add one shovel of coal to the white ash atop the fire's muted cherry glow. I had learned from several supervised trial runs that I shouldn't carelessly toss the coal but should sprinkle it evenly around the perimeter, for the fire was a minor miracle of thermodynamic balance.

If it was treated too roughly it could fall through the grate to the ash pit. There was a lever designed to shake the ashes through, but it had to be manipulated with great care. Too little effort meant nothing fell through; too much and you dumped the entire fire.

Banking the fire for the night was even more complex. Just the right amount of coal had to be added, the exact quantity of ashes extracted. Nor was there lying abed early the next morning, for the fire had to be stoked and revived for another day.

All those ashes accumulated in tin bushel tubs that had to be hauled to the fields and spread neatly for future soil augmentation. I didn't much like that job, or care much about the soil quality. But any notion of getting out of it—or any other farm chore—was just pie in the sky.

**RICHARD LONDRAVILLE**
**VENICE, FL**

Richard and his sister Mary Ann enjoyed a snow day below, but no one ever enjoyed tending the furnace, like the woman at right.

# GETTING THROUGH TOUGH TIMES

## A friend in need is a friend indeed

On a brighter day, Bill watches over the turkeys on his parents' farm.

### FLOCKING TO THE FOWLERS

An early winter storm was much worse than the forecast. In the '50s, weather was frequently a best-guess science.

"Sweetheart," Dad whispered to Mom, "I've got to get out of bed and go check on the turkeys." When Dad left the house, Mom worried that he wouldn't be able to make it to the farm. The snow was whipping around the little white frame house at 40 miles per hour, and there were deep drifts.

At 7 a.m., Mom was ready to call for help when Dad's truck slid into the driveway. He nearly collapsed on the kitchen floor. "Call Bishop Gurney," he stammered. "Have him tell the congregation to come up to the farm and get a free turkey for Christmas dinner.

"Near as I can tell, we have 500 frozen birds," he said, shaking his head in defeat. "Give me a minute to get warm and cleaned up." With seven children to feed, he knew the loss would be financially devastating.

That morning Bishop Gurney relayed the tragic story. Then he called other local bishops and urged them to tell friends and neighbors where they could get a turkey.

As the sun burst forth, hundreds of cars drove up the snowy road to the Fowler farm. Friends viewed the scene in sympathy. But the mood changed as more people arrived. Every turkey was claimed.

Nearly all of the birds, which still had to be cleaned and plucked, were paid for in cash. With the realization that the tragedy was being salvaged, neighbors talked and even laughed. Someone placed a donation can on the hood of Dad's truck. Often more was proffered than what the birds would have cost at the store.

Mom and Dad humbly thanked the Lord as they counted hundreds of dollars and hundreds of friends.

**BILL FOWLER**
**ST. GEORGE, UT**

## TRACTOR'S LASTING LEGACY

For years now, we, the Orrell family, have spit-shined and hand-cranked our antique John Deere tractor to prepare it for Christmas parades, and every year we hear people say how remarkable it is that "the Deere still runs." What's remarkable to us, though, is the history behind this piece of machinery and what it means to Davie County, North Carolina.

In the late '30s, family and neighbors in Advance, North Carolina, helped each other and shared tools during the harvest. On Feb. 16, 1937, the farmers in Advance agreed to set up the Potts family's steam-driven tractor—the only one in Davie County—in exchange for some harvested Kobe lespedeza, a grass used for hay, as well as some seed to use next season.

At about 10 a.m., something went horribly wrong. The vehicle's steam engine blew up without warning, hurling large chunks of metal and sheets of iron hundreds of yards. The explosion could be heard for miles.

Harvey Dinkins, a *Winston-Salem Journal* newspaper reporter, described the scene like this: "The force of the explosion was almost incomprehensible. A large section of garden palings was picked up near the point of the blast and literally blown to splinters .... Gearings off the engine proper were hurled about like leaves in the wind." The running gears of the steam engine, which he said was the size of a school bus, were "stood on end" by the explosion and landed on a truck parked more than 6 feet away.

Three people were killed that day, and at least one more suffered injuries. There would've been another person there, Paul Potts, but his mother, Ida, had an eerie feeling, perhaps a mother's intuition, and she didn't allow him to go that day.

As the community mourned the loss of loved ones and neighbors, crops sat in the fields waiting to be harvested. How would families who depended on selling the crops make ends meet?

My grandpa James Orrell and my parents, John and Maybell, weren't about to give up. The three sat down by an oil lamp and calculated the pennies they would need to pinch to buy a new tractor. And pinch they did.

This workhorse tractor couldn't be just a piece of machinery; it had to be depended on by both our family and others in the area. Several days after their meeting, my family went to Martin Brothers in Mocksville, North Carolina, and bought a new 1938 John Deere tractor, among the first rubber-tire tractors ever made.

In the following years, Grandpa and Dad took the tractor to many farms to plow and harvest fields. So it's not just that this Deere still runs. It's that we can honor those no longer with us.

**LYNN ORRELL OWENS**
**ADVANCE, NC**

The Orrells' 1938 John Deere helped their community survive tragedy.

## THE BRIGHT SIDE OF SNOW

In February 1958, I was a senior at Solanco High School in Quarryville, Pennsylvania. One day it started to snow and didn't stop until everything was covered in huge white drifts. Our road was closed, and the snow still kept coming down.

We had to shovel our way to the barn each time and then shovel our way back to the house. Every farm job took longer because of the drifting. The snowplows finally came a few days later, but before long another big snowstorm hit us. The power went off and we had to milk the cows by hand.

There were some special benefits, though. Our neighbors came over for home-churned ice cream made with the milk that we couldn't ship. We also enjoyed seeing a neighbor travel by snowshoe across our fields. The beauty of the wintry landscape was well worth the extra work we had to do!

**RHODA MELLINGER**
**WILLOW STREET, PA**

## THE SINGER SAMARITAN

My grandmother inherited 40 acres and a three-room cottage in rural Fayette County, Illinois, from her father. Eva Baker, my mother, was born there in 1925, when her two sisters were 9 and 12 years old.

Money was tight, but the family never went hungry. Grandma had an enormous arbor of Concord grapes from which she made delicious jelly. She also canned applesauce and apple butter, made from the fruit of the orchard that my grandfather had planted in the '10s.

Lila treasures her grandma's Singer.

They milked a couple of cows, raised some chickens and butchered a hog every year. My mother said she spent hours hoeing weeds in the big vegetable garden.

The 40 acres and the hard labor kept the family fed, but it didn't clothe them. For that, Grandma relied on a very old sewing machine that was barely working.

In the spring of 1939, on a rare shopping trip to Vandalia, Grandma stopped in a store that sold quality sewing machines. Her eyes fell upon the Singer 15-88, a treadle model with an oak cabinet. The price was $95—without a stool.

She knew it was more than she could afford, but the salesman said she could make time payments and take the machine home that day.

After much discussion, Grandpa agreed to pay the salesman $5 down and $2.50 a month, interest free, for 36 months. It was one of the happiest days in Grandma's life.

Every month my grandparents scraped up the money. It wasn't easy. In addition to raising my mother after the older girls left, they'd also taken in a grandson. One month in 1941, they couldn't make the payment.

Soon a warning letter came from the store. They promised to pay, but they couldn't that month or the next. Three months after that first unpaid bill, a man came to pick up the Singer. As Grandma watched him drive away, she felt hopeless.

She fussed with her old sewing machine, which she'd banished to the back of the closet, but finally gave up the relic for an old-fashioned needle and thread.

The day Grandma broke down and cried over a needle prick, my mother, even at 16, knew she was really crying over the loss of her Singer.

But early one summer morning, as Grandma stepped out onto the porch, something caught her eye. It was her cherished machine! A note on top read "Paid in full." My family never learned the identity of the good Samaritan, but Grandma was forever grateful for the gesture.

I learned to sew on Grandma's Singer, and my mother gave it to me when I married.

Rearing five children and working haven't left me much time to sew, but when life slows down I plan to get reacquainted with my Singer.

That sewing machine is special to me because it's part of my family heritage and it reminds me of the value of small acts of kindness. Thank you to the generous person who paid off my grandma's Singer.

**LILA BIRCHFIELD**
**ELGIN, IL**

## FROM BOUGHS TO BEDS

We were a Cajun French family living in Louisiana in the '40s. Papa was a sharecropper, and we were very poor. I remember Papa and my brother hitching the horses to the wagon and pulling moss off the trees along the bayou. They brought it home, stuffing the moss into what used to be a feather bed. The winters were very cold, and there were cracks in our walls. Beneath many quilts, I snuggled onto my moss mattress. I was a happy child—I didn't know any better.

**LILLIAN HOLCOMB**
**PUEBLO, CO**

## THE OLD THUNDER MUG

In 1964, our family of seven was living in a house without water or bathroom facilities.

The washhouse and bathrooms were about half a block away, which made them quite inconvenient to reach during the night. So one day, my father-in-law suggested, "You need a good old-fashioned thunder mug."

I went to several types of stores asking for a "thunder mug," all to no avail. No one had heard of such an item. Finally, some knowing soul said, "Ohhh—you mean a chamber pail?"

Of course! Why hadn't I thought of such a discreet name for it?

**JAN STAMPFL**
**BURBANK, CA**

## MILK DELIVERY BY BOBSLED

In 1936, when our family lived on a farm outside Belvidere, Illinois, we had a major snowstorm in February. The snow drifted, the temperature dropped to 20 below, and there were no plows.

My dad had milk that he needed to get to the dairy, and I had to get to high school, so Dad hooked his team of horses to our bobsled and we went over the fence tops to town. We stopped once at a friend's home to warm up, and then Dad took me to another friend's house in town. I stayed there for a month!

Every weekend Dad checked on me. I had fun in town, because my friend and I got to go to the movies on weekends, a treat for me.

Every spring, the schoolyard would flood. To get into the schoolhouse, you had to take off your socks and shoes and wade to school. The boys would fall into the water and get sent home to change clothes, shortening their days.

**GLADYS SNYDER**
**BELVIDERE, IL**

## FARMING AND FRIENDSHIP ACROSS THE POND

My great American barn story does not start in the U.S., but it has to do with Americans.

I live in Germany. I am 67, and I was born on a big farm near Munich. I grew up on three different farms where my daddy was the administrator. I had a sheltered, happy childhood. After the awful second world war, cities were ruined and farms were troubled, but people were satisfied that the reign of terror had ended.

The first priority of the American military government in Germany was nourishment of the people. We got CARE packages with necessary supplies of food thanks to the good Americans who helped us when we were poor little kids. At that time, I thought our country must belong to America because so many U.S. soldiers were here. Those very friendly GIs were often around our farm in the woods on maneuvers and exercises. Sometimes the GIs rested under the trees, talked to us and taught us kids some English words, and they always gave us candy and chewing gum. Kids back then couldn't buy candy from a store or a vending machine, so it was a real treat.

Karlheinz Dettweiler in Texas circa 1982.

In return, we kids looked after the soldiers and supplied them with fresh milk that we snuck from our cow barn. Our dear mother also missed some of her preserves. Those young fellows sure liked the milk and homemade food we gave them.

When there was a big problem, the good Americans always helped us. One day our barn caught fire. It was a dangerous situation, because a fire can jump to other buildings and the house. Our daddy and his staff were busy with the rescue of the animals, and the little fire department from the next village wasn't able to help put out the fire. But then a very big fire truck from the Air Force base about 7 miles away came along and extinguished the fire. Thanks, U.S.!

Years later, in 1982, I drove a tour bus of farmers and ranchers from Texas to visit several European farms and the agriculture exhibition in Paris. It was a very nice tour with very nice people. One of the ranchers invited me to visit, so I went to his ranch in Angleton, Texas, with my wife and 4-year-old daughter. We experienced ranch life, and I also helped work a little bit. As a farming man, you can always help on a farm if you like. I returned alone for a longer visit in 1999. My rancher friend was sick, so I helped his son make hay. I was 20 the last time I'd driven a tractor, but once you learn, you never forget it.

In 2013, I traveled to New Holland, Pennsylvania, to meet my friends Leonard and Dolores. We'd met on a bus tour in 1985. The little parish where I grew up had many Mennonite farmers, so I was impressed with the working methods the American Mennonite and Amish farmers still have. My grandfather worked like the Amish do on his leased farm in Bavaria until he gave it up because of his age in 1955. I miss the many little farms we had after the second world war, but farms here are going in the direction of bigger and bigger. Farmers now face a real challenge to produce more and more every year. We shall see whether this development is good.

During my stays in America, I met a lot of friendly, wonderful people, and I'm looking forward to my next visit. Until then, regards to all the good Americans I met. And thanks to all the farmers in the whole world, whether they have a little farm or very big farm. They are doing a good job every day.

**KARLHEINZ DETTWEILER**
**HAIMHAUSEN, GERMANY**

This 1938 photo shows 6-year-old Walter on the family's farm in Norway.

## COUNTRY BOY DURING WORLD WAR II

My mother, my sister and I came to Norway from Bridgeport, Connecticut, in 1936, when I was 4. We were planning to return to the U.S. in April 1940, but Norway was invaded by Germany that very month, so we could not get out of the country. I'll never forget the German planes that flew low across the sky early in the mornings. Soon after the invasion, the German military took over our school and used it as a base. We had to row over a river and walk a long way to a private house for school. All citizens were also ordered to turn in their radios to the authorities. It was a sad day for my sister and me because we liked to listen to a children's program every evening.

The last four years we were in Norway, we lived in one small room in a log cabin far out in the country. The winters were cold and snowy, and food and clothes were hard to come by. One winter, my sister and I stayed indoors because we didn't have shoes. When I was 8 years old, we had a box of crayons and wrote "God save the king" on a wooden wall. This was not allowed, and the next day, the sheriff came to question us.

Toward the end of the war, English planes came at night and dropped strips of silver paper to confuse the German radar. I found it out in the fields and hanging in the trees. I still have some.

May 8, 1945, was a fantastic day: War was declared over! All the flags were out, and it was not long afterward that we got the radio back too! We returned to the U.S. in October 1946 and docked in New York at night. It was wonderful to come out on deck and see all the tall buildings. Until then, I was used to only country living.

**WALTER LARSEN**
**STAVERN, NORWAY**

## A ROUGH THREE WEEKS

The blizzard of 1954 started with big snowflakes as we fed cattle in south-central Montana. By the end of feeding time, we could hardly see through the driving snow. By midafternoon, there was 2 feet of snow.

By 5 o'clock my father had tied ropes to trees in the yard so we could cover the 300 feet to the barn without getting lost in the whiteout. The thermometer closed in on 35 below zero.

By morning we had 4 feet of snow and the temperature had bottomed out at 60 below.

We started the small John Deere tractor in the garage and worked our way to the big John Deere in the barn. Hooking a chain to it, we pulled it until the oil in the transmission warmed up enough to get the tires rotating. Then we pulled the big tractor around until it started. This was an everyday event for the next three weeks.

To feed the cattle, we made a track to follow in the snow. We left a doughnut hole space in the bales on the wagon so the rider avoided wind.

No one could get to town, and the only meat in our freezer was pork chops. After eating them three times a day for three weeks, it was years before I could look at another pork chop.

After three weeks we ran out of food, so Dad had to start the D-6 Caterpillar. It was four hours before the big diesel engine roared to life. It took the rest of the day to clear the road to the main highway 5 miles away.

The school wanted to hold me back a grade for missing so much work, but I made it all up. I'll always remember that country blizzard, when I was as cold as I will ever be.

**RAYMOND HOEM**
**BUHL, ID**

## THE MILK STRIKE PITTED NEIGHBOR AGAINST NEIGHBOR

Gordon Raddatz of Oshkosh, Wisconsin, tells his son Wesley about his 70 years in the dairy business.

**Wesley Raddatz:** *Dad, what is your first memory of your Wisconsin dairy farm?*

**Gordon Raddatz:** I was born in 1918, and the earliest memory I can recall is of the delivery of my father's first tractor, in 1922.

But another special memory is from when I was 9 years old, and it was my task to get the cows from the pasture for milking. My favorite cow would let me sit on her back—she let me ride her to the barn while the other cows followed us! It wasn't long before she wouldn't even come to the barn unless I rode her there.

**Wesley:** *You were a teenager during the Great Depression. What do you remember about farming in that era?*

**Gordon:** Low prices of a dollar per hundred pounds of milk (that's about 11.5 gallons) spawned militant groups like the Wisconsin Milk Pool to call violent milk strikes. This resulted in the governor of Wisconsin declaring a moratorium on milk marketing for several days. Deliveries were allowed only to hospitals and people with small children. Picketers halted milk trucks, forcing them to dump their loads in the street.

Such tactics pitted neighbor against neighbor and friend against friend. Barns were burned, and cheese-factory equipment became mysteriously contaminated with kerosene. Fierce competition forced the price of milk to a low of 5 cents per quart. Fortunately, a lot of milk-marketing cooperatives formed around then to help farmers deal with the harsh realities of the free market.

**Wesley:** *How did World War II affect your farm?*

**Gordon:** When the war began, I was operating the farm with my father and had enough production units for a deferment from the draft. But shortages made times tough for everyone, and new trucks or tractors were available only for the defense industry. We kept going as best we could.

In 1944, an opportunity arose for me to buy a route hauling milk to the White House

Aug - 1927.

Milk Co. in Winneconne, which supplied condensed milk to the A&P food stores nationwide. I acquired a 1939 Dodge truck from the previous owner after it had been hit by a train. Because of the war, parts were hard to find, and I had to run it with a cracked engine block for nearly a year, patched by a piece of steel bolted over the hole. I sold the route in 1950, when I decided to expand into Chicago.

**Wesley:** *That was around the time some major changes started to occur, right?*

**Gordon:** Yes. Our herd's production levels advanced dramatically after artificial

Gordon Raddatz spent his life on the family dairy farm in Oshkosh, Wisconsin. Eventually he graduated from riding cows (left) to running his own truck route in the '40s (below), supplying milk to the White House Milk Company and A&P food stores nationwide.

insemination became part of my farming practices in the early '50s. The dairy-herd bull was a dangerous animal but a necessary part of maintaining the herd. Bulls have an unreliable temperament, and many farmers were killed or injured while handling or moving them about the farmstead. Fortunately, I don't remember any really close calls.

**Wesley:** *Thanks, Dad. That's where my memories of growing up on the farm begin.*

**GORDON RADDATZ AS TOLD TO WESLEY RADDATZ**

## THE FROZEN SCHOOLMARM

In May 1951, I completed a one-year course that certified me to teach in a country school. That summer I was hired to teach—and live—in the Horseshoe Bend School, 9 miles northwest of Okaton, South Dakota.

My cot and camping stove were in one corner of the schoolhouse and my "indoor plumbing" was under the bed. The only running water came from a hand pump in the entry. The building had no electricity or telephone, but it did have a new oil heater to keep the chill off. The students and I sat huddled around it on the coldest days of the worst winter I've ever seen.

We had snow on the ground in December, but the weather didn't get really bad until January, when the first big blizzard hit. It closed the school for a week while the snowplows cleared the roads. Then school resumed until a February blizzard piled snow on top of snow. The drifts were 10 and 12 feet deep, and we lost another week of school while the roads were cleared.

Classes resumed for two or three more weeks before the worst blizzard of all hit in March.

I've never seen snow accumulate as fast as it did that day. Parents came early to pick up their children. The family that came the farthest got stuck in the snow before they made it home, I learned later. Luckily, it was in their own driveway.

Meanwhile I was stuck at the school, completely alone. I had a battery-powered radio, but I couldn't listen very long without running down the battery. So I did a lot of reading.

With drifts up to 18 feet deep, even a bulldozer couldn't push the snow up the hill east of the school. They had to drive the Caterpillar across the fields to the top of the hill so they could push the snow downward.

By the time they got the roads open, I was living on crackers and jelly.

And when the snow finally began to melt, the roads turned to gumbo mud and became nearly impassable again! Even so, one morning I decided I needed a break, so I walked 5 miles to visit my sister and her husband on their farm. One of their neighbors gave me a ride back on the hood of his Ford tractor.

That fall I went back to college so I could teach at a school in town.

**DARLENE WOODS CHAMOIS, MO**

Willow branches are a popular choice for dowsing rods, but Tom—above with his brother Rick on Dad's drill rig—used copper rods and geological maps.

## A RARE AND DUBIOUS TALENT

My father, George Middleswart, and his partner, Walter "Pete" Annett, used to dig wells in Iowa around the town of Martensdale with a horse-powered boring machine.

Dad pulled a four-wheeled drill rig built by the Lisle Corp. of Clarinda, Iowa, from job to job with a flatbed truck he made from an old wood-frame school bus. He kept the two front seats and side door so my brothers and I could ride with him—essentially building an extended-cab truck decades before Detroit made one.

A huge Belgian gelding workhorse named Dan provided power to the drill. He was harnessed to a large oak singletree that turned the entire wood-and-steel drilling platform in circles. When the 30-inch-by-4-foot steel auger was full, Dan pulled it up to the surface and we'd dump the dirt around the machine using a small gantry.

The key, though, was drilling in the proper location. Some farmers hired water witchers, also known as dowsers or diviners, who used a forked willow stick or two L-shaped copper rods. They typically guaranteed the farmer that they'd find water or refund their fee, which ranged from $10 to $100. The farmer was still stuck for the cost of a dry hole, though.

Dad was scientific about locating his wells, keeping careful records of water depths and soil types. He hated it when we showed up at a farm to find oak stakes with strips of orange cloth, because they marked the spots where a witcher told the farmer to drill. While witchers did detect water from time to time, Dad felt their success was spotty.

But one day he decided, if you can't beat 'em, join 'em. He made a set of L-shaped copper witching rods and showed my older brothers and me how to use them. Soon we pulled in to a farmstead and found the dreaded stakes with orange cloths. Dad knew from his records that there was little chance of finding water under those flags. Plus, the well would be a long way from the buildings and electricity.

So Dad told the farmer he would witch a well closer to the farmstead for free. Then he explained that his fourth son was struck by lightning, leaving him with an uncanny ability to find water. He handed me the copper rods and told me to let them cross south of the windmills by the old fenceline.

Sure enough, we hit water right there, and plenty of it. Dad had dug a well for the neighbor the year before, so his journal told him he'd find that same aquifer at 58 feet—and he hit it right on the nose.

That was the beginning of my short but fruitful career as a water witcher, which involved crossing those rods wherever Dad's geological journal said.

Dad's well machine is now at the Midwest Old Threshers Heritage Museum in Mount Pleasant, Iowa. My friend Bob Whipple restored it, and each year he harnesses up his Belgian gelding and demonstrates it at the Old Threshers Reunion. Surprisingly, though, he has yet to invite me to witch him a well.

**TOM MIDDLESWART**
**MARYVILLE, MO**

## MOTORING IN THE MODEL A

This winter, as you climb into your cold car, shiver, turn the key and mumble about how winter can't end soon enough, I hope my reminiscing will cheer you up.

Back in the '30s, the temperature sometimes reached 30 below on our family's central Nebraska farm. Going to town for supplies meant starting up the Model A. The engine would be so cold that the oil in the pan was the consistency of heavy glue.

The oil and the engine had to be warmed before you could even hand-crank the engine, and it wasn't long before we had the complicated procedure down pat.

First you filled a pan with corncobs soaked in coal oil, slid it under the engine and set it on fire. If you didn't accidentally burn the insulation off the wiring, you could turn the ignition switch on and put the gearshift in neutral. After setting the spark, throttle and choke for a cold start, you were ready to get out and crank the engine.

By now the flaming corncobs would have warmed the oil enough to make cranking possible. You grasped the crank handle with your fingers and thumb. If you forgot this particular grip, the engine had to kick back only once to make you remember forever. Something about dislocating a thumb is truly memorable.

With the engine running, and being sure the radiator's drain cock was closed, it was time to play the fill-the-radiator game. The trick was to gradually add water, pouring quickly enough to keep the engine from overheating yet slowly enough to keep the cold metal from freezing the water.

You never, ever let a radiator full of water freeze. Which brings us to the last thing you needed to do before moving: Cover part of the radiator with cardboard. Otherwise, as you drove along, the rush of 30-below air would freeze the water in the radiator.

As you motored along, you'd want to keep an eye on the system, because once the car warmed up, it would keep warming up, and if you didn't stop and remove that piece of cardboard, it would go right ahead and overheat. While this was far from the dreaded frozen-water-in-the-radiator situation, it wasn't a good place to be, either.

So you'd burned your cobs, watched your thumb and yanked your cardboard. But getting to town didn't mean you were home free. It was more of a crossroads. Once there, you could:

A. Turn the car off and attempt to shop faster than the water in the radiator could freeze.

B. Leave your trusty Model A running until you were ready to go.

C. Shut the car down, drain the radiator and, when you were ready to head home, start the whole process over from scratch. (This was not a beloved option.)

Whatever you decided in town, once you got back home you made certain you opened that drain cock and emptied the radiator. And that was all there was to making a quick trip into town!

**LLOYD BRESLEY
SUMMERSVILLE, WV**

In the '30s, farmers like Lloyd and Roe Hatley (left) mastered the art of starting a Model A in winter.

Clockwise from top left: Harold poses with his first car in 1947. Some years earlier, Harold hugs his sister, Alyce, near the family barn where he once ran away from home for an entire day. Harold and his wife, Marian, hold daughters Nancy and Susan, born just 11 months apart.

June 1-1947

## WHAT DEPRESSION?

Harold Moore tells his daughter Susan Moore Dangelo about growing up in hard times.

**Susan Moore Dangelo:** *Where were you born?*

**Harold Moore:** In Wilkes-Barre, Pennsylvania, on Dec. 5, 1924.

**Susan:** *Why did you move from Wilkes-Barre to Johnson City, New York?*

**Harold:** My dad, Harold Sr., bought some farmland in Johnson City and also went to work at the Endicott-Johnson shoe factory there. He would get up at 5 a.m. to milk the cows, go to work and then come home and milk the cows again. He made $5 a week.

**Susan:** *What was your new house like?*

**Harold:** They took the old house apart in Wilkes-Barre, piece by piece, saving even the nails, and rebuilt it in Johnson City. It was just a shack. There was a kitchen, a living room, and one bedroom for Mom and Dad. My sister, Alyce, slept on the couch, and I slept on the kitchen floor next to the stove, where snow came up between the floorboards. There was no electricity or running water. We had an outhouse and a well outside, plus chamber pots.

**Susan:** *What was the Depression like?*

**Harold:** What Depression? We were poor. We didn't know any different. It affected the rich people and the people in town, but we lived on a farm with 1.5 acres of vegetable gardens. We never went hungry, even if it meant eating potatoes and bread for dinner. You don't miss what you never had.

**Susan:** *What kind of jobs did you have around the house as a child?*

**Harold:** Alyce and I picked corn and cucumbers from the garden and sold them door-to-door. We sold corn for 2 cents an ear.

**Susan:** *Where else did you work as a kid?*

**Harold:** During fifth and sixth grades, I got a job as school janitor because my dad was on the board of trustees. I had to raise the flag, sweep the floors, fetch two buckets of well water every morning, and start the furnace in winter. I was paid $30 for the year.

**Susan:** *Did your family do anything unusual for money?*

**Harold:** During Prohibition, Dad and his brothers made and sold moonshine. Mom hated it. Once when Uncle Fred was visiting, Mom went into town for the day. She got back early to find Dad and Fred making moonshine in the washbasin. She immediately pulled the plug and started chasing them around the house with a mop.

**Susan:** *Have you had any dangerous jobs?*

**Harold:** Once I was the meat manager for Loblaws in Johnson City. We'd cut up chickens while blindfolded to see who could do it fastest. I won. And I never lost any fingers.

**Susan:** *One last question, Dad. When did you get your first credit card?*

**Harold:** Around 1946, I got a card from Montgomery Ward. I used it to buy my parents their very first refrigerator.

**HAROLD MOORE AS TOLD TO SUSAN MOORE DANGELO**

## STONE COLD NIGHTS

Oh, no! Grandma is lining up bricks on top of the wood-burning stove in the kitchen. That means it will be below zero tonight.

Grandma tells my aunt and me to put on our coats, go upstairs to the bedrooms, plump up the feather ticks and add extra blankets to the beds.

Trudging up the stairs, watching our breath turning to fog in the cold air, I remember the warm summer day when we repaired the feather ticks. What fun! Whenever we plucked ducks or geese to sell at the local grocery store, we saved the down in big sacks. That summer, we took the feather ticks out to the lawn, opened one end and stuffed handfuls of down into them until we couldn't fit one more feather in. Then Grandma sewed the ends closed. The lawn was white with feathers that escaped, and our hair and clothes were sprinkled with bits and pieces.

Upstairs we hear trains rumbling along the Mississippi. The cold, crisp air carries the sound of train whistles screaming warnings at the crossings in our town of Moline, Illinois.

Carefully, we shake the ticks and level them off with a broomstick. After replacing the usual blankets, we add extra wool quilts Grandma has made of worn-out clothing. Then, out of the storage room we drag the horse blankets made from the hides of horses and ponies that have died. Each bed is covered with one of the heavy blankets. I sneeze as we make up the last of the beds, because the horse blankets are very dusty. My bed is covered with one made from Blackie, a Shetland pony; its coat was long, black and shaggy.

Getting ready to go to bed, we stand by the stove and put on flannel pajamas, two pairs of socks, our coats and stocking caps. Each of us taking a brick wrapped in a towel, we run upstairs and put the bricks in our beds, where our feet will be. I climb on a chair and step into the bed, being careful not to push down the edges of my feather tick. Then I lie down and pull the blankets completely over my head. With my finger, I make a little path for air to reach my nose and mouth so I can breathe. That hot brick feels good by my feet, but I still shiver until the blankets are warmed by my body heat.

Nothing could be better on a freezing cold night than a warm brick, a feather tick and dusty Blackie.

**MARY LOU SCHAECHTER**
**MOLINE, IL**

Warm memories of Grandpa and Grandma Ruefer's farm are kept by Mary Lou. Both are shown circa 1943.

# THE DUST BOWL

## Surviving one of the most difficult times in farming history

### THE DIRTY '30S

Doris Sinden tells her daughter, Susie Buckley, about how the Dust Bowl nearly killed her.

**Susie Buckley:** *Where were you born, Mom?*

**Doris Sinden:** I was born in central Kansas and raised on a farm near the Home on the Range Cabin, where the words to our state song were written by Dr. Brewster Higley. It was said that on a still night, my grandfather could hear Dr. Higley sitting outside his cabin playing his fiddle.

**Susie:** *What did you do for fun as a girl?*

**Doris:** Each Saturday, I was allowed to trim my grandfather's mustache. I earned a dime for this. Come evenings, we would drive into Athol to do our Saturday night trading. I loved going to the little general store and spending my dime on candy!

**Susie:** *Can you describe a difficult time in your life that you survived?*

**Doris:** The time known as the Dirty '30s was disastrous to our area. I was 11 or 12 when we suffered through the terrible dust storms. We put wet sheets up around our doors and windows to try to keep the dust out, but to no avail. The sun would be blocked out by the dust, and our chickens would think it was night and go roost even in midday. People would get lost and have to use fences to find their way back to shelter. My sister came down with what was called dust pneumonia. She went to a hospital 15 miles away for care. I caught it as well but was too ill to be moved. As when I had scarlet fever as an infant, I was not expected to survive. But somehow I did.

**Susie:** *What was your first job?*

**Doris:** I moved to the small town of Harlan, Kansas, in my sophomore year of high school. I worked in a couple's home, keeping house for them. It was at Harlan High School that I met my future husband, Eddie. I graduated in 1939, and we were married in 1941. Eleven months later, my husband went into the Air Corps. Because of a shortage of males in our small town, I found employment at our local post office. I worked there until my retirement.

**Susie:** *Did you enjoy the work there?*

**Doris:** Yes. What I enjoyed most of all took

Doris Sinden (above) on her father's central Kansas farm. Susie (pictured with Doris, right) is her only child.

place during the war years. I would make special trips down to the office and look for letters from servicemen. I delivered them to family members personally, which gave me a great deal of satisfaction.

Now, at 95, I am blessed to spend time with my daughter and son-in-law, my two grown grandchildren, and my six great-grandchildren. God has been good to me!

**DORIS SINDEN AS TOLD TO SUSIE BUCKLEY**

# When Crops Are on the Tough Side

## ...it's the OLIVER *Self-Propelled*

The smooth, steady hum of an Oliver Grain Master is sweet music in any field. But, it's when your crops are on the tough side . . . when thick, towering weeds threaten trouble, that the threshing superiority of the new Model 33 Self-Propelled shows up. And, that's when this Oliver Grain Master pours out an *extra* margin of profit for you by *saving more grain . . . getting it out faster* and *cleaning it better.*

If you're the grower of any combinable crop, or a custom operator, it will pay you to visit your neighborhood Oliver dealer before the harvest season begins. You can check for yourself the combination of features that accounts for the great capacity of Oliver Self-Propelled . . . that makes it so easy to maneuver.

The 12-foot, hydraulic header lifts and lowers on the "go." Six forward speeds give you ground travel rates from a creeping crawl to almost 10 miles an hour to meet changing field conditions. Besides, you can control threshing speed and forward motion independently with the double-clutch power take-off mechanism. A 6-bat, semi-revolving reel reduces shattering . . . an 8-inch auger unloads the 45-bushel tank on the "move". . . the husky, 6-cylinder engine is located at "waist height" for quick servicing. The Oliver Corporation, 400 West Madison Street, Chicago 6, Illinois.

**1950**

# OLIVER

## "FINEST IN FARM MACHINERY"

The Oliver Corporation
400 West Madison Street, Chicago 6, Illinois
Please send me catalog describing the modern advancements on the Oliver Model 33 Self-Propelled Grain Master.

Name..........................................

Post Office...................................

Rural Route........State.....................
F-4-3

## HOWLING BLACK MONSTERS

In the unbearable days of the dust storms on the North Dakota prairie, the wind would not be still, whistling through our house like a cat crying day in and day out. Even at night we would wonder if one of our cats was caught someplace.

I was 6 years old when I started at our country school, some 2 miles from home. One day a student alerted the teacher to rolling black clouds on the ground in the distance. The teacher said, "Stop everything you're doing, get your things and go for home, and don't you dillydally along the way."

We kids had always been told to follow the fence line to our gate so we wouldn't get lost. The dust behind us looked like some black monster ready to pounce. We flew over the ground so quickly I don't think we even left footprints. We'd stay close together, one behind the other. Mother was waiting at the gate just as the wind hit us. Oh, how glad we were that she was there!

There wasn't a thing in the house that wasn't covered by Mother Nature—black dust all over and dirt drifts on the windowsills and near the doors. When you walked around the house, the dust would rise in a swirl and tag along with you.

It got so dry that the earth would crack open. We kids put long sticks down into the cracks to see how far they'd go. Some of them were a foot or more deep and 2 or 3 inches wide.

Worry took its toll on everyone, but we were fortunate to have a homestead where we could stay.

**DOROTHY BEHRINGER**
**SIREN, WI**

## PESTICIDE ON THE PLAINS

I grew up in rural Kansas and walked more than a mile to a one-room school. One day when I was in third grade, the dust began to build in the morning and got heavier by the minute.

The teacher closed the school and walked her son and me home. As we got closer, I could see that Mother had the lamp lit. It was so dark the chickens had gone to roost. That dust storm lasted a couple of days.

I don't know if the grasshoppers came before or after that, but the sky turned dark with them as well. My dad and I went to the county courthouse and got banana oil, which we mixed with poison and sawdust and applied to the top of fence posts to kill the insects.

**WILMA BROOKS**
**MANHATTAN, KS**

## HUNGRY HORDES DESCEND

In South Dakota we had swarms and swarms of grasshoppers. I was just a kid in the first grade when Dad turned to us seven children, pointed and said, "Look back at the sun." We couldn't see much of the sun through the dust in the air and the thousands of grasshoppers in flight.

When the insects landed, they ate everything in their path and covered the wooden fence posts. They even chewed on the posts, along with my horse's mane and tail!

The five of us who were in school at the time got there in a cart pulled by a team of horses. My folks gave the teacher strict orders not to send us home early; they wouldn't know we were coming, since not many people had telephones. The horses knew the way home if we momentarily lost our direction in the dust, and one day we got home just before it really got bad. You would've thought it was night for the darkness.

**DARLENE PRICE**
**PRAIRIE CITY, SD**

LAKIN, KANSAS, 1935 Three kids head off to school with books, lunch pails, goggles and homemade dust masks in an image from Ken Burns' film *The Dust Bowl*.

# CHAPTER 7

# A LOVE OF THE COUNTRY

*Whether you have always lived in the country, grew up there and left, wish you could go back, or simply love the idea of living there someday, read on: You'll enjoy accounts of those who truly embrace country living.*

# GOING BACK TO THE COUNTRY

### Once you've been there, you never really leave

## HAND-ME-DOWN COUNTRY DREAMS

After World War II, my father, Leo, came home and married the woman he'd thought about the whole time he was overseas. Together, he and my mom, Mary, somehow scraped by on Dad's paper route earnings and raised their six children.

As you can imagine, we never had much to go around. One thing we did inherit was my father's vision of someday owning some land or even having a farm.

Growing up, we spent every weekend and vacation at my Aunt Albertine's farm. Dad loved tinkering in the little cabin he and his buddy Joe had built. We kids fished, caught frogs and turtles, and roamed around 80 acres to our hearts' content.

My dad eventually did buy a 1-acre lot with an old house on it and planted a small garden. By that time, though, it was getting hard for him to work or even enjoy the property.

Dad passed away in 1992. My mom couldn't maintain the place on her own and eventually moved to an assisted living center.

After Mom died we were surprised to learn that my parents had set aside a few dollars for their retirement. We grown children divided what remained, and I soon decided to use my portion to buy the farm my father always dreamed of.

In 2009 my wife and I set out on a search for land. Eventually we found and bought 10 acres of rolling hills with a clearing and lots of trees.

Now Susan and I can't wait for the weekends to go to the farm to cut grass and make improvements. We like building campfires, hiking and taking photos of wildlife.

This property is much more special than Susan or I could have imagined. It offers us the peace and quiet my dad loved so much.

I feel God's presence here, and my parents', too. I know Mom and Dad are always with me in spirit, proud that the dream is real.

I use my time on the farm to prepare mentally for the next medical exam and sort out life's challenges. My father's dream is now mine. This love of the land carries me through each day, as it did for him.

**JERRY CHRISTEN
WEST CHESTER, OH**

Jerry hangs this sign when he visits the farm; wildflowers abound (left).

Delores (above) tells a great story about oxeye daisies (left).

OXEYE DAISIES: HENRY WESTHEIM PHOTOGRAPHY/ALAMY STOCK PHOTO

## WEED INSPECTOR

As a teacher, I'm glad when summer work provides extra income. But I'm especially grateful for the summer I worked as a weed inspector for the Department of Agriculture in British Columbia's Peace River Regional District.

The farmers in the district are supposed to recognize and control noxious weeds such as sow thistle, Canada thistle, tansy, wild oats and yellow toadflax. Even oxeye daisy looks pretty in meadows and yards but can seriously harm crops.

After initial training and passing an exam to prove I could identify harmful plants, I was hired to check farmland, forestry roads, recreation areas and trails, oil patch leases and even garbage dumps—which were frequented by bears.

I loved the area assigned to me in northern British Columbia. It stretched from Fort St. John—near Mile 50 on the Alaska Highway—north to Mile 250 and then west and east 60 miles from the highway in each direction. It was like a small fairy-tale kingdom with homesteads hidden away in the wilderness.

A few people complained about unwanted government interference; after meeting one especially grumpy man, I started parking my car facing the road in case I needed to make a hasty exit. But most people valued our service and cooperated.

On one road that I wasn't even sure was a road, I met a woman from Germany in a Hansel-and-Gretel-type house whose husband had ventured into town for supplies. I was the first visitor she'd seen all summer. She served delicious cookies and tea in a china teapot. I will never forget her.

And one day, two visitors from Denmark joined me as I explored a remote stretch north of the mighty Peace River. We came across a beautiful homestead with a well-built log barn, an attractive home and a large rail-fenced yard filled with lovely flower beds. As I drove in, the owner ambled forward to meet me.

He and his wife had immigrated to Canada from Germany and had carved this showplace out of the wilderness. Though I had my required photo ID around my neck, weed inspectors don't wear uniforms or drive government vehicles. I leaned across his fence and said, "You have a beautiful place here, and your flowers are lovely! But do you know that these oxeye daisies are harmful noxious weeds that have to be controlled?"

A broad smile lit his face. He rested tanned arms on his top fence rail and replied, "Don't tell the weed inspector."

"I *am* the weed inspector," I confessed.

The rancher whooped with laughter and opened his gate to wave us in. "Run tell Grandmother to put on coffee and serve cookies," he told one of the children playing in the yard. "We have guests."

We all enjoyed ourselves. Then he and his wife listened to my instruction, accepted brochures and complied immediately. I love remembering those visits and the vast, remote landscapes from the best, most unforgettable summer job I ever had.

**DELORES TOPLIFF**
**MAPLE GROVE, MN**

## FARMING AT 56

I grew up in the city, but I have deep roots in the country. The Shelby County, Illinois, census stated that Rezin Whitlatch, my great-great-grandfather, "went to farming on land he purchased in 1865." I also found pictures of my grandfathers, one plowing behind two mules and the other casting seeds on the farmland where my mother grew up.

But when Mom married and moved to town, she wanted her four daughters to be cultured—which to her meant piano lessons and ruffled dresses. I liked to climb trees, catch crawdads in the creek and collect bugs, but I hated piano lessons.

Daddy, on the other hand, fished and raised worms for bait, and we had a large garden and meat rabbits. Being city girls, we refused to eat our "pets."

By the time I was old enough to remember trips to my grandparents' farm, the chickens were down to a small flock and most of the livestock and horses had been sold. But I have memories of my aunts gathering in the kitchen to put up freshly picked produce. We drank from tin cups and feasted on delicious homemade biscuits, strawberry preserves, and smoked ham and bacon.

Away from city lights, my sisters and I discovered skies full of stars. We slept in feather beds underneath handmade quilts, learned to swim and took hikes down the gravel road to visit our great-grandparents.

As a teenager I always dreamed of owning a log house and raising chickens. It bothered me that I was the first generation not to grow up on a farm.

I took the farming dream with me to college, but after graduating I moved forward in the world of office spaces, pretending it was the life I had wanted all along.

Then, when our sons were grown, my husband, Randy, and I moved to Tennessee, and hope rose again. We began to plan for the day we could afford a bit of land.

Seven years later, our real estate agent, Donna, came across a house she thought we'd be interested in. One look and I was ready to buy—but it needed a lot of work.

> **WE SLEPT IN FEATHER BEDS UNDERNEATH HANDMADE QUILTS, LEARNED TO SWIM AND TOOK HIKES DOWN THE GRAVEL ROAD TO VISIT OUR GREAT-GRANDPARENTS.**

Karen Shaw always knew she was meant to be a farmer.

The previous owners had applied taupe paint to the exterior logs and chinking and had covered up the interior exposed logs with paneling.

I decorated our new home with precious heirlooms, and I now own a rabbit named Sunshine and lovely chickens whose eggs I eat and sell. I tend vegetable gardens, can and freeze whatever I grow, and cook meals that remind me of home. We also maintain a worm farm just as Daddy did, compost organic matter and collect rainwater.

One of my greatest joys is working at Trevecca Nazarene University's Urban Farm in Nashville. I tend the organic gardens; raise pigs, goats and chickens; and care for tilapia in the aquaponics system. I've also become a beekeeper and I teach soap-and-salve-making classes. In the summers I help run camps for students in middle and high school.

As I get closer to the age when most people retire from their jobs, I feel that I have just begun to live. My 89-year-old mother laughs when I tell her I'm taking yet another class, but I can tell she's proud of me.

When the university's urban farm manager introduced me to a group of students as "one of our farmers," I thought, "Who, me?" At age 56, I can't wait until the next census comes around so I can write down "farmer" as my occupation, the same way that my great-great-grandfather did.

**KAREN SHAW**
**GOODLETTSVILLE, TN**

Taking care of animals and gardens (near left and center) at a university farm and living in a log home (below) give Karen pride and contentment. Her family's pantry is stocked with colorful homegrown produce (above).

## UNEARTHING THE PAST

On a chilly autumn morning, I gathered my trowel, a spade and several bags of spring-flowering bulbs and headed to the far corner of the yard. This was our first year on our little farmstead, our lifelong dream come true.

It was heavy going, digging a new flower bed in the dense clay soil, and one section of particularly thick sod gave me much trouble. I struggled to remove tenacious roots and rocks. I also found shards of broken crockery and rusty pieces of old tools—relics of days gone by. I worked with zest, putting rocks in one pile, debris in another.

When I paused to catch my breath, I spotted it. Although it was caked with soil, one rock appeared quite different from the others. Slender and about 6 inches long, it was an elegant tool, a whetstone used for sharpening a scythe. I knew I had dug up a treasure.

It must have lain undisturbed for decades in the quiet corner that was once a field and is now the edge of a lawn. When the farmer discovered the whetstone was missing, the whole family undoubtedly went looking for it. Back then, replacing a good whetstone was an unwanted expense. But it remained hidden where it fell, and eventually the searchers gave it up for lost. I scraped away the mud carefully.

Impressions of the farmer's own fingers were worn into its surface, a rough testament to years of hard, productive work. It fit my own hand comfortably. I wondered about when the farmer first noticed it was missing. Had it fallen out of his pocket as he worked?

As I turned it over, I imagined him standing the scythe on its end and using a keen eye and practiced strokes as he ran the whetstone along the curve of the blade. Maybe he stopped to look up at the sky, gauging whether he could finish cutting before the rain began. Or perhaps it was the end of the day and, putting the scythe across his shoulder, he walked to the house—hot, weary and ready for supper.

From the property deed, I know the names of the farmers who had worked our land. Which one lost this stone? Was he cheerful or dour, easygoing or stern, generous or greedy? Did he find joy among the trials of life? Did he look with hope upon the coming harvest, or was he beset with worry? Like the rest of us, he likely felt all those things at one time or another. Whoever he was, he labored hard. The stone bears testimony to that.

**ANNE CARRINGTON MCHUGH**
**VIROQUA, WI**

Anne uses the old whetstone she found in her yard to keep her gardening tools in good shape.

## THE PERFECT POT...OR NOT

After we married, my husband and I moved to rural Larimore, North Dakota. I didn't know much about country life, but I'd enjoyed visits to Grandpap's farm.

The first winter, my husband installed a wood-burning stove. Ours was probably the only house that had its windows wide open when it was 20 below out, but eventually we got the hang of regulating the stove. I pictured myself stirring homemade soup on my vintage stove. All I needed was a soup pot—an old one, with character and charm.

So I headed to the first spring auction at a neighboring farm. Young and old stood around trailer beds stacked with boxes. Some were sorting through items, some were searching as if on a mission. Trying hard not to look like a newcomer, I started poking around.

A small carton nearly tripped me as I moved along the side of a trailer. There, lying on its side, with dents and dings, was my soup pot with a lid, a handle and lots of personality.

The auctioneer looked out across the crowd and began. He went through a lot of things I didn't want, but then he finally held up the white enamel pot. I held up my auction card and won! Was I the only one who thought this pot a find?

As I took my treasure from the auctioneer, a young woman with a baby on her hip asked, "What are you going to do with that?"

I launched into my woodstove story and told her that I was looking for this very thing for soup. She smiled slightly, turned to the farmer on her right and repeated our conversation. He stared at me, then told the story to a younger man nearby. They both looked at me and chuckled.

Soon it seemed all the people were craning their necks to look at me and shake their heads. As I headed for my car, the young woman sidled up to me and in a rather confidential manner said, "You do know that is a chamber pot, don't you?"

A what? I had never seen a chamber pot before, and now I was holding one in my hands. Guess I wouldn't be stirring up soup in it after all.

I took the pot home and planted red geraniums in it. They grew exceptionally well.

**PATTY ANNE O'HARA
WAUSAU, WI**

Rex Gogerty and wife Kathleen have been living the farm life since 1949.

## 160+ YEARS ON THE FARM

Our house is packed with memories. Kathleen and I have been living good times and hard times here since we moved in as newlyweds back in 1949. My grandparents began building dreams on this prairie farm in the 1890s, when they built a four-room frame house here. That replaced a log home my Great-Granddad Bernard had built when he and Lydia homesteaded here in 1856. For family members, it's not just a home but a rustic shrine.

Many young folks ask about living on a farm home back in the good old days. "At first, running water in our home meant running to the well to fill a bucket" is Kathleen's favorite line for granddaughters who wouldn't know a cistern from a swimming pool. She also explains that central heating meant doing school homework around an oil-burning heater. The chimney running through the upstairs bedroom provided the only heat to shivering schoolkids.

Eventually we added a living room and a basement bedroom. Neighbors came with plenty of muscle to excavate the room. The cozy dig became a mini bunkhouse for our three boys. Later came central heating, air conditioning and TV. Even so, those hardscrabble years when the children were small remain some of the most memorable.

Our five children helped with the chores, including milking cows, feeding pigs and walking beans (pulling weeds in soybean fields). Of course, outdoor work and play often tried the homemaker's patience. Kathleen held back the tears when she saw the boys in muddy boots running to the back door. She managed to put on a happy face, a practice she has continued for generations of kids who savor her homemade bread and chocolate chip cookies. "Sometimes I watch our great-grandchildren playing in the yard and wonder where the years have gone," she says.

Some family members and their friends come to visit from their homes in Japan, Turkey and Germany. Like our local friends, they enjoy the laid-back lifestyle. The kitchen is the hub of our home. Family photos decorate the walls. Backyard evergreens and wildlife beckon beyond glass doors. A coffeepot that's always on and the oak leaf table with a plate of sweet rolls add to the atmosphere.

We've considered moving, but we would miss the winter wind and drifting snow, the pheasants' call as spring arrives, and wagonloads of corn signaling the fall harvest. What's more, on a clear summer day, we can see our hometown from the front porch. Most of all, we'd miss friends and family walking in our front door to spend an hour or a day in what we still call Grandpa Bernard's home.

**REX GOGERTY**
**HUBBARD, IA**

## ESCAPE FROM NEW YORK

In Southern Appalachia it takes some folks a while before they stop regarding city-raised people like me as suspicious, but that's fine—because it also takes us country newcomers some time to acclimate to rural living.

When I moved to the Blue Ridge Mountains 10 years ago I resolved to do whatever was necessary to fit in among my neighbors. I even took bluegrass banjo lessons hoping to be able to attend local jam sessions.

The first question other residents asked in our holler, as I learned to call my neighborhood, was: "Y'all aren't from around here, are ya?" With a bit of help from a friend who's lived here all of her life, I learned to reply, "No, but I got here as fast as I could."

I was born and raised a mere 11 miles from New York City, but I never felt quite at home there. Maybe I inherited a rural living gene from my southern father, who moved to find work.

One of the biggest differences that I encountered was the friendliness of people. For years, I lived in apartment buildings where I did not know the neighbor across the hall. In the city, kids learn not to speak to strangers.

That's a far cry from my mountain home, where it is considered rude if you do not acknowledge everyone you see. It took me a while to learn to smile at strangers and to respond to the one-finger wave from drivers coming down the road.

Now I look forward to going into a shop and having the clerk ask me how I am and sound as if he means it. Even when I go to the doctor, people in the waiting room get into conversations.

Often when I'm talking to my new neighbors, I tell them they're lucky to have lived in such a beautiful place all of their lives. I hope they never take for granted the clean air and water and the forests and wildlife that surround us. I live in a natural wonderland, and I appreciate it every single day.

**LISSA BROWN
ZIONVILLE, NC**

## IT'S NICE TO BE BACK

*Here is a letter that my father, Charles Berdo, wrote upon returning home from World War II:*

Life is really wonderful. Out of the Army in September 1945, I am finding an unlimited number of jobs on our 800-acre farm, idle for three years. Barns to be painted, fences to be built, weeds 8 feet tall to be plowed into the soil, livestock to be bought. Already, the combination of the goodness of bountiful nature guided by hard work is to be seen on our land. Fat Hampshire pigs farrowed since my return play in our fields. Fifty-two Hereford heifers have grown sleek and fat within a month on the lush fields of grass untouched by livestock for three years. After four years in the Army, it is a real pleasure to watch the heifers lie stretched out in the pastures enjoying the warm Indian summer sun. Fortunately, my 10 horses and two tractors and all of our machinery were waiting for me. I can't express the joy I have in getting to work with them again.

So my return from the war to normal living is unfolding. I am awaiting the arrival of my wife from England, and we are looking forward to our future together on the land. The postwar era looks rosy indeed.

**JAYNE CUSTER
WAYLAND, IA**

# FOND MEMORIES

Nostalgia for the good old days on the farm

## THE LAND LIVES WITHIN HER

The dreams came in the busiest, most stressful times in my life. I'd go to bed, toss and turn, and finally fall into a dream world. I'd walk out the front door of my house, cross the empty lot and walk behind the greenhouse, where the pavement beneath my feet melted into the gravel driveway of my grandparents' farm.

My heartbeat would instantly slow and my soul would be at ease. As I rounded the corner, there were my great-grandparents Ione and Ralph, side by side, waving at me (I called them Grandma and Grandpa). Later I'd wake up calm, refreshed and ready to take on the day.

The first chance I got after having the first dream, I headed to my grandparents' farm across the Mississippi River in Maiden Rock, Wisconsin. It was my way of thanking them for teaching me to love the land. Many times I didn't tell my family I was going there. It was my secret, my joy.

Listening to the hum of the country and the birds singing, I imagined I heard the noises that used to spill out of the barn. I saw my mother and aunt stacking hay. I could even hear

Grandma Ione calling her family for dinner as the sun sank in a beautiful summer sky.

I'll always remember Grandma and her big black purse, which seemed to hold everything she treasured. She hid candies and cards and who knows what else in that Mary Poppins bag. Thanks to her recipes, her food comforts us to this day.

To me, Grandpa was the embodiment of a grandfather. He always had us laughing. He could fall asleep anywhere after a meal. While everyone else talked, you just had to look over to find Grandpa's head slightly dipped, his eyes closed and a soft snore coming from his direction.

I never really got to see Grandpa work the dirt, but I saw love for it in his eyes and on his weathered, wrinkled hands. His tools fit in his gifted hands as if they were specially made with each contour and callus in mind.

I wish I could have seen Grandpa walking in from the

An expecting Jodessa visits the farm with her husband Adam.

field after a long day of labor, a day that made him happy. Even when he was older and walked with a cane, he got up early in the morning to make his rounds, because the land lived in him.

My husband, Adam, and I still visit the farm together. One weekend we camped on the knoll by the barn, which is slightly tattered but holding steady. We had an unending view of the fields in front of us and the comfort of the old buildings behind us. With a toasty fire burning at our feet, we watched the setting sun paint the sky in golden ambers and rich reds.

We live just an hour from tiny Maiden Rock, but it seems a world away. Below the farm, houses teeter on the rocks and hillsides of the Mississippi River bluffs. When I look out over Lake Pepin, I can almost make out the beach where my family spent summers boating along the bluffs. And I see the old brick schoolhouse where my grandparents fell in love.

The life I lead is miles and lifetimes away from the one Grandma and Grandpa led on this farm. Still, I try to weave my memories of that way of life into the fabric of who I am so that I never forget where I came from.

When our daughter is born, Adam and I hope to instill in her a deep respect for our families' roots, traditions and history. We'll walk the land with our child, and we will tell her stories that can't be found in children's books—true stories that will sound like a faraway dream to her precious little ears.

**JODESSA WALDHAUSER**
**INVER GROVE HEIGHTS, MN**

*"I never really got to see Grandpa work the dirt, but I saw love for it in his eyes and on his weathered, wrinkled hands."*

Grandpa's barn (below), in Perry County in southern Illinois, was once a picture of progress. In time, the family (right) grew up and the farm went quiet, but they still savor the memories.

## THE LIFE OF THE FARM

It's pretty rough around the edges, but this old, weathered barn was once the life of Grandma and Grandpa's farm. I can still picture walking into the barn, with its impressive red paint, through a small door in the north wall. The entryway is next to the large doors that once let hay wagons in to be unloaded. I can see the big hallway with its set of stables housing Grandpa's horses—Ole Harry and Tony. The gentle horses loved to stick their heads across the board into the hallway and have their noses scratched.

Just past them is a larger room, the corn bin. Grandpa didn't have a combine to shell his corn, so he picked the ears and shoveled them into the bin. He spent hours each day there, sorting ears for the animals. Larger ears went to the pigs or were shelled for Grandma's hens. The cows got the nubbins, or stubby ears. If there were not enough nubbins, Grandpa cut big ears into smaller pieces, using a wooden box with a corn knife attached to one end. I loved helping throw the corn into the cows' trough.

To the right of the corn bin is a small room that housed the hand-cranked corn sheller. It was fun to drop ears of corn into the hopper as my aunt or uncle turned the crank. Farther down, a small stable provided a home for the inevitable late calf or two. The calves spent the winter in there, eating hay and corn from a trough that opened to the big hallway.

The barn's northwest corner held another small stable, used for any cow that needed a little extra care. The south end of the barn was where Grandpa's eight dairy cows came in for the winter; I can still see the stanchions where the milking was done by hand, and I remember petting the cows' velvety heads while they ate.

Next came the pigpen for the mother sow and her piglets. I liked watching the little ones run and hide in the fresh straw when they heard me coming. Along the west wall and back toward the entryway, a small grain bin held oats.

Wooden ladders reached down from the big loft that held hay and straw. It was fun to climb and play among the bales, and finding farm cats sleeping in the warm hay was even better.

Nowadays, the barn is home mostly to mice, and the swallows are the only ones hiding in the hayloft. That old barn was the story of American agriculture 60 years ago, but I know we must progress to continue to feed the world. We'll savor the memories of yesterday as best we can, and learn from them to make tomorrow better.

**HELEN MAYER
CUTLER, IL**

## THAT OLD DUSTY ROAD

During my childhood, many country roads around my hometown of Sedalia, Missouri, were made of dirt. I can still feel it between my toes, ground to a soft, fine powder by traffic. I can close my eyes and see myself and my friends walking barefoot in our loose-fitting bib overalls, no shirts or shoes. A stick fishing pole is over my shoulder, and a small cloud of dust puffs up at each footfall. We are on our way to some fishing hole that will require us to walk several miles into the country on both tar and dirt, dreaming of hooking a big fish (something that seldom happened!). Along the road are trees and bushes, some with gooseberries as big as my thumb or other wild fruit, which is why we didn't carry any food—but you can bet one of us had a saltshaker in his pocket.

When you drive these roads now, the trees and bushes that fed us have been cut or sprayed out of existence. Thank heavens I have my many memories of those old dusty roads that were hard on drivers but great for barefoot little boys.

**JACK MILLER**
**SMITHTON, MO**

## ONE "YEE-HAW" TOO MANY

My heroes have always been cowboys. The words of that old Willie Nelson song ring very true for me. Early on I favored Roy Rogers, Gene Autry and Hopalong Cassidy. Then I moved on to John Wayne and Clint Eastwood as my tastes matured.

But I finally figured out that all my heroes were just playing the part, except for one. My uncle Leland Hallmark was the genuine article, from the soles of his worn boots to the top of his hat—which he put on whenever he left the house.

My earliest memories of Uncle Leland come from visiting him and his family on a ranch in the Hill Country south of Llano, Texas. It was a beautiful place for a kid whose main passion, other than baseball, was to ride horses.

I was full-grown when I found out Leland didn't own the ranch; he was the foreman. But it didn't matter to me. He made his living on the back of a horse just like my other heroes. My little brother, Glenn, was equally crazy about cowboys, and we thought Uncle Leland must have hung the moon while sitting on top of his horse, Cricket.

My only problem with Leland was his cowboy hat. It was always bent in strange directions. It was dirty. And worst of all, it wasn't white. Whenever we visited I made it a point to fix his hat for him. I preferred the Roy Rogers look, so I worked real hard on his hat every night.

And every evening when he came home from work, the hat would be a mess again.

One day Leland left before sunrise—with a freshly arranged hat—to gather all the cows that needed treatment from the local veterinarian.

He was gone all day. Toward sunset, Glenn and I were sitting on the porch, sipping cool water from the well, when we saw Leland working a small herd of cows toward a corral. We got so excited we nearly fell over running to the rail fence to welcome him home, yelling at the top of our lungs, "YEE-HAW! RIDE 'EM, COWBOY!"

The look on Leland's face was only slightly less surprised than the look on the faces of all those cows. I've never seen that many cows run in that many directions in all my life. It was so exciting, Glenn wet his pants. Granted, it didn't take much for Glenn to wet his pants back then.

Our momma came running with a look on her face that scared us. We didn't know why she was mad at us, but we ran and hid anyway. She finally found us in the barn. Leland didn't make it back home with the cows for another four hours, so she had plenty of time to explain her anger.

Leland, on the other hand, didn't seem too mad at all. He handed me his hat, ate a quick bite of supper and went to bed. Because that's what heroes do.

**RUSSELL MIHILLS**
**HURST, TX**

Uncle Leland, with his favorite horse, Cricket, was the real deal.

## FROM THE FRONT PORCH

I can see so many things clearly from my front porch. Like the big old Black Angus bull way down there under that cottonwood tree. He's been busy swatting flies with his tail and playing tag with the blistering sun all day. The light cuts sideways and holds on hard while that burning fireball sinks into the Pacific Ocean. The bull will rest easy soon—a rush of cool air always comes down the canyon at dusk.

I can see the big cedar with the tree house that my grandson and I built years ago. I can still see us up high, pounding nails and laughing about Grammy telling him every half-hour or so not to fall.

From this old porch, the rusty metal roof of the barn looks to have been part of the landscape forever. For a hundred years or more, in the heat of summer and cold of winter, it has provided shelter for every manner of creature. All found rest within the big, musty sanctuary. Beams of sunlight stream like lasers through the knotholes, and the sound of laughing children chasing one another over bales of hay echoes forever in my memory.

I can see into the past from this old porch. I see the look of delight on my grandfather's face when I'd come to visit him, seldom as it was. His words were kind and his love absolute. I smell mesquite in the air; I hear the wind in the hoodoos and the trickling sound of the Red River's Prairie Dog Fork as it passes in front of the old ranch house where I was born.

Grandparents, parents and siblings have all gone on, but their image lingers on this porch. I can hear voices of the past floating in the soft breeze of twilight. Reaching out, I take the hand of my darling. We sit and hold on to each other in the quiet shadows. Our hands are weathered and wrinkled, yet hers are forever tender. The image of a beautiful young girl stands facing me as I place a ring on her finger. Fifty years of her unwavering assurance provide the energy that sustains me.

The future is shrouded from view as always, and the number of sunsets we'll see remains unknown. Though one evening the cool air will come down the canyon, the heat and pestilence will give way, and we'll forever rest easy.

**KERRY TAYLOR**
**LIVERMORE, CA**

## DADDY'S FOUNTAIN OF YOUTH

My daddy, Elvin Elliott, has always had a passion for farming. Even though he turns 82 this year, he'll be out on the tractor this summer, happily making hay for his 50-cow beef herd.

At 81, Elvin still looks forward to making hay each summer.

Last year I took a vacation day from work to shoot photos of Daddy and my brother Terry, who takes time off every year to help with haying. Terry says it's still a vacation for him because he enjoys being out in the fresh air, driving a tractor and helping Daddy. As I watched Daddy rake the hay into neat windrows while Terry ran the baler, I thought about how lucky I was to grow up on our farm.

My mama, Uzelia, was a city girl, but she supported Daddy's dreams and became his best farmhand. They started in 1961 on a rented farm, tending 18 acres of tobacco and milking 18 cows in three stalls Daddy built in the tobacco barn. Daddy worked third shift at Burlington Mills to pay the bills. In 1975 they bought their own farm, and eventually milked as many as 130 Holsteins.

It was my job to drive the cows to the barn and bottle-feed the baby calves. Sometimes I'd have as many as 15 calves—and they all wanted to be fed at the same time. To keep them from crowding up, I used to tap them lightly on the nose with a stick. Before long they all knew to wait their turn. I'd feed two, and when they finished, two more would come up.

My favorite haying memories are of break time, when we'd get "square nabs" peanut butter crackers and a Coke. We made square bales back then, which took a lot more hand labor than the big round bales Daddy makes now. It was hard, hot work.

We sold our milk to Pine State Creamery. When it went out of business in 1989, Daddy sold his Holsteins and got the beef cows. And now, even though he's been farming for more than 55 years, Daddy has no intention of retiring anytime soon. And why should he? He's doing exactly what he loves.

Every Sunday we get together at our parents' house for lunch after church. Most Sundays, 19 or 20 family members are there. God has truly blessed our family.

**ANITA VANERELLI
OXFORD, NC**

## AUNT AND UNCLE'S FARM WAS LIKE ANOTHER WORLD

In 1968, when I was about 7 years old, my folks took my brother David and me on a trip to Texas to visit relatives. We lived in Los Angeles, California, and I was quite a city kid. We went to a small town outside Fort Worth to visit my mom's Uncle Charlie and Aunt Ida on their farm.

It was all wonderfully new and different to me. Uncle Charlie was a lean, grizzled old fella in overalls, a cotton shirt and a straw cowboy hat. Aunt Ida was an older woman in a gingham dress, an apron and a fabric bonnet. Their farm had a little of everything—crops of corn and grain, berries and grapevines on the fences, pigs, chickens and more. My aunt kept a country kitchen, and my mother told me Uncle Charlie expected the same menu every day: eggs, bacon, sausage, biscuits, preserves and homemade gravy each morning—and fried chicken, potatoes, green beans, corn, biscuits and pie for lunch and dinner.

Aunt Ida wanted to do something special for her citified great-niece. She took me to their watermelon patch and let me pick a melon. She cut out the heart of it for me to eat and threw the rest to the hogs. Then we continued eating our way through the orchard. I felt rich because I had never had more than a slice of watermelon before—and certainly not a feast like this!

I learned that watermelon meat comes in a variety of colors, including red, orange, yellow and pink. Imagine that! Aunt Ida could not have thought of anything that would've impressed me more.

I met my cousins for the first time. Rhonda, the oldest, was a year ahead of me, and her sister Renee was my age. One day, we decided to visit the farm's bull, which we'd been told to leave alone in his pen. Well, can you guess the one thing we wanted to do? The three of us ended up inside the hay-filled barn adjacent to the bull's pen—separated by only a door held in place by a thin piece of wire. We began feeding hay to the bull through the crack of the door. He enjoyed the extra food and began pressing against the door to get more. The door appeared to be giving way, and the three of us hightailed it out of there. Later on, when the grown-ups were heatedly discussing how the bull could've gotten into all that hay, we were silent!

The rest of my trip was fascinating, but I couldn't wait to go home and tell my friends about it.

**CHERYL BONNER
MIDDLEBURG, FL**

Cheryl is wearing the red dress in this family photo.

2 GIRLS ON LEFT - ME; RENEE
NOV 1969

BOTTOM ROW: RHONDA, DAVID
& FAR RIGHT - RUSTY

**LITTLE HELPER** "I love being outdoors in the fall," says Carol Jacobs Norwood of Myerstown, Pennsylvania. "The crisp, cool air and the falling leaves make it special. When I was a little girl, I often helped my parents with yard work. Here I am raking leaves with my father, Bill Jacobs, in 1958 on our farm in Gardenville."

# CHAPTER 8

# PASTORAL SCRAPBOOK

*Peruse this charming chapter of heartwarming photos, and you'll see folks of all ages sharing smiles. Memories of country living, favorite farm animals and more remind us how fast the years fly!*

# HOME ON THE RANGE

Farm living was the life for them

### ▲ ALL THEIR CHILDREN

Joseph and Elizabeth Kraft must have had quite a time keeping track of their kids. "I love this fabulous photo of my mother, Angie, and her 14 brothers and sisters," says Jennifer Davis of Minneapolis. "At far right is the oldest, Leonard, born in 1930. Then come, from right, Bill, Lorraine, John, Rose Schmitz, Mary Ann Tubbs, Ken, Betty Page, Kathy Henry, Karen Atkinson, Rita Pigarelli, Angie, Jim, Jerry and Ron. I think the setting was the family farm in Minnesota."

### ◀ HERE, CHICK CHICK!

Since 1951, Gay Dawn Downs of Burley, Idaho, has had one favorite chore: feeding the chickens.

## ▲ ROOM ENOUGH FOR KIN

"This beautiful 18-room farmhouse in Greendale, Wisconsin, belonged to my great-grandparents," writes Beverly Biba of nearby Greenfield. "My mother, Hilda Boldt, and her sister and parents lived there for three years while building a home."

### GOATS ON THE GO ➤

"As a country boy in 1938, I trained my goats, Lightning and Dynamite, to pull me in a wagon," writes Harold Roquet of Ottumwa, Iowa. "With their help, I hauled firewood, oat bundles and hay. I even drove Lightning and Dynamite 1½ miles down the dirt road to school one day. They performed as well as any team of horses."

### ▲ DIGGING IN THE DIRT

Patricia Althiser of Elmwood, Illinois, loves the different expressions on the kids' faces as they toil in Grandpa Rodgers' vegetable garden in Farmington, Illinois, in 1973. The excited work crew (from left), siblings Bob and Sally Althiser and cousin Clete, pull their weight amid the corn and cabbage.

### LONG JOE 2ND
"Here is my grandfather Earl Arnold Stanley standing on Long Joe 2nd shortly after the 2-year-old Poland China boar won the blue ribbon at the 1919 Illinois State Fair," writes Debra Stanley of Makanda, Illinois. Long Joe 2nd was a favorite among the judges and breeders at the fair. "Grandfather Earl later said, 'They spoke of him as being the greatest boar they had ever seen.'"

### BLUE-RIBBON LAMB ▶
Raymond Jackson, age 7 in 1950, showed this lamb at the Kern County Fair in Bakersfield, California, as part of a 4-H club. The poised young duo won a blue ribbon.

### ◀ TRUE RANCHER'S UNIFORM
"Under that ragged, sweat-soaked, soil-spotted hat is a man with as much character as his headwear," writes Helen Belnap of Roberts, Idaho. "He was not just a neighbor but a real neighbor, there to help, visit or just gossip. He was a rancher, owning horses, cows and a band of sheep. A cow dog followed at his heels everywhere he went, even to the small shed where he could be heard shouting at umps on TV. Above all, he was a family man. His family came first—always."

### "I WANT TO SIT NEXT TO KATHY!" ➤

"On the first day of school, it was tradition to take pictures of our four children, Paula, Greg, Kevin and Kathy, at our home in Otter Lake, Michigan," says Barbara Mohr, now of Millington. "Our farm was 8 miles from the school, so it was quite a ride for them. When it was Kathy's turn to ride the bus for the first time, there was arguing going on as to who was going to sit with Kathy on the bus. I told them, 'I am going to the grocery store, and when I get back, I want this situation settled.' When I returned, Paula had composed a document with some legal terminology like 'whereas' and 'therefore.' The paper listed who would sit by Kathy for the first few days, and they each had to sign it. Paula then posted it on the bulletin board. I was impressed, to say the least, since there was no arguing or fighting!"

### ▲ HURRY UP AND STRIKE A POSE

Harold and Bill Fisher (far left and third from left) sulk with their cousins Jack and Allen Gray when a photo shoot interrupts playtime on their Centerville, Pennsylvania, farm in 1932.

### ▼ CHUG, CHUG, CHUGGING ALONG

"My dad loved his gardens, and sometimes he let me ride with him on the old Doodlebug (an International truck that he remade into a tractor)," Jean Bradford writes via Facebook. "Later he got a used John Deere, and I can still hear the sound of it chugging along. Here's a photo of us on the Doodlebug in 1963; I was 6, and Dad was 66."

### ▲ SOMEONE GOT YOUR GOAT?

This circa 1910 photo shows siblings W.T. (left) and Frankie Welch on their West Virginia farm. "The goat was an orphan, given to my father by the sheriff," says Imogene Grimmett, W.T.'s daughter. "Grandpa built it a little wagon, and together, Dad and his goat did all kinds of work around the farm."

*"When I was 3 in 1965, my brother Lyle set me on top of the sheep, who were so intent on eating, they didn't even realize I was there," Sally Lee writes of farm life near St. Paul Park, Minnesota. "Not a baaad place to grow up!"*

EIGHTEENTH NATIONAL 4-H CLUB CONGRESS
STEVENS HOTEL, CHICAGO, ILLINOIS, DECEMBER 6, 1939

## ▲ YOUTH WILL BE SERVED

"My father, Wesley Anderson, won a trip to the 1939 National 4-H Congress," says Roland Anderson of Plymouth, Minnesota. "For a boy from the Minnesota 'sticks,' attending a big convention in Chicago was the highlight of his young life."

## ◀ THE BEST PANCAKES AROUND

"Grandma Seely was famous for her pancakes, and my 6-year-old son, Dale, just loved eating them," writes Glenyce Croasmun of Marienville, Pennsylvania. "As he waited for the school bus on this spring morning in Redclyffe, in 1960, Dale wandered over to our family's big old maple tree and checked the can collecting sap. Soon the bus arrived and off he went to school, dreaming of sweet maple syrup and Grandma Seely's pancakes."

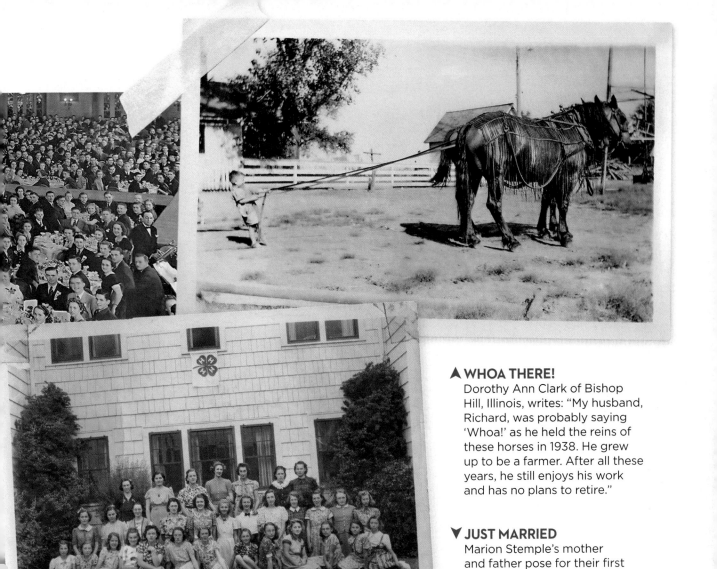

### ▲ WHOA THERE!
Dorothy Ann Clark of Bishop Hill, Illinois, writes: "My husband, Richard, was probably saying 'Whoa!' as he held the reins of these horses in 1938. He grew up to be a farmer. After all these years, he still enjoys his work and has no plans to retire."

### ▼ JUST MARRIED
Marion Stemple's mother and father pose for their first wedding picture, in 1916, after driving back from the ceremony. The pastor of a small church married them while standing on the running board!

### ▲ 4-H CAMP FUN
"Oh, what happy memories! Back in 1940, I went to 4-H summer school at Oregon State College in Corvallis," says Loraine Stephensen of Mesa, Arizona. "For a small sum, 4-H club members from all over the state gathered for five days of fun activities. We lived in the fraternity and sorority houses and dormitories. My sister Fay Wilkinson and I joined the girls at Delta Delta Delta. Fay and I are in the center row, sixth (me) and seventh (Fay) from the left."

Working with horses was second nature for Judy Pearce, here riding in costume for the Santa Barbara Old Spanish Days Fiesta in 1958.

## SADDLED WITH RESPONSIBILITY

I landed my first job in 1958 at the San Ysidro Ranch in Montecito, California, working in the stables. The ranch, which was also a hotel, was a favorite with stars like Angela Lansbury, whom I got to meet when her family went riding there.

Since my own family didn't have a car, I rode my horse to work. At the stables, I fed and watered the animals, mucked out the stalls, and groomed and saddled the horses. I also guided guests along the scenic trails. It was the perfect job for a horse-obsessed 16-year-old.

**JUDY PEARCE
CARPINTERIA, CA**

## ▲ PET BUNNIES

"My husband, Bud, treasured this photograph of his cousins Shelby and Maurice Worley for many years," writes Lillian Phelps from Bickleton, Washington. "The boys looked so serious holding their pet bunnies. I believe the photo was taken on their farm in Poplar Bluff, Missouri, during the '20s."

### ◀ DODGE BROTHERS

"My father, Roy Krentler (left), is pictured with his brother Glenn in this photo taken in 1969 in Hanover, Pennsylvania," Doris Keller writes from Manassas, Virginia. "My dad planned to refurbish the 1915 Dodge Brothers automobile behind him but passed away before he could complete the restoration."

### MAKING CHICKEN FRIENDS ▶

"My parents kept several chickens for eggs, and some for the skillet to help feed our family near Denver," writes William Sheets of Franklin, Nebraska. "I was next to the youngest of seven children, and this 1945 photo shows me, at age 5, with the chicken I'd selected to be my pet. I carried her from one place to another when she wasn't busy laying eggs. This particular chicken became the family's dinner at some point—so I made friends with another one."

### FARMERS' BREAKFAST ▶

"This photo of my parents, Charles and Catherine Cywinski, was taken around 1947 at their 80-acre farm in the town of Glenmore, Wisconsin," says Marcella Cywinski of Green Bay. "A Maxwell House photographer had come to get a picture of a real farm couple having coffee."

## ▲ PONY POWER

"In the summer of 1949, my late father, Lyle Herrington (the first rider on the left), engineered a chuck wagon for the Calgary Stampede Parade in Calgary, Alberta," writes Audrey Herrington of Madoc, Ontario. "Four Massey-Harris Pony tractors were the horses, controlled by the drivers in the wagon who held the reins. Four outriders on Pony tractors flanked the horses, just as it's done in a real chuck wagon race. This float received the award in the industrial section. I don't know how he did it, but my father was truly a man ahead of his time."

## ◄ RURAL ROOTS

"Each summer during the early '30s, my cousin Mary Jane Roth visited our farm in Parke County, Indiana," writes William Swern of Rockville. "She was a city girl from Lafayette, but she became a regular farm girl around us."

### ◄ LOVELY STORE-BOUGHT FINERY

"The three Busby sisters—Rosalie, Marles and my mother, Ilah Mae—proudly show off their new store-bought dresses in their front yard in 1934," says William Horton of Forsyth, Illinois. "Times were hard for farmers in Nodaway County, Missouri, during the Depression, but my mother's family had dignity, food, a home and lots of love."

### HERE, THERE, EVERYWHERE ►

"This 1929 Ford Model A pickup came in handy for all sorts of jobs on our family's farm near Milan, Michigan, including moving the privy," writes David Cranson of Payson, Arizona. "The outhouse was used on our farm until my daddy, Ford, built a new house with indoor plumbing and moved the old privy to a nearby lot where my brother, Kenneth, was building a house. The photo shows the final move in the early '50s to a lot where my wife, Jo, and I built our house."

### ◄ ROUSTED FROM THE ROOST

"My brothers, Henry (left) and Walter Hackshaw, and Grandma's rooster look as though they mean business in this photo taken in the early '20s in Concord, New Hampshire," writes Betty Lou Lynch of Cheshire, Connecticut.

# WINTERTIME ON THE FARM

## Cold weather led to heartwarming moments

### ▲ MOM POWER

"We were lucky enough to grow up on a farm in Gardenville, Pennsylvania, where we had lots of wide open space," writes Carol Jacobs Norwood of Myerstown. "Our mom, Cita Jacobs, would take a turn pulling my 3-year-old sister, Maureen (above, center), and me around after we got a ride from our dad, Bill. No matter who was powering us, it was always a lot of fun. That's quite a toothy grin I have. It always seemed that the snow was piled high. Of course, we were happy to get a day off from school—what kid wouldn't be? This was the winter of 1961. You can see for yourself that the mounds of snow (left) were really tall, much taller than we were, anyway! That's me on the left and Maureen on the right."

**FRIENDS OR FOES?**
"This is my dad, Don Kretzer, at the family farm in Ross County, Ohio, in about 1938. I suspect the turkey was soon to be dinner," says Becky Ward of Bainbridge.

### ◄ MILK RUN
"This photo was taken in early spring 1940 as my sister, Linda (on right), and I carried Karo syrup pails to get milk from our neighbor's farm in rural Echo, Minnesota," says Ruth Gjermundson of Echo.

### MILES IN THE SNOW ►
"The air was bitterly cold when my sister, Barbara, and I left our farm on Beaver Island, Michigan, for school in 1936," says Rod Nackerman of Lake Orion. "We didn't have a car, so we had to walk 2 miles. The snow was so deep in spots that we walked on top of the fence posts. We wore coats our mother, Grace, made from old adult coats and carried lunch pails made from Karo syrup containers."

### ◄ BEST DRESSED
"My grandfather built this barn in 1934. Its bright red coat really shines in winter," says Bill Bosley of Beaver Falls, Pennsylvania.

**Pioneers of the *First* factory-built LP gas model TRACTORS**

**1951**

**TO GIVE YOU**
★ **MORE POWER**
★ **GREATER ECONOMY**

MINNEAPOLIS-MOLINE U TRACTOR, factory-built to use LP gas, gives you positive assurance of realizing all the advantages offered by LP gas fuel—butane or propane or a mixture of both . . . SMOOTHER PERFORMANCE . . . MORE POWER . . . GREATER ECONOMY!

MORE POWER OUTPUT—The high anti-knock rating of *100 octane plus fuel* permits a high compression ratio. Ask your dealer for facts. LP gas steps up the horsepower of the already powerful U about 10 per cent. Since MM factory-built LP gas tractors have high compression and *cold* manifolds, more power is realized and fuel consumption is cut to the very minimum.

EVEN LONGER ENGINE LIFE than usual on the already famous, long lived MM U tractor. Because LP gas is a dry gas it burns clean and eliminates carbon deposit and crankcase dilution . . . lubricating oil lasts several times as long due to less contamination, washing of lube oil from cylinder walls is eliminated and uniform bearing pressures are maintained because of the longer power impulse. Vibration is also lessened and the tractors run much cooler.

GREATER ECONOMY in maintenance costs is realized with all MM LP gas powered tractors and it is a fact that these tractors are great money savers, especially in areas where LP gas prices are favorable.

MM LP GAS TRACTORS ARE SAFE — Factory-equipped with special cylinder heads, special carburetors, and special tanks heavily built to resist pressure with a safety pop-off valve which meets the requirements of all states.

UNI-MATIC POWER is available as extra equipment and gives you smooth, accurate, hydraulic control of mounted or pull-behind tools. It features a double-acting jack with exclusive safety lockout, constant running engine-driven pump, and break-away couplings.

See your friendly MM dealer for the complete facts on MM LP gas tractors available in Universal and Standard models. Four kinds of power are available on these tractors: drawbar, power take-off, belt, and Uni-Matic. Ask your dealer or write us for additional literature on the *first factory-built LP gas tractors.*

For Row Crop Cultivation MM Visionlined LP Tractor, with Quick-On — Quick-Off attachments, offers maximum utility and minimum operating and maintenance costs.

MM LP Tractors help progressive farmers further lower production costs . . . realize greater returns.

Cultivating or Harvesting, MM's LP Tractors operate even more economically . . . deliver more power!

the *First* FACTORY-BUILT LP GAS TRACTOR

Quality Control in MM Factories Assures Dependable Performance in the Field

**MINNEAPOLIS-MOLINE**
MINNEAPOLIS 1, MINNESOTA

**Mighty Model "G"**

**FLASH!**
MODEL G NOW AVAILABLE FOR LP GAS—ASSURING CHEAPER POWER BY THE HOUR

★ FACTORY BUILT LP GAS TRACTORS SINCE 1941

# THEN & NOW

Remaking cherished country-living photographs

THEN

...AND
NOW

## ▲ TWO FARM BOYS

"Brothers relax outside their Bennington, New York, home before their milking chores in 1940 in the top photo. On the left is my brother-in-law, Donald Rudolph, 10, and on the right is my husband, Richard, 15," writes Jean Rudolph of Akron. "Below, 75 years later, Donald has bought that farmhouse from his dad and rents out the land. The brothers still get together to relax and talk but no longer have milking chores."

1941

◄ **GROWING UP**
"On our parents' farm in Stow, Ohio, I (far left in both photos) had plenty of jobs, as did siblings Bill, Anna Marie and John Holley," writes Charles Holley of Greeley, Colorado. "We hoed, harvested and picked apples, peaches, strawberries and raspberries. Of course, no eating while picking." Reunited on Bill's Ohio farm in 2011 (left), the "kids" can eat all the berries they want now.

**THEN**

**...AND NOW**

▲ **TOUGH GUYS**

"My brother and I grew up on a farm in Gallitzin Township, Pennsylvania," writes David Kurash of Lakeland, Florida. "The top photo was taken in 1939 with me standing on the left and my brother, Richard, seated on the mower. We still have a mower like it on the farm and took this re-enactment photo 50 years later, in 1989." (Now get to work on that grass, Richard!)

**SITTING STOVE SIDE** This stove looks as if it could heat up a room in no time! The slide is one of many from the '50s and '60s inherited by Dorothy Bentz of Torrington, Connecticut, from an aunt and uncle.

## CHAPTER 9

# FARM-TO-TABLE

*Featuring fresh ingredients, comforting flavor and all the down-home satisfaction you can imagine, there's simply nothing like country cooking. Call the gang to the table and dig in to these delightful tales of farm-fresh foods.*

# FARM-FRESH FLAVOR

## Enjoying the fruits of their labor

### THE PORK CHOPS ARE IN THE MAIL!

Electricity was slow in coming to our small community of Kintyre in Emmons County, North Dakota. So until the Rural Electrification Administration (REA) finally got around to us in the late 1940s, families had limited options for storing meat. They could butcher it themselves in the fall and can it, salt it or store it in ice caves. Or they could rent a lockbox in the local frozen-food locker plant.

My father managed Kintyre's locker plant, which was also a farmers co-op. He'd cut up and package hogs, beef, lamb and venison. Sometimes he would drive the co-op's van out to the farm, slaughter the animal and bring it back to the storage cooler until it was time to cut it up. He also had a shed where he could cure the hides and prepare them for a buyer who came from somewhere and hauled them away.

Our community was an interesting mix of Swedes, Finns, Norwegians and Germans, many of whom were first-generation Americans. Each group had its own church, social activities and customs for butchering and cooking meat. Many German families, for example, seldom had the beef cut into steaks and roasts; they wanted these portions cut and marked as "soup bone."

Farmers would give Dad instructions about how they wanted the meat cut and packaged. Then the cuts would be wrapped, quick-frozen and stored in the farmers' lockers. On Fridays, my dad would receive postcards from many of his patrons who lived on the rural mail routes around town. These cards might say something like, "Dear Rof (or Ruf or Raf—Dad's name was Ralph), Please send 3 pac hamburg, 4 pac porckchop, 3 soup bone."

So on Saturday morning, Dad would pull the customers' cuts from the locker boxes, wrap them with butcher paper and tie them with heavy string. He'd weigh each bundle to determine how much postage it required and attach the stamps. Each patron who used this delivery method kept an envelope in Dad's desk that contained an assortment of stamps. They'd replenish their meat-mailing stamps whenever they came to town.

Dad would then carry the packages—sometimes as many as 10 or 12—across the street to the mail carrier's Jeep. The postmaster would come out and cancel the stamps. Then the mail carrier would drop off the meat along his route, placing packages beside the mailboxes.

Surprisingly, I don't recall ever hearing of a single problem associated with this delivery method.

**JOHN SISCO**
**SPRINGFIELD, MO**

If you couldn't get it in the mail, you probably didn't need it.

Mary (left, with family dog Mutt) and her sisters loved farm life.

## IF YOU DIDN'T WORK, YOU DIDN'T EAT

If you ask kids where their food comes from, you may hear "from the store" or "from a restaurant." That was not the case when I was growing up. My sisters and I knew exactly where our food came from, having had a hand in the production, harvest, preparation and preservation of it.

My parents, Joe and Ruby Kranawetter, my three sisters, Nancy, Kay and Carol, and I lived on a farm in Cape Girardeau County, Missouri. We raised chickens, cattle, hogs and rabbits that provided meat for our table. As kids, we were expected to help feed and water these animals, tend them when they were sick, and run after them when they escaped.

Our cows provided plenty of milk and cream. We sold most of the cream to the local dairy and churned our own butter with some of the remainder. Mama used skim milk to make cottage cheese. Daddy also used extra milk mixed with ground feed to slop the hogs.

Eggs were served for breakfast every morning and also contributed to our income, as we raised several hundred chickens and sold hatching eggs. When the hens got older and a new batch of chickens was ready to move into the henhouse, we had butchering days. We learned about science without even realizing it.

Hogs provided the main source of meat for us. A well-stocked smokehouse was a must for our family until Daddy bought a large freezer in the '60s. The enchanting place was filled with the sweet smell of sugar cure. Rows and rows of sausages, hams, shoulders and bacon and crocks of lard provided security for the cold months.

We couldn't wait for that first meal of thickly sliced ham, mashed potatoes, Mama's milk gravy and light-as-a-feather biscuits.

Most of the rest of our diet came from Mama's garden and nature. Mama decided what to plant and Daddy took care of plowing and fertilizing, which required the use of our horses and a two-bottom plow until we got a tractor.

Hoeing, weeding and harvesting involved all of us, and we knew it was no use to complain, as we certainly enjoyed eating. Daddy read the passage in the Bible, "If any would not work, neither should he eat." We were especially attentive to our favorites—melons, popcorn and peanuts.

Mama let us girls pick flower seeds to plant near the garden edges. "Pretty flowers are God's way of rewarding us for hard work," she said.

We also made frequent treks to the woods and fencerows. Blackberries, elderberries, dewberries, persimmons, wild grapes, wild plums, walnuts and hickory nuts were just a few of the God-given foods free for the taking.

Helping produce our own food supply taught us life lessons: the appreciation and conservation of nature, the rewards of hard work, and the fact that sharing and caring make life worth living.

**MARY KOEBERL RECHENBERG**
**JACKSON, MO**

Myrtle's grandsons Brian (left) and Nicholas (right) personally devoured their own lamb cakes on their first birthdays, per family tradition.

## LAMB CAKE LORE

Making lamb cakes has been a tradition in my family ever since the '20s, when my mother, Signe Jensen, brought a heavy cast-iron mold home to our small dairy farm.

I was 9 years old at the time and remember watching with great interest as she poured a raisin-studded batter into the lamb-shaped mold and baked it. After it was done, she carefully took the warm cake from the mold. Later she'd spread frosting on the lamb, then sprinkle some shredded coconut on top to give it a fluffy coat.

From then on, the lamb cake reappeared for special occasions, particularly Easter. But the little lamb was always so cute, no one wanted to eat it. So sometimes instead, we would put it in a place of honor inside a glass cabinet until the coconut "wool" started to turn yellow.

I inherited my mom's treasured lamb mold when I became a mother myself. But instead of making the special cake only at Easter, I started my own family tradition with my son, Dennis. I baked him a lamb cake for his first birthday, surrounded it with small candies, then set it all in front of him. He dug right in—literally! Dennis had so much messy fun with that cake that when my first daughter was born, I also made her a lamb cake of her very own.

The tradition lives on with my grandkids, who get a lamb cake to dig their little fingers into on their first birthday. I'm not sure what my mom would think about how I turned her tradition on its head, but the kids definitely enjoy it!

**MYRTLE HIPKE**
**RACINE, WI**

## ONE POTATO, TWO POTATO...

When I was growing up in Iowa in the '30s and '40s, we had a very large bin of potatoes in the cellar. The contents not only carried our family of six through the winter but also provided seed potatoes to plant our half-acre the next spring.

One of the chores for us kids was to rub off the potato sprouts as they grew. One by one we rubbed the skin, put the potato aside, picked up the next and repeated the process until we'd cleaned the whole bin—only to do it again in a month or so when the sprouts reappeared. My brother and I used to see which one of us could find the longest sprout. It was usually on a potato that had fallen behind the bin.

The reward? Eating potatoes all year: mashed, fried, scalloped or in Mom's potato salad.

**ELSIE MASTELLER ROSE**
**BRANSON, MO**

## BREAKFAST AT GRANDMA'S

Grandma and Grandpa lived in the hills of Kentucky. When I stayed there, I slept in a bed over their porch and I would wake before the sun was up. Grandma would already be up, and I would smell sausage frying.

They had one flashlight, and Grandma would give it to me and tell me to go gather eggs from the chicken house. There were always just enough eggs for breakfast. It wasn't until years after she died that I figured out that before I got up, she would take the eggs to the chicken house so I could gather them for breakfast.

When I'd return, there'd be coffee for me. It was mostly cream and sugar, but it made me feel big. I would sit with my coffee and watch her cook.

**BOB GOINS**
**WHITMAN, WV**

1946

*Blended Right for Pleasure Bright!*

## Enjoy the Taste that's Mellow as a Sunny Morning

You, too, will prefer SCHENLEY Reserve for its smooth, rich flavor. Quality ingredients skillfully blended have made it America's largest-selling whiskey. Try SCHENLEY Reserve soon. Blended Whiskey 86 proof. 65% grain neutral spirits. Schenley Distillers Corp., N. Y. C.

## SCHENLEY
### RESERVE
PRE-WAR QUALITY

## HOW DO YOU LIKE THEM APPLES?

In the late '50s and early '60s, my family made cider. We enjoyed drinking it and also sold it for 50 cents a gallon. Given the price of gasoline at the time—25 to 30 cents per gallon—that might seem like a lot. But when you factor in the time spent picking apples and the cost of preparation, we probably never really made money.

People came from up and down our street and sometimes miles away to get a jug of our cider. There were three reasons it was different from others: First, my father insisted we wash all the apples we used. This practice was not the norm—waiting in the long cider-mill lines on Saturday mornings, we saw many apples that were rotten or dirty go through the cider press. Second, we used five varieties of apples, all grown in our orchard: Winesaps, Cortlands, McIntoshes, Jonathans and Granny Smiths. Most others used only one or two varieties. Third, we had a secret ingredient: The apples we used were very juicy but generally spicy-sweet or even a little tart. To give our cider more sweetness, we added Bartlett pears from our orchard. About 10 percent of the pressed juice was actually pear juice. Our cider was just plain better because of it.

Cider mills were plentiful during those years. The apples were placed in a hopper above the cider press, and the operator put a large cheesecloth-type fabric inside a wooden framework. The apples were covered, and then a press would squeeze out the juice. It flowed into a holding tank, and the operator would measure how many gallons we had. The cider was then transferred to our two 50-gallon barrels.

Once we got the barrels home, we would tack up our "cider for sale" sign. It didn't take long for the word to spread—we had people knocking on the door until late in the evening to get a jug. We drank some every day during the season, which generally lasted from September until about mid-November, at which point we would be sold out.

I can't argue against pasteurization, but cider today simply doesn't taste as good and lacks that tantalizing nip. Hmm...maybe I should make my own again!

**WAYNE STEPHENS**
**WOOSTER, OH**

## GRANDMA'S MINCEMEAT

In 1906, my grandma was born on a farm, the second-youngest of eight children. Her family raised or grew everything they ate, and everyone had chores.

When I was young, I always helped my grandma, my mom and two of my grandma's sisters whip up a big batch of mincemeat. Mincemeat is a wonderful pie filling with cooked ground beef, chopped apples and raisins for body, plus spices and other juices for flavor. It took all day to make: We ground the beef very finely with a small hand-crank grinder and cooked it, peeled and chopped nearly a bushel of Jonathan apples, and then mixed and simmered the stuff to perfection.

When the mincemeat was finished, we packed it into glass quart jars and sealed them using a pressure cooker. One quart makes a nice, full pie, and everybody who helped make the mincemeat took home several jars. This all-day project produced anywhere from 20 to 30 jars of mincemeat, and the sealed jars would keep for years in the basement.

I made the mincemeat once as an adult, and it turned out just like Grandma's. I love it! Every holiday season, I think of her because she always had our entire family—20 to 25 people—over to her house to make mincemeat for pies.

Grandma originally wrote the recipe on an envelope, and I love to look at her handwriting and remember her life on the farm. I grew up close to her, and I now live in a new house on the same property. Her house is gone, but she will always be here.

**CONNIE HAMMOND**
**FORT MADISON, IA**

| DISH | MINCEMEAT | PREPARATION TIME NUMBER OF SERVINGS SOURCE OF RECIPE | |
|---|---|---|---|
| | 5 qts. apples, chopped | 1 qt. brandy or wine |
| | 3 qts. cooked ground beef | 1 cup vinegar |
| | 3 qts. sugar | 1 tbs. black pepper |
| | 2 qts. raisins | 1 tbs. salt |
| | 1 qt. suet or butter | 2 tsp. cinnamon |
| | 1 qt. fruit juice or cider | 2 tsp. pumpkin pie spice |
| | 1 qt. molasses | Juice of 3 lemons |

Put everything into a pot at once.

Cook until apples are done.

STYLECRAFT, BALTO. 30, MD.  PRINTED IN U.S.A.          REFILL NO. 801 R

Making kraut was serious business for Barbara's mom, Cecelia Karas (here with a truckload of cabbages).

## THE KRAUT KETTLE

As far back as I can remember, the white kettle with red trim sat on our stove. I was in grade school when a friend asked me what was in that big pot. "Sauerkraut, of course," I said. That's when I learned that not every family had a kettle for kraut on their stove all day, every day of the year.

While cooking, Mom would tell one of us, "Turn the sauerkraut on." Whoever did the job knew to check first that there was enough liquid in the kettle to heat the kraut. If the kettle was in the dish rack, you had to get a new jar of home-canned kraut, open it, dig out the kraut with a fork and add water. I always enjoyed a sample of the raw kraut. I'm not sure today's food-safety experts would approve, but it was a tasty treat at the time.

The raw kraut needed a little extra time on the stove the first time Mom cooked it. Heating it up after that took only a few minutes. When the kraut in the kettle had been reheated several times, Mom would change the recipe. I loved when she added onions—they made the kraut less strong. Dad loved it when she added cracklings, the crisp remains left over after we rendered and preserved lard in the fall. Dad never tired of kraut.

Making sauerkraut was a major job for the whole family. First we scrubbed and dried our tools: cabbage cutter, 12-gallon crock, kraut tamping post, a wooden board and a heavy stone. Cabbages were hauled in the wheelbarrow, and we all stood ready at our stations. I don't remember getting formal instructions; we learned by watching our parents.

The unwritten recipe was this: three cabbages, cut and salted as needed until the crock was full. Dad insisted on salting the cabbage. One year Mom did it, and he complained all year that the kraut wasn't right. After that, we made kraut only when Dad was around to season it.

After the cabbage was shredded and salted and it was dumped into the crock, my job was to tamp it with the wooden post. The tamper broke through each layer of cabbage, making a sucking noise as I pulled it out. I liked to think the cabbage was speaking its own language.

When the crock was full and tamped enough (Dad was the expert on this, too), we slipped a specially cut and shaped board into the crock on top of the kraut. A huge rock plucked some years earlier from the field went on top of the board as a weight, and then the mixture was left to ferment for several weeks. Finally, Mom canned the kraut in quart jars.

Sauerkraut was always a part of my childhood. Now it has become one of those treasured family memories that I share with my children and grandchildren.

**BARBARA PIEHL
NORTH BRANCH, MN**

Winter work in the sugarhouse makes syrup that tastes wonderful all year long.

## SWEETS OF SPRING

When I was a child in the late '20s, our family of eight moved from Sedalia, Missouri, to a small farm in western Kentucky. The 80 acres were part of the homestead my mother's relatives settled in 1794.

We had a garden, orchard, chickens, turkeys, pigs, horses and Jersey cows. We sold eggs and cream in town to buy what we needed at the grocery store. With everyone working, we always had plenty to eat.

Still, as spring approached, we started to dream of pouring maple syrup over our breakfast biscuits instead of sorghum molasses. That meant everybody had to help make it. The two older boys attended high school in town but were home on Saturdays to cut wood for the house and sugar camp. The younger children went to a country school and were home, so they helped carry sap to the camp.

A group of maple trees grew on a hillside not far from the house. At the bottom of the hill on flat ground near a stream was a furnace made of native rock, with a chimney several feet high. The front was shaped to fit three large iron kettles. The largest kettle sat in front directly over the fire. Two 50-gallon barrels placed near the furnace held the sap we called sugar water.

After getting the furnace ready, we brought the buckets and spiles down from the smokehouse loft to be cleaned. The spiles were checked to see if we needed to cut any new ones from the slender willows that grew along the creek.

When the weather was just right for the sap to run, Mother carried brace and bit, hammer and nails to the camp. The children followed along with buckets and spiles. Sometimes the buckets were loaded onto a homemade sled pulled by faithful old mule Jake. He traveled along a road that ran at the top of the hill. Each tree got three to five spiles, according to size.

We also got ready for the first day of boiling by placing blocks of wood in front of the fireplace to seat those who took care of the fire and kept the kettles filled. At noontime during the boiling, Mother went to the house to prepare lunch. Sometimes she would bring a pot of soup or some ham to cook over the fire, but we mostly took turns going to the house to eat.

When the syrup was the right consistency, the fire was banked and the syrup was poured through a clean cloth into a shiny milk pail to be carried to the house to cook some more.

We poured the syrup into quart jars, which we sold in town for a dollar each. One businessman always wanted a gallon.

Sometimes a little leftover syrup would be cooked until it sugared. We children loved that. If there was enough, it was poured into old iron muffin pans to harden into cakes. We'd use it to flavor sugar syrup later in the year.

It was a sweet time. But each year when the sap started to taste sour, we knew it was time to close the furnace and store the spiles and buckets in the smokehouse loft to wait for another spring.

**VIRGINIA MCNEELY RICE
SPRINGFIELD, MO**

JOHN H. KNOX

## JARS OF GLASS

Upon a dusty kitchen shelf up high
Treasures once holding peaches for pie,
Empty jars colored both clear and green,
Now displayed proudly to be seen.

Their history lies in hands that worked
In orchard, in garden and within the earth,
To harvest and fill each to the brim
In the heat of a long-ago country kitchen.

Jars given to Mother from Grandma and Aunt
To preserve the bounty in sealed can;
Arrayed warm and clean out of the canner,
Filled with treats of all kind and manner.

Memories of picking, digging, gathering
into bucket or pan
Blanching, peeling, washing, scraping by hand,
While Grandma and Mother talk and laugh
Filling sterilized jars into the boiling water bath.

Now finished, they rest on counter and table,
Contents visible, no need for a label.
We watch and listen for the pop that sealed
The bounty for a future winter meal.

Opened in winter when times were lean,
These jars recall many a comforting home scene.
Now, empty jars of glass rest in beautiful array,
Holding reminders of another day.

Recalling Aunt Mattie, Grandma and Mother,
Preserving summers' bounty
one season to another.
Arrayed on cellar shelves colorful to see,
Now resting on mine,
empty mason jars clear and green.

**SHERRON FIELDS**
**BEDFORD, IN**

## COUNTING COTTONTAILS

My friend Dean Bowman and I were sophomores at Esbon Rural High School 69 years ago when a typical Kansas snowstorm swept into the area. About 4 inches had piled up by the time we finished our lunches and, though there was no wind yet, the school superintendent feared there would be blowing and drifting snow. So school was closed for the day, and the country kids went home on the bus.

On the way, Dean and I sat together, laughing and looking out the window at the white wonderland. The bus driver let us off a mile west of the Bowman place for fear that drifting snow would prevent him from finishing his route. We were delighted to have the afternoon free. Everything was so white, with downy flakes caressing our ruddy cheeks. Trudging along toward home, we mapped out our afternoon. We would hunt rabbits!

We stopped at the Bowmans' place to get Dean's gun and ask his mom's permission. Then we walked the mile-plus to my house, cleared our plans with my parents and picked up my Stevens rifle and a supply of cartridges. We walked until we reached a wooded, bushy area along the creek, just east of a cornfield where a lot of grain had been missed in the harvest. This was a grand situation for many rabbits—nice fat corn-fed rabbits—living among the creek-side gooseberry bushes.

We hunted the afternoon away with our .22-caliber single-shot rifles, and our success was phenomenal. We each had so many cottontails we could hardly carry them, so we secured them on a pole that we carried between us on our shoulders. Everyone appreciated rabbit meals in those days; it was good meat that helped lower the grocery bills. In my mind, fried rabbit with potatoes and gravy was fit for a king!

**GAIL COLSON**
**MANKATO, KS**

# FOOD FOULS

## Mishaps happen in farm kitchens, too!

### GRAVY BY THE SLICE

I've been thinking a lot about my dad lately, remembering the hide-and-seek games he played with us around the granary and the barn in the '30s.

Dad enjoyed having his children josh him occasionally so he could register a comeback—usually more droll than snappy. But he never was one to get involved in lengthy or philosophical conversations.

He didn't say much, one way or another, about food, but he did lick his lips over good pork chops. We used to get a side of pork from Uncle Will, Dad's younger brother.

For some reason, only Dad, my brother Bob and younger sister Marjorie were at home one winter evening. That put me in charge of cooking dinner.

After everyone gave me lots of advice for preparing the pork chops, potatoes and canned tomatoes, they sat down at the table and began talking. That left me, about age 12, alone to make gravy. I had no experience—Mother didn't like us to help her cook, only to clean up and do dishes.

When I asked, Dad said he didn't know how much flour was needed for thickening the gravy. He didn't want to miss out on a favorite part of the meal, however, so he hesitated for a moment and then said, "Aw, just mix some flour into some water in a pint jar, and stir it into the brown crusty stuff in the frying pan. Add a half-teaspoon of salt."

I'm sure I didn't pour off any of the fat, and I probably added a quarter-cup of flour. What I produced was a grayish, greasy mass that defied being poured or ladled into the gravy boat.

Dad, seeing my teeth cutting into my lower lip, said, "That looks like rib-hugging gravy. Slice off two pieces for me. I'll put one slice under and one slice over my potatoes. I'm hungry for a good gravy and potato sandwich."

There was absolute silence as I stood there with tears welling up in my eyes. Maybe Bob snickered quietly.

"Here, use my knife," Dad offered.

"I want a gravy and potato sandwich, too," Bob said, turning gallant with a second order.

I had to smile on hearing a loud round of laughter as I put a slice of that gravy under and over the mashed potatoes on our plates. That was the best gone-wrong-to-right supper. I could have hugged Dad!

**JEAN CREA GORDON**
**RICHMOND HEIGHTS, OH**

Cooking for Dad was a rite of passage for country girls like Jean and this young chef.

OLD VISUALS/ALAMY

## LEARNING TO LOVE A CORN-FED LIFE

I'm from Germany, and that's where I met and married my husband. We left in 1949 and settled in Idaho, where my in-laws owned a farm.

During a Sunday dinner at their home, I declined to take any corn. When my mother-in-law asked me about it, I told her that we didn't eat corn in Germany—we fed it to the pigs. That comment didn't go over so well.

Months later, after I had found that I really liked corn, we had dinner at my in-laws' again. I took a big helping of corn, which my mother-in-law noticed right away.

"Well, I certainly am glad you joined us pigs!" she said with a smile. We all had a good laugh.

**HILTRUD WILMOT**
**SYRACUSE, UT**

## WHAT A JAM!

My mom and dad married in 1928 and lived on a farm southeast of Bolivar, Missouri. Being a young bride, Mom decided to make her first batch of jelly. She put it on to cook in the early morning. Well, it was getting close to midday—time for her to start making lunch—so she set her jelly aside because it hadn't thickened.

Dad came in for the midday meal, then went back to the field. Mom put her jelly back on to cook. She cooked it and cooked it, but it still didn't thicken. Not wanting Dad to know her jelly had failed, she threw it behind the chicken house.

When evening came, Dad came in and said, "I don't know what that old hen is caught in behind the hen house, but she seems to be high-stepping, raising one foot and then the other." Embarrassed, Mom slipped out with a water bucket and washed the hen's feet. Then she got a shovel and threw sand and gravel on the mess.

Every time I think of this story I laugh. Later on, Mom learned how to make really good jelly.

**PATRICIA TINDLE**
**BOLIVAR, MO**

## SHE PUT A BUG IN HIS EAR

My 3-year-old nephew came blackberry picking with us one summer. We each had a bucket, and when it was full we'd pour the berries into a large tub and head back to the fields to pick more.

On our second round, we went to empty our buckets, but to our surprise, the tub was almost empty. That's when my mother spotted my nephew with blackberry juice running down his chin and covering his shirt.

My mother told him we have to wash off the bugs from the berries before we eat them. When he heard that, my nephew looked as if he was going to be sick. We didn't lose any more berries. That night, Mother made a blackberry pie.

"None for me, Granny," my nephew said. "I'm full of bugs."

**MARGARET WORLEY**
**WATERTOWN, TN**

## THE SWEETEST CAKE

I recently opened a book of Mom's that brought her as close to me as if she stood at my shoulder, although she's been gone for years. It's called the *Searchlight Recipe Book*, published by *Household* magazine around 1943.

I don't remember Mom baking when I was small, and I think the reason was, having married in the depths of the Depression, she never had supplies to bake with. When supper consists of water gravy on water biscuits, you don't waste time imagining chocolate cake. The first cake I remember her baking was when I was 7.

We lived in Washington, where Dad was working in the shipyard. We had money enough to buy the cookbook, but since World War II was going on, Mom must've saved up our rationing stamps for a very long time to get enough cocoa, sugar and butter.

The dense chocolate aroma filled our little project row house. I was proud of Mama, and I brought two kids from next door over to see the cake. But they were already jealous because my mother was home all the time with me—their mothers worked in the shipyard. They slid corner-of-the-eye looks at each other. I heard Helen whisper to Scotty that it was a "homely" cake.

Their vocabulary was better than mine. I thought that since "home" was in it, homely had to be a good thing. I asked Mama what it meant. "Oh, it means plain and kind of ugly," she replied.

Well, sure, the fudge frosting got a little hard

> **THE DENSE CHOCOLATE AROMA FILLED OUR LITTLE PROJECT ROW HOUSE.**

and gouged out a few chunks of cake when Mama spread it, but it wasn't ugly! I was so mad, I made Helen and Scotty go home.

Before long, my folks bought 10 acres with a shack to live in and nut and fruit trees. Dad would come home after working eight hours and put in eight more turning it into a house and a farm.

In addition to making a home, plus caring for my toddler sister, my baby brother and me, Mom grew a big garden and preserved in mason jars.

Dad fixed up the house, but Mom made it a home. Between the two of them, they did the job so well that I loved to hear the wind howl at night, because it reminded me how cozy and snug I was inside with them.

Improving the house meant money was tight. Mom adapted the *Searchlight* recipes to use ingredients our farm provided. We had filbert and plum trees. No matter what nut was called for, Mom used filberts. A recipe might specify dried apples or peaches, but it got dried plums.

Decades later, I turned to the *Searchlight's* cake chapter. There, in the margin alongside the recipe for One-Egg Cake, was Mom's faint handwriting from a lifetime ago, doubling the measurements needed to turn a one-layer, one-egg cake into her two-layer homely cake with fudge frosting.

Yes, it was homely, Mom, in the very best meaning of the word.

**DONNA SCOFIELD**
**YAKIMA, WA**

Today, Donna shares Mama's "homely" cake with (from left) grandchildren Jasper and Adria and great-grandson Roman.

**DAD KNEW A GOOD EGG** "My father, Ed Krumland, ran a business in Columbus, Nebraska, for more than 50 years, beginning in the '20s," says Ethel Sutton. "He bought cream, eggs and poultry from local farmers and resold them to companies that supplied those items to grocery stores and restaurants. Having grown up on a farm in the area, he was familiar with the merchandise and many of the farmers. To determine the amount of butterfat in cream, my father used a Babcock tester. He then paid the farmers according to the butterfat content. The eggs were candled before resale, which meant they were viewed with a light to determine the quality of the white and yolk."

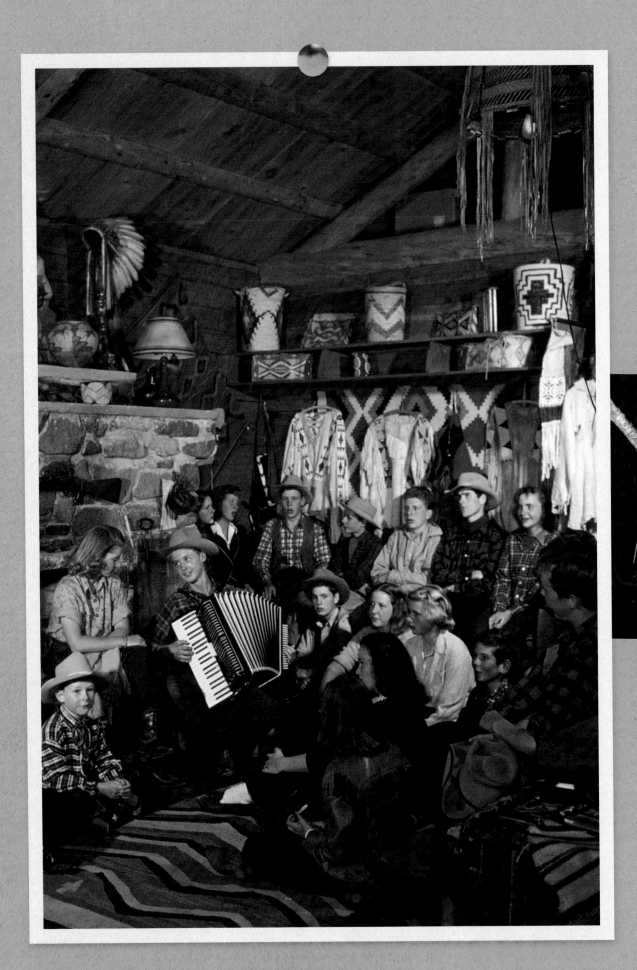

## CHAPTER 10

# HOLIDAY CHEER

*Christmas, Thanksgiving, Halloween and Easter
are definitely memorable experiences on the farm.
From Mom's peanut brittle to tales of the headless
horseman, these recollections of holiday fun
are sure to make you smile.*

# CHRISTMAS ON THE FARM

## Warm memories of the most wonderful time of the year

Listen carefully at midnight on Christmas Eve and you might hear the barnyard animals talk.

## DO YOU HEAR WHAT I HEAR?

When I was 5 years old, everything was possible, especially at Christmas. That Christmas Eve, my three brothers and I sat around the brightly lit and overdecorated tree while Mother brought us hot chocolate and cookies.

"There's a legend," she said, "that on Christmas Eve, a wonderful thing happens, but only if you believe." We scooted a bit closer.

"If you give all the animals extra feed and you're very quiet," she said, leaning in, "at midnight, for just one minute, all the animals in the world can talk."

"The animals can talk?" I asked in a whisper. How wonderful!

"If you can stay awake long enough, we'll all put on our coats and boots and go to the barn later," Mother promised.

Shortly before midnight, we bundled up and followed Mother into the night, the snow crunching under our boots. The sky was never so clear, the stars twinkling like a thousand diamonds, the moon a luminous pearl.

The animals seemed surprised to see us. We threw hay and oats into the mangers, then stood quietly, holding our breath. Mother pointed at her watch and nodded. It was midnight!

We strained to listen but heard only animals chewing and the occasional snort from a horse.

"I guess we didn't hear them," Mother finally said. "Maybe my watch was wrong and we missed it. But we can try again next year."

We all should have been disappointed, but we brimmed with excitement. Next Christmas, we might be the only people in the world who ever heard animals talk!

The snow sparkled in the moonlight, the pines cast dark shadows, and the icy pond shone like an enormous silver mirror. The boys started throwing snowballs at each other, and Mother and I joined in. It was magical, being out after midnight and playing in the snow with Mother. She seemed so young as we ran after the boys, all of us laughing so hard that we could hardly keep from falling down.

Every year after that, we repeated the ritual. Midnight on Christmas Eve we'd gather in the barn, smiling at one another, waiting for the animals to talk.

We grew older, and still we all walked to the barn late Christmas Eve. The smell of the hay, the warmth from the animals' bodies, the solid strength of the huge barn—every detail added to this singular moment we treasured in the harmony of farm and family.

The year before my brother left for college, I tried not to cry, knowing our whole family would probably never be wholly together on Christmas again. One by one we moved away, and while we often came home for the holidays, it was never again all of us at once.

After I married and we had our own children— a daughter and three sons—I began re-creating Mother's Christmas magic on our small Missouri farm. It quickly became a tradition to take turns saying that the clock must be wrong and we must have missed them by just a few minutes, but that we'd try again next year. Somehow, the years flew by and then it was my children growing up and moving away. Once again, I tried not to cry.

But then more years passed, and before I knew it my first grandchild, Colt, was 5, just as I was that first magical night. My son Pete and his wife, Rebecca, brought Colt and 3-year-old Shiloh, my second grandchild, for their first holiday on the farm that year.

It was early evening when I fixed hot chocolate and we all sat around the Christmas tree. I smiled and said quietly to Colt and Shiloh, "There's a legend that something wonderful happens every Christmas Eve, but to see it, you have to believe..."

**APRIL KNIGHT
FEDERAL WAY, WA**

## A PIECE OF TINSEL

Growing up, we never had an artificial Christmas tree—or a cut one. Instead, before Christmas, my parents would haul in a balled or potted evergreen that we'd plant later. Daddy said it made "good cents." Mother said it was a meaningful tradition.

Vivian still has the family piano.

After we got the heavy tree into the house, Mother would conceal the bulky container with white flannel to make it look like snow. Daddy would string the lights, and over the tree's boughs, my sister and I would drape red and green paper chains, strings of popcorn and cranberries, and other baubles we fashioned out of shiny milk-bottle caps. Then we would hang tinsel, weaving one strand at a time.

After we finished we'd gather around the piano to drink eggnog and sing Christmas carols.

On a warm Saturday after New Year's Day, we'd all go into the backyard, pick a site and plant our Christmas tree, making sure to water it well to protect it against the January freezes.

Each year, the yard got a little woodsier as we continued to add new spruce or pine specimens. On summer afternoons it was fun to find birds' nests in the branches and recall "this Christmas" or "that Christmas." Best of all, on nice warm evenings, we loved to sit in lawn chairs and watch fireflies flit in and out of the branches, as if trying to create their own Christmas tree light display.

One summer afternoon—some 40 years later—I drove by that childhood home and slowed down. The new owners were working in their yard, but when they saw me they came over to talk. When I told them that I had grown up there, they took me on a tour. The porch, front door and fireplace looked the same. The kitchen had been updated, and the screened-in back porch was now a four-season room. When we walked into the backyard, I caught my breath and fought back a tear. I was standing in a forest. The couple explained they were from California and loved the evergreens.

When I walked over to admire a spruce, a glint of silver caught my eye. I could hardly believe it: A strand of weathered tinsel was still wrapped around a branch, sparkling in the sun.

Through almost half a century, that remnant survived, much like my fond memories.

**VIVIAN STEWART
PIEDMONT, OK**

## CHRISTMAS MAPLES

I grew up on a farm outside Port Clinton, Ohio. I was the youngest son, with four brothers and four sisters, plus a girl my folks took in when she was in sixth grade and raised along with us.

By the late '60s, most of us were married and had families of our own. My wife and I had two kids; I worked full time and also had a part-time job on a tree farm.

One day, while we were visiting my parents in late summer or early fall, Dad mentioned he'd always wanted a Crimson King maple tree for the yard. Mom agreed that they were pretty.

Like many parents, mine were hard to shop for, so I figured this was a great opportunity to get them something they'd appreciate. I also thought that if they wanted one tree, two would be even better. I checked the price at work and decided that it was a bit more than I could afford—but all of my siblings agreed to chip in.

In northern Ohio, you don't plant maple trees at Christmas, so we decided to surprise Mom and Dad with a special Christmas in October before the ground froze. We asked my aunt if she'd help

> **ON THE CHOSEN SUNDAY, WE ALL MET AT MY HOUSE AND LOADED THE TREES INTO A PICKUP TRUCK.**

us with the deception, and she called my parents in advance to say she was coming for a Sunday visit. Then my sisters and sisters-in-law went into action, planning a big holiday turkey dinner.

On the chosen Sunday, we all met at my house and loaded the trees into a pickup truck. I even dressed up as Santa Claus—though at the time I weighed about 140, so all the padding in the world couldn't make me look like St. Nick.

Then off we went, nine or 10 cars loaded with people and food, plus the pickup.

When the caravan arrived at my folks' house, Dad came barreling out the back door, convinced something was wrong. He and Mom were amazed when we told them why we were there.

When Christmas rolled around, of course, we couldn't go to our parents' house empty-handed, so Mom and Dad got double presents that year. Almost half a century later, I still drive by the old farmstead and smile when I see those big, handsome trees and remember giving a special gift to special people at Christmas.

**ROBERT ALLEN
PORT CLINTON, OH**

## MAMA'S PEANUT BRITTLE

Homemade peanut brittle was one of our family's Christmas traditions during the Great Depression. Mama always made it for Papa and us six children. Today's store-bought variety doesn't compare to Mama's freshly made brittle. I can still picture Mama hefting her huge iron skillet to the cookstove, dumping in sugar and stirring gently. It never burned as she deftly moved the pan from hot to cooler places, letting the sugar slowly liquefy.

Next came the peanuts, which Papa harvested from our field with the mule. He stacked the vines in circles to dry and then stored them in an empty crib. In late November, we would sit in a tiny semicircle in the cold, drafty barn, picking the nuts off the vines. Sometimes a mouse would burst into our midst, making us kids scream, but Mama would calm us down. She fed the bare vines to the cows, saying the vines made the milk taste so much richer.

At the cookstove, stirring the golden sugar syrup, Mama folded the peanuts we had just shelled into the molten mixture. The final ingredient, baking soda, made the amber liquid foam up and nearly overflow. After blending everything thoroughly, Mama poured the mixture onto buttered platters, then took them outside to cool.

Seated around the table inside, we watched raptly as Mama held up a big piece of candy and tapped it with a spoon, shattering it. Soon a great pile of shining peanut brittle made the most beautiful sight I'd ever seen. Mama always used this moment to remind us that anything worth having was worth the work and wait. As we reached in to select the perfect piece, we knew she was right.

**MYRTLE BEAVERS
DESTIN, FL**

Store-bought varieties just don't compare to homemade peanut brittle.

## A CALF FOR CHRISTMAS

With no electricity on our farm north of Charleston, Illinois, Christmas Eve 1940 was far different from what it is today.

The holiday didn't affect the dairy cows, which still had to be milked by hand, and often we had to chop ice in the water troughs so the cattle could drink. Sometimes we even had to perform gymnastics in the snow or on the ice just to get bales of hay and grain to the animals.

We went to church that night in a drafty old car with an anemic heater and an engine that was reluctant to start at much below 20 degrees. Over our good clothes we wore heavy coats, gloves and hats.

Just 5 years old, I was excited to be part of the children's pageant. With the church dressed in its finest and all our favorite old hymns ringing out, each of us felt the joy of Christmas in our hearts.

Back home, as we turned on the living room's kerosene lamps, I contemplated the arrival of Santa Claus. Around 8:30 p.m. Dad told Mother he was going to look in on a cow that was due to calve at any time. Always eager to see a little calf, I found an excuse to go along.

Putting on my winter wear, I waited while Dad lit a kerosene lantern. He took my small hand in his as we headed toward the barn. A bright moon shone down, and our steps squeaked in the heavy snow. As we opened the barn door, the familiar, agreeable smells of cured clover hay and cattle greeted us.

The dim light revealed a new heifer calf on a pile of straw next to her mother. Dad seemed pleased to have a Christmas calf and was in a mood to reminisce.

He related a childhood story: that at midnight on Christmas Eve, all the cattle would lie facedown in the manger as if bowing before Baby Jesus. I asked if he'd ever gone to the barn at midnight to see it. He never had, but allowed that it certainly could be true.

As we returned to the warmth of the house, I pondered Dad's story and other mysterious things, like why Santa never left tracks in the snow. I secretly vowed to return to the barn at midnight. Of course, I never made it, being far off in dreamland when the clock struck 12 a.m.

As I grew older, I solved the mystery of Santa, but the mystery of Christmas remains: that God's son was born in a most humble and unlikely place.

**JACK PIERCE**
**MATTOON, IL**

Family jamborees, like this one and Barbara's, are a wonderful rural tradition.

## CHOIR OF ANGELS

One of nine children in a very poor family, I grew up on a south Georgia farm. Like our neighbors, we raised our own food. Our parents showed us lots of love while teaching us about hard work and honesty.

One Christmas memory stands out above all others, from back when I was about 8 years old. We had cut a small tree to decorate with handmade ornaments and pinecones, which were all we had, and placed it by the fireplace. In our hearts, we hoped Santa would bring us presents, although we knew there was little chance for that.

But there was no doubt that we would feast. As he did every year, Dad butchered a hog. Early on Christmas Eve, the delicious aromas of ham, greens, chicken and stuffing filled the house. Mom baked pies and cakes, and we had fresh fruit and nuts.

But the thing that made this Christmas so special came next. Suddenly, out of the blue, two cars pulled into the driveway. The cars were full of aunts, uncles and cousins from our dad's side of the family. They had driven up from Florida to surprise us.

What a time we had! They were all musicians, and they made such a happy group as they sang and played their guitars for us. We kids sat around in wide-eyed enchantment until we fell asleep. Mom made makeshift beds for everyone on the floor, and nobody minded because we were all together.

Santa did visit us after all, bringing us one toy each. On Christmas Day, we happily shared them with our cousins. But as much as we'd hoped and hoped for gifts, the love and closeness of family made us happy in a way no presents could.

I remember waking all warm and cozy by the fire Christmas morning, then crawling out from under the covers and up into my dad's lap as he sipped his coffee. Together we watched a beautiful sunrise.

**BARBARA CHILDERS
ATLANTIC BEACH, FL**

Marcia (above, at age 6) waited in the big barn (left) as her siblings finished their chores on Christmas Eve.

## ALL IS CALM, ALL IS BRIGHT

Snow fell as I ran toward our red barn, telling two terriers, "Santa's coming, Santa's coming!" The dogs sensed my excitement and circled around me.

I was 7 years old that Christmas Eve in 1952, and as I did my chores on our Ohio farm I wondered if Santa would fix my sister Betty's old doll crib and buggy for me. Dad had sent them to Santa at the beginning of Advent.

*I hope, I hope,* I told myself as I rushed to the barn and plowed into Betty, who was carrying a straw bale for the calves.

"Watch where you're going!" she protested. "Why are you in such a hurry?" Then she smiled knowingly. "You know we can't go into the house until Santa turns on the Christmas tree lights and all the milking and feeding are done."

After I fed the calves, I cracked open the door of the barn and saw that night had come. A 40-watt bulb in the corner of the barn shed a faint light on the falling snow. The flakes drifted gently down, forming a misty curtain in front of the house.

My breathing slowed as I watched the snow fall. I wondered: Jesus was born in a stable. Did He have snow on His birthday? Did the animals keep Him warm with their breath and body heat? Jesus got gifts from the wise men.

The barn seemed to breathe a response to my questions with the sounds of the calves rustling the straw, the rabbits thumping their hind legs and the cows lowing. All the ordinary sounds

I heard every day became charged with the presence of something I couldn't name. I felt a sense of peace settling all around.

At that moment, the Christmas tree lights came on, the colors hazy through the falling snow. I stood entranced. I wanted to stay with that feeling of being part of it all. Presents? I would be happy with whatever I got.

My brother Dave looked out the door with me. "Hey, the lights are on! Jim and Betty have only four more cows to milk. Won't be long now. Come on!"

"Isn't everything beautiful, Dave? The snow, the lights, the barn?" Dave had already walked away and didn't hear me. "Yes, it is," I said softly.

Anticipation mounted as all four of us kids ran to the house. The Christmas tree's soft lights bathed the living room in a warm glow. Then I saw my gifts. The repainted doll crib and buggy; the new sheets in a flower design like the one on the sack our flour came in; matching pillowcases finished off with a crocheted edging that Mom put on all her fancy work; my favorite doll with a new nightgown made of the same flannel as mine; and a dress and cap made of the same material as my school dress.

As I played with my doll and put her in her new bed, I saw my parents sitting on the couch, watching. They looked content. Again I felt the same presence as in the barn, only then I knew its name: love.

**MARCIA DAHLINGHAUS**
**GOLDEN VALLEY, AZ**

 **Everybody knows the sign of good coffee**

Perfect timing for a neighborly invitation. The long cold miles ahead will seem shorter after a heart-warming cup of truly good coffee . . . full-bodied, fragrant Maxwell House. The *only* coffee with that famous "Good to the Last Drop" flavor. Behind that finer flavor, there's a secret . . . a closely guarded recipe for certain fine coffees, and how to blend them for *more* richness, *more* mellowness, *more* deeply satisfying goodness. Because it offers the <u>best</u> in coffee drinking pleasure, more people buy and enjoy Maxwell House than any other brand of coffee—*at any price!*

*Now in Instant form too!*

*Products of General Foods*

*TUNE IN . . . "Father Knows Best" . . . delightful family comedy starring Robert Young . . . NBC, Thursday nights*

*Maxwell House . . . the <u>one</u> coffee with that "Good to the Last Drop" flavor!*

# SEASONAL CELEBRATIONS

## Family and friends turn all holidays into occasions to remember

Trick-or-treating was extra spooky on dark rural roads.

### THE LEGEND OF SKUNK HOLLOW

Halloween night found us kids scurrying along dark, heavily wooded roads. A full moon peeked around tall trees, sometimes illuminating the path before us, other times casting eerie shadows that both scared and thrilled us.

Trick-or-treating was difficult around our rural Pennsylvania farm because of long walks between houses. Kindly local farmers knew this. Instead of a quick exchange at the door, they invited us in to warm up around a woodstove. They fortified us with big helpings of homemade goodies and fussed over our costumes.

The longest haul was along Hollow Road, from my house to the Kulp farm, but it was my favorite. The road had no official name, but we knew it as Hollow Road. Dad called it Skunk Hollow to tease his friend Mr. Kulp, who lived at the end.

To us kids, it was the legendary Sleepy Hollow. We named it after the short story by Washington Irving that featured the famous fictional headless horseman character.

Five of us, ranging from 7 to 10 years of age, were trick-or-treating together one particular Halloween. We scared ourselves silly by telling stories about the headless horseman, who surely lived in the woods.

As we neared the Kulp farm, we heard crashing and snorting among the trees. The sound of galloping hooves was headed straight for us. Frozen in fear, we were too scared to run. A creepy coldness ran up the back of my neck. Henry, age 7, finally broke the trance, running and screaming for all he was worth toward the Kulp farm. Seconds later, two deer leapt out in front of us. After catching our breath, we laughed about how little kids like Henry could be scared of deer.

By the time we got to the house, Mrs. Kulp had calmed Henry. She herded us into her kitchen and plied us with apple-butter glazed doughnuts and hot cider. As we were leaving, she stuffed bags full of treats into our arms. Mr. Kulp saw we were tired and took us home. We arrived filled with the warmth of good food and the knowledge that, as long as we had caring neighbors, we were safe from headless horsemen.

**PAT ARBEITER**
**GRAND JUNCTION, CO**

## FIVE MONTHS OF THANKSGIVING

Preparations for Thanksgiving began early on my family's sheep ranch in Northern California's Anderson Valley. While my cousin and I were riding our ponies over the dry, grassy hills and swimming in the Navarro River, Mother, Grandma-Ma, Auntie Gert and my older cousins began the annual ritual of canning in the old homestead's summer kitchen.

The summer kitchen filled one end of a long, enclosed back porch. It had a counter with a white porcelain sink; cupboards cluttered with canning pots, sieves and funnels; a worktable covered with checkered oilcloth; and an ancient woodstove. A large pantry with shelving stood just beyond the old stove's brick firewall.

By mid-July, the summer kitchen was running full steam—literally! Peas were always the first to be processed. Everyone Grandma-Ma could recruit sat on the back porch steps shelling the peas into large pans as we wished we were out swimming. Then came the cherries. Grandma-Ma and Mother packed them into pint jars, while Aunt Gert separated the riper cherries into a large pot to be made into a delicious jam, which to this day is my favorite.

Peaches and apricots followed shortly. Apricots needed only to be washed, pitted and packed into jars. Peaches, the family's favorite, were carefully blanched in the old black enamel kettle, then skinned, halved and packed. They were stored in a place of honor in the center of the pantry, shimmering golden in the light of the room's sole 100-watt bulb.

Then came string beans, beets, corn, cucumbers and two giant Red Wing crocks stuffed with shredded cabbage slowly fermenting into sauerkraut. After the tomatoes were canned and the late summer apples stored, my cousin Skip and I helped Grandma-Ma and Aunt Gert hang bouquets of fragrant oregano and lavender high on the pantry walls. By fall, ropes of onions and garlic hung at the ends of the shelves; crates of apples, potatoes, squash, pumpkins and walnuts lined the floor.

I loved helping Grandpa search for the perfect

Ray's family gathers to enjoy Thanksgiving at the old farmhouse in the late '40s.

branch of California bay leaves to hang over the pantry door, which he believed kept away the bugs. The bay leaves also found their way into Grandma-Ma's winter soups and stews.

With the coming of November rains, Grandma-Ma filled the remaining shelf space with Folgers coffee cans packed with her famous fruitcakes—along with a bottle of brandy for the finishing touch. The pantry's aroma of spices, apples and bay leaves drifted into the house, announcing the Thanksgiving season.

The weekend before Thanksgiving, aunts, uncles and cousins began to arrive, and we all took up temporary residence in the five upstairs bedrooms and an old cabin in the redwood grove behind the house. My uncles helped Grandpa catch up on repairs around the ranch; my aunts baked every conceivable type of pie and bread; and we cousins played checkers, card games and Monopoly in the front room, clustered as close to the warm woodstove as possible.

With four leaves extending the dining table into the front room, Grandpa would say grace, thanking God for the bounty stored in the barn and the back-porch pantry, which smelled of spices, apples, California bay leaves and a hint of brandy.

**RAY PRATHER
ROCHESTER, MN**

## THE BEST-LAID PLANS

The year might have been 1970 or earlier, when my brother, Greg, and his wife, Linda, invited us to their new home for Thanksgiving. My husband, our two little girls and I lived on our little farm in the Catskill Mountains with a few horses, goats, chickens and dogs. My brother's house was at least 3½ hours south, but it would be such fun to see the family. I sure did miss them.

That week I baked bread and my famous apple pies and made a bucketload of coleslaw. I added several jars of my homemade green tomato pickles to the menu, and my husband picked up some delicious local apple cider.

My good friend Martha, who lived a few miles up the road, promised to feed our horses if we didn't get home in time for the late feeding. Her folks and sisters were driving up from the city for Thanksgiving, so she bought the biggest turkey she could find. While Martha cleaned her house and got ready for her company, I peeled apples, kneaded dough and shredded cabbage for coleslaw.

Everything was ready for our early-morning departure. I fell asleep thinking of the fun we would have.

I bounced out of bed at the first sound of the alarm. When I put the coffeepot on, I noticed movement outside the window above the sink. I turned on the outside light and saw snowflakes. The unexpected flurry was 15 inches deep and still falling.

There would be no trip. The car wouldn't get out of the driveway. I let the family sleep peacefully and tried to get over my disappointment—no relatives and no turkey. I quietly put on my coat and boots and trudged through the snow to take care of the animals.

The girls were in their rooms pouting when our party line rang a few minutes before 9 a.m.

"Bummer, huh?" Martha said.

"It is!" I replied. "At least we have lots of apple pies, bread and coleslaw. Are your folks going to try to come up from the city?"

"Oh, no!" she said. "It's even worse in the city. Maddie was supposed to bring dessert and salad. We don't have much else! Just the turkey!"

"Hey!" we both said at once.

I packed the coleslaw, pickles, bread, cider and apple pies. We secured the food on our toboggan and spent almost two hours breaking a trail through the fluffy new snow.

No one complained about the long walk or cold, wet feet. We got to Martha's just in time. That day, we talked about the things we were thankful for: health, happiness, wonderful friends, warm homes, good neighbors and enough food for an army.

The return trip in the sparkling, snowy twilight was so peaceful. I've enjoyed many Thanksgivings since, but the memory of that snowy one is the clearest of all. It taught me that God could turn disappointments into surprise blessings. I am so thankful I learned that lesson.

**JOYCE CARROLL**
**ACCORD, NY**

Joyce and her family broke
a trail through fluffy snow
on foot one Thanksgiving.

## UP ON THE HOUSETOP, CHICK, CHICK, CHICK

One of my most memorable Christmases had nothing to do with a perfect gift or a pretty tree. It all goes back to hatching guinea fowl eggs for a science project in which—despite an earlier declaration that we wouldn't interfere with nature—Mom helped the first hatchling when it had trouble. The little keet's legs were bent, so she gave it physical therapy, picking up the chick several times a day and straightening its legs. Knowing Mom, I'm sure she prayed, too. To our delight, the bird grew up to walk just fine.

We were sad when our guineas had to go live at a friend's farm, but when we moved to a rural home in Virginia years later, one of the first things we did was buy more. We raised 10 keets to adulthood, and we couldn't have been more pleased when two paired up and hatched their own little family. Lennie and Jennie were inseparable and protective of their small but active brood.

The guineas developed a daily routine that included an early-morning and a late-afternoon romp on our roof. Back and forth they ran between our two chimneys, much to the dismay of those wishing to sleep in.

Just before Christmas a few years ago, we were about to eat breakfast when a strange sound came from the living room. We left our pancakes to investigate and found that the noises were coming from the fireplace.

Dad reached in and very carefully slid open the vent over the gas logs. Flapping all the way, a soot-smeared, slightly perturbed female guinea plopped out and hopped down. Just like that, we had a feathery intruder.

Now, guinea fowl are not tame by any means. When people pull into our driveway, whether to deliver a package or evangelize, they take one look at them and decide to stay in the car. "What are those things?" they yell. "Turkeys?"

And now there was a hen in the house. We ran and threw open the front door, but it was too late. The sooty bird strutted confidently down the hall, well on her way toward the master bedroom. We scrambled after her as she purposefully ambled into the bathroom and hopped right up on the countertop. Mind you, we made a sizable mob: my mom and dad, my four sisters, one brother and me. But this didn't faze our petite feathered houseguest, who strode the counter with the grace of a tightrope walker, knocking nothing down, then bounced into the bathtub. She took it all in for a thoughtful moment, then decided she'd had enough and neatly sprang right out.

Like the born performer she was, the hen led her parade—our open-mouthed, wide-eyed family—back through the bedroom and across the living room. And then, with utter aplomb, she sauntered out the front door. She returned to the waiting flock looking as unflappable as if every morning she enjoyed a spin through the house after breakfast.

Mom and Dad quickly got caps for the chimneys, so now the guineas can run around the roof, and we're assured there will be no more fowl impressions of Santa.

**HANNAH HELMER**
**DINWIDDIE, VA**

## FAMILY TRADITIONS

We would always have Thanksgiving at my grandfather's farm. All the sisters, one brother and their kids would show up. Aunt Louise always fixed a huge turkey in the wood-burning stove, and the rest of the sisters would take care of everything else. After the meal, some of the older guys watched TV while others hunted. We kids played touch football. Later on, all the kids drew names for Christmas gifts. I can still smell the coal-fired furnace and Grandpa smoking his cigars.

**JACK TIGGLEMAN**
**VIA FACEBOOK**

## THE EASTER BUNNY LEFT HIS MARK

When I was 5 years old, in 1965, my family lived on a small farm southwest of Madison, South Dakota. My mother was a true "Mrs. Clean," and everyone, including the Easter Bunny, wiped his or her feet before coming into the house. The night before Easter, my folks dyed and hid the eggs. Then my mother took a clean white cotton dish towel and painted multicolored bunny tracks all over it with the leftover dye. She laid it in front of the door and painted more tracks up toward the doorknob. I was so excited when I woke up and saw where the bunny had wiped his feet—and with evidence like that, you just had to believe in the bunny!

**DONNA OWEN**
**MADISON, SD**

**SUNDAY BEST** "When we moved to a 320-acre farm in Jefferson County, Florida, the first several years were tough but we always managed to give our children Easter outfits," says Charles Cocroft of Monticello, Florida. Charles shared this darling photo of him with his children, Janine, Billy and Carl, taken before heading to church in 1966.